202

THINGS YOU CAN MAKE AND SELL FOR BIG PROFITS

202
THINGS TO MAKE
AND SELL
FOR BIG PROFITS

JAMES STEPHENSON

EP
Entrepreneur.
Press

Managing editor: Jere L. Calmes
Cover design: Beth Hansen-Winter
Composition and production: Eliot House Productions

This publication is designed to provide accurate and authoritative information in regard to the
subject matter covered. It is sold with the understanding that the publisher is not engaged in rendering legal, accounting, or other professional services. If legal advice or other expert assistance is
required, the services of a competent professional person should be sought.

Library of Congress Cataloging-in-Publication Data
    Stephenson, James, 1966–.
        202 things you can make and sell for big profits/by James Stephenson.
        p.   cm.
    Includes index.
    ISBN 1-932531-69-6 (alk. paper)
      1. Entrepreneurship. 2. New business enterprises. 3. Small business. I. Title: Two hundred
two things you can make and sell for big profits. II. Title.
    HB615.S74 2005
    658.4'21—dc22   2005007913

Printed in Canada

11 10 09 08 07 06 05   10 9 8 7 6 5 4 3 2 1

CONTENTS

CHAPTER 4

Everything Else You Need to Know _____ 55

The Best Places to Sell the Things You Make _ _ _ _ _ _ 73

CHAPTER 6

The Best 202 Things You Can Make and Sell for Big Profits _ _ _ _ _ _ _ _ _ _ _ _ 97

Things You Can Make and Sell for Big Profits

Things You Can Make and Sell for Big Profits

PREFACE

Are you the creative type? Are you someone who likes to work with your hands? Are you someone who constantly looks for ways to improve products? Are you unhappy with your present job? Are you someone who likes to face new challenges? Are you a big thinker? If you answered yes to one or more of these questions, chances are you are the type of person who would enjoy, excel, and ultimately find success and financial prosperity by starting and operating a business making and selling products. In doing so, you would join the millions of other women and men across the nation who have taken control of their lives and fulfilled their dreams of self-employment.

Hundreds of years ago, the Industrial Revolution changed the way most products were being manufactured, taking production out of the hands of the individual craftsperson and putting it into the hands of factory laborers producing mass quantities of the same product. Today, technology has driven the manufacturing industry to even higher levels of efficient production, making all sectors of manufacturing sharply competitive. How then can you start a business making products and compete against manufacturing companies with bundles of loot to spend on technology or against foreign manufacturers with considerably lower labor costs? The answer is simply specialization and handcrafting.

Specialization means making a product really well and selling it to a specific segment of the target audience willing to pay for quality and better features. This is known as seeking and serving a niche market. Likewise, there will always be a marketplace for handcrafted products. Look no further than to the motorcycle enthusiast for proof. Unquestionably, the United States, Japan, and Germany have a stranglehold on motorcycle manufacturing, producing everything from economy models to fully decked-out highway cruisers, selling millions of new motorcycles every year. Yet, there are numerous pint-sized companies manufacturing and selling handcrafted motorcycles that have customers lined up at the door, waiting for as long as two years to get one and more than willing to shuck out $100,000 for the privilege of owning one. You can buy mass-produced hand soap at any grocery store, yet specialty hand soap makers continue to flourish. You can buy mass-produced furniture at any furniture retailer, yet custom furniture manufacturers continue to flourish. You can buy mass-produced clothing on just about every street corner, yet independent fashion designers are doing exceptionally well. The reasons are simple: all have learned to provide a better product and have taken the time to seek consumers looking for a better product.

Making and selling products also offers flexibility. You can make and sell products full time and replace, or even increase, your current income. You can make and sell products part time to help pay your way through college, pay down the mortgage, or save for your kid's education. You can make and sell products to supplement your retirement income so you can enjoy your golden years to their fullest, pursuing the things you never had time for in the past. All of this is easily within your reach and can be achieved by starting and operating your own business making and selling products.

My objective in creating this book is clear: identify the best products to make and include the information and tools that you need in order to successfully market and sell your products for maximum profitability. There are numerous books available on making products, but *202 Things You Can Make and Sell for Big Profits* is the only book that lists the best products to make and the best ways to sell them for maximum profitability. This book is the most up to date and is packed with resources. The information included has been specifically developed to take you through every step required to start and run a business for success and profit.

After completing this book, you will have acquired valuable information and knowledge on all the critical topics, including legal and financial issues, business planning, setting up shop, sales and marketing, and the best 202 products to make and sell for big profits.

Getting Started

Who can make and sell products? Everyone can! Everyone is qualified because everybody knows how to make something, or with basic training can quickly learn how to make a product(s) that can be sold for a profit. If you want to earn extra money, work from home, turn a hobby into a moneymaking venture, or start and operate a full-time business, you'll learn how. Operating your own business, even a small manufacturing business, also gives you the potential to make more money than working a traditional job, and again you'll learn how. There are also a number of advantages associated with making and selling products—minimal financial risk, low investment, ability to work from home, flexibility, and many tax advantages. You will discover them all in this book.

Don't worry if you lack business skills and experience in areas such as time management, selling, and bookkeeping because this book shows you how to capitalize on your current skill set and knowledge to get started right now and to learn business skills over time and with hands-on practical experience. You will also learn about financial compatibility, finding a good match, level of time commitment that best suits your needs and ambitions, and information to help you decide if you should start a business, buy a business, or buy a franchise.

Legal and Financial Issues

Inside you will discover information that demystifies all of the tough legal and financial issues, such as what licenses and permits are needed to start your business and how these can be obtained. You will also learn about legal business structures—the sole proprietorship, partnership, limited liability corporation, and corporation—and the advantages and disadvantages of each.

Do you need insurance to make and sell products? Yes. You will learn what insurance coverage is needed to best protect your assets and where you can get it. You also will learn how much money is needed to start your new enterprise and what funding sources are available to you. This book shows you how to start your new venture on a shoestring budget and where you can get the money you need to get rolling. Money management issues are discussed. You will learn how to set up your books, work with accountants and bookkeepers, and open commercial bank accounts. You will also discover how to establish merchant accounts so you can provide your customers with convenient purchase payment options, including credit cards, debt cards, and electronic money transfers.

Setting Up Shop

To make products, you need a base of operations. Depending on the products you make, setting up shop can mean anything from converting a spare bedroom into a candle-making room to leasing a factory to mass produce a complete line of patio furniture. The advantages and disadvantages of working from home, leasing a factory, or renting a storefront so you can make and sell products, are discussed. An operating location can also be on the web, so this book shows you what you need to know to get on the internet and start doing business there. Topics such as building your web site, selecting the right domain name, and registering with search engines are all covered.

Setting up shop also goes far beyond a physical location and includes things such as equipment and tool needs, transportation, office furniture, technology, and communication devices. In other words, you need to know how to organize your workspace so that you can maximize efficiency and productivity, and inside you will learn how to achieve both. To start, operate, and grow a business takes a team, and here you learn who makes up that team as well as valuable information on creating and projecting a professional business image on a budget.

Everything Else You Need to Know

An entire chapter is devoted to everything else you need to know to start, operate, and grow a business, with a host of additional helpful information to put you on the path to long-term success and profitability. All ventures need a business and marketing plan, regardless of whether you plan to build a global manufacturing empire or just make wind chimes at home to sell at weekend flea markets. You can use the information in this book as a road map to guide you through the process of creating your own business plan in step-by-step format.

Product pricing is also important because if your prices are too high or to low, people might not buy because of perceived value and quality issues. Therefore, I will teach you how to price your products for profitability. Likewise, often what separates the winners from the losers in business is the level of service for customers. Your ability to survive in business will be based on many factors, but one of the biggest is your ability to retain customers and foster long-term and profitable selling relationships. You are shown how to do that with a smile. Advertising can motivate people to buy your products or can be a complete waste of time and money. Teaching you what you need to know about getting the biggest bang for your advertising buck makes sure that won't happen.

The Best Places to Sell

Making a great product is only half the job; selling it for big profits is the rest. That is why an entire chapter is devoted to helping you learn basic selling techniques as well as the best places to sell the products you make. You will discover how to sell from home utilizing interior showrooms, exterior display, and in-home sales parties, as well as simple and cost-effective advertising methods such as classified ads and fliers to promote homebased sales. If your approach to marketing and sales is to rely on "walk in traffic" to generate new sales, you will need to rent a storefront location or sell factory-direct. If that is your plan, you will learn how to pick the best location and merchandise your products for maximum profitability.

What if you are a big thinker with dreams of going global and selling your products wholesale to small retailers and multinational chain retailers? Can this book help? Don't worry, we have you covered by showing you how to sell your products in mass quantities on a wholesale basis. There are also tons of ways to promote and sell products online. You will learn about three—eBay, e-auctions, and internet malls. You will also learn how to sell your products at a number of other great locations such as flea markets, craft shows, trade and consumer shows, and community events.

The Best 202 Things to Make and Sell

This is where the fun begins. Chapter 6 is completely devoted to informing you about the best 202 things to make and sell for big profits. You will find a description of each product featured, why it is a great product to make, what you need to know to get started, and how to effectively market and sell the products you make. You will also find hundreds of valuable American and Canadian resources throughout this chapter, including private corporations, business associations, web sites, publications, products, services, and lots more, all of which have been included to help get you to the next level.

All of the web links, telephone numbers, and mailing addresses featured throughout the book were active at the time of writing. Over time, some information may have changed or may no longer be available. In an effort to ensure resource information remains beneficial and active for the long term, great efforts were made to find the most reputable businesses, organizations, publications, and individuals, but this is not an endorsement of any. It is the responsibility of entrepreneurs to do their own due diligence to make sure they are doing business with reputable firms and individuals and purchasing quality products and services.

The following are the resource icons used:

   δ   A mouse icon represents an online resource web site address.

   ☎   A telephone icon represents a resource's contact telephone number.

   📖 A book icon represents a book or other publication that offers further information.

   ★   A star icon represents a franchise or business opportunity.

■   ■   ■

202 Things You Can Make and Sell for Big Profits is the most authoritative and comprehensive book available of its kind. It gives you the ability to identify the best things to make, to learn how to get started, and to find the information and tools you need to sell the products you make for maximum profits. Harness the power of this book by putting it to work for you today.

GETTING STARTED WITH THINGS TO MAKE AND SELL

Who can make and sell products? We all can! Everyone knows how, or can quickly learn, to make items that can be sold for a profit. Making products to sell truly knows no boundaries. Anyone with a desire to earn extra money, work from home, turn a hobby making crafts into a profitable part-time venture, or operate a full-time business can make and sell a product— regardless of age, special skills, and business experience. The purpose of this book is simply to give you the basic information that you need to start and operate such a small business and help you identify the best product(s) for making big profits.

In Chapter 1, you will discover the advantages associated with making and selling products. You will learn how you can capitalize on your existing skills, pick a time commitment that is right for you, and understand the importance of financial compatibility. You will also learn about the pros and cons of starting a manufacturing business from scratch as opposed to buying an existing business or franchise—and lots more!

The Money You Can Earn

How much money do you need or want to earn making and selling products? Operating your own business, even a small manufacturing business, gives you the potential to make more money. Why? Simple duplication. When you work for someone else, there is only you and only so many hours in the day to work for a wage. When you operate a business, you can duplicate yourself and hire employees to make more products and salespeople to sell those products. You also have the ability to find more like your customers so they can purchase your products. You can even duplicate your business model and open in new geographical areas to sell more products to more customers to earn more profits.

The expansion of the internet also gives entrepreneurs access to a global audience of buying consumers. The internet has made it easier for the small business owner to market and sell products in the global marketplace by utilizing online sales venues such as eBay, internet malls, and e-storefronts. Only a decade ago selling products outside of a specific geographic location was not a option for most small business owners because of the time and costs associated with penetrating far-off markets. Now with the simple click of a mouse you can promote and sell your products to consumers worldwide—again offering the opportunity to make more sales and earn more money.

There are certainly upper limits to how much money you can earn making and selling products, at least on a small scale. But at the same time, your ability to earn an above-average income will be determined by your ambition and motivation, not by trading hours for a wage. If you are prepared to work hard and smart, there is a better-than-average chance you will earn more making and selling products than you are, or can, working at your current job.

The Advantages of Making and Selling Products

There are a number of advantages associated with making and selling products. You have the potential to earn more money. But perhaps the biggest advantage is you become your own boss and take control of your future, which is unlikely to happen when you work for others. Consider a few more advantages associated with starting a business making and selling products.

- *Low investment.* The majority of product manufacturing opportunities featured in this book require only a minimal investment to get started. In fact, there are many product manufacturing opportunities listed in Chapter 6 that can be started for only a few thousand dollars in total investment, but have excellent growth and profit potential.
- *Minimal financial risk.* Because almost all of the money you spend to get started goes into buying inventory and equipment to make products, there is limited financial risk involved. If you decide to quit, simply sell off the raw materials, equipment, and completed products to recoup all or most of your investment.
- *Homebased.* For people who want to work from home, making and selling products is a great choice because many of the products featured in Chapter 6 can easily be made at home, and with few if any expensive alterations to your current home. You can turn your garage, basement, or a spare bedroom into the workspace you need to make the products.
- *Flexibility.* Pick your time commitment and make and sell products part-time, full-time, seasonally, or only occasionally. You can set your own schedule and level of commitment as determined by your goals and objectives, not your boss's.
- *Tax advantages.* Operating a legal manufacturing and sales business has numerous tax advantages and business write-offs, especially if you operate the business from home These tax advantages will leave more money in your pocket at the end of the year and less in the tax man's.

Capitalizing on Your Skills and Knowledge— and Finding a Good Match

Don't worry if you lack business skills and experience in areas such as time management, selling, and bookkeeping. Yes, these are all important skills to have, but at the same time they are skills that can be learned with time and practice. More important is the question, "What skills and specific knowledge do you have that can be capitalized upon and put to good and profitable use in your new manufacturing venture?" Everyone can make and sell products, regardless of business experience or special skills, because training is available that can teach you how to make any product. At the same time, your skills and knowledge are by far your best business assets. People all have specific skills and knowledge that is valuable;

however, they just do not understand their true value until they take the time to identify those special skills and specific knowledge. For instance, if you possess carpentry skills, these skills can be used to start a business manufacturing products such as gazebos or furniture. If you have a green thumb, this skill can be capitalized upon to grow and sell trees, shrubs, flowers, herbs, and even Christmas trees. Or, if you are very knowledgeable about fishing, this knowledge can be utilized in a fishing tackle manufacturing and sales business, even if you have no actual experience in manufacturing fishing tackle.

You also have to think good match when it comes time to decide what products you want to make and how these products are to be sold. Skills and knowledge are very valuable, but if you are not healthy enough to make and sell the products, then that would not be a good match. Three additional points to consider in terms of a good match include: Are there any specialized training or certification requirements for making or selling the products? Does the product match your personality type and level of maturity? And most importantly, would you enjoy making and selling this product? If you think not, then don't start. You can't stay motivated and rise to new challenges if you do not like what you are doing.

Financial Compatibility

Before you decide to get into business manufacturing and selling products, there are two financial compatibility issues to consider—your income requirements and the amount of money you have to start or buy a business. You first must figure out how much money you *need* to earn to pay your personal bills—housing, food, transportation, health care, and so on. If you need to earn $50,000 per year to make ends meet, it makes no sense to start a picnic table manufacturing business. Sure, it may be possible to earn $50,000 a year building and selling picnic tables, but it is not a realistic expectation. The product(s) you decide to make and sell must have the potential to meet your income needs. Keep in mind that if you need to earn only a few extra dollars every week or if income is not your motivation for starting a small manufacturing and sales business, income potential will be less of a factor in your decision-making process.

The second financial compatibility issue concerns investment capital. Not only do you need money to start or buy a business, buy equipment and tools, and buy inventory, but you will also need additional money over and above your initial investment to use as working capital to cover operating expenses until the business achieves positive cash flow. The time frame for achieving positive cash flow varies by the type of product being manufactured and how it is sold; it can take a week, month, or even a year. This is one reason why business and marketing planning, as well as financial forecasting, is so important. The information you research and record will answer questions such as the time it takes to reach a point of positive cash flow.

Ultimately, financial compatibility is important in terms of starting a business and deciding on what products to make and sell. If you cannot afford to start the business and do not have the financial resources to pay operating expenses until the business breaks even, you will probably have to look at alternative options, such as starting part time, choosing a different product to make, or waiting until you have saved sufficient money to meet your initial funding requirements and working capital needs.

Making and Selling Products Part-Time

For many people making and selling products on a part-time basis is the best way to get started because it enables you to reduce risk by limiting your financial investment. Starting part-time also allows you to test the waters to make sure that being self-employed making and selling products is something that you enjoy and want to pursue. If all goes well, you can transition from your current job and devote more time to your business each week until you are working at it full-time. Other advantages to starting part-time include keeping income coming in from your regular job, taking advantage of any current health and employee benefits, and building your business over a longer period of time, which generally gives it a more stable foundation for long-term growth. If it turns out that you are not the type of person who is comfortable being self-employed, you have risked little and still have the security of your job.

Having a part-time business may be all you want. Not every business has to be operated full-time. Each person has to assess his or her own situation and choose a level of commitment that best suits. For instance, you may only want to generate extra money every month to help pay down the mortgage, save for retirement, put yourself or kids through school, or pay for travel and leisure activities. If so, making and selling products part-time can help you reach your goals.

Making and Selling Products Full-Time

You can jump in with both feet and start your new manufacturing business full-time. This option would appeal to people without a current job, those facing layoff, homemakers, and to people who are confidant in their ability to operate a successful business. The downside to starting off full-time is risk. If you leave your job, you risk loss of current employee benefits and loss of income. But it is possible to minimize or entirely overcome these effects by planning and saving for your new business well in advance of leaving your job.

The upside to starting full-time is potential rewards, which can be many. There is the opportunity to make more money than you can at your current job, to gain control of your future, to build equity and financial security, and to have the personal satisfaction that comes with being your own boss. Overall, the decision to start or buy a business full-time will largely be determined by issues such as your current financial situation, family matters, health, personal risk-reward assessment, and your goals, objectives, and ambitions for the future. Jumping in full-time will definitely appeal to the truly entrepreneurial, those who have clear visions of their futures and plans to get there ahead of the pack.

Making and Selling Products to Supplement Your Retirement Income

The 50-plus age group is the fastest growing demographic in the United States and Canada. Retirement businesses have become extremely popular, sometimes even a necessity, because the rising costs of living quickly erode retirement savings and income. The result is lots of people heading into retirement need a little extra income to cover expenses and provide an adequate lifestyle, or to maintain their preretirement lifestyle.

Even if retirement income is not a concern, making and selling products can be a great way to have fun and stay active as you slip into the golden years. People are living longer and healthier than in the past. Because of this, many are seeking new challenges, and starting and operating a business is a great way to embrace new challenges. In fact, many innovative retired entrepreneurs have learned how to have the best of both worlds by combining a business manufacturing and selling products with their travel plans. Some often spend part of the year making products at home, and the balance of the year traveling around the country and selling their goods at flea markets, fairs, trade shows, and right from their RVs at campgrounds.

Starting a Manufacturing Business from Scratch

You have three options in terms of how you get into business making and selling products: You can start a manufacturing business from scratch. You can buy an existing manufacturing business. Or, you can buy a franchise specializing in manufacturing products. For many reasons, the most common option is to start a business from scratch. First, depending on the products you intend to manufacture, operating location requirements, and equipment needs, less money is generally needed to start a business from scratch. It is more than possible to start a manufacturing business with excellent profit and growth potential with an initial investment of $1,000 or less. Second, many people choose to turn a hobby such as woodcrafts or sewing into a business. Third, if you want to make and sell products only part-time or seasonally, there is little sense in buying a business and paying a premium. By starting a business from scratch rather than buying a business, you will have lower investment, products that you want to make, and the ability to choose your level of commitment in terms of time and location.

The disadvantages to starting a business from scratch are the same things that make starting a business attractive—lower initial investment, little regulation, and quick start-up. Because you can literally decide what type of product you are going to produce today and be open for business tomorrow, you may leave no time to properly research and plan the business. Also unlike buying an operating business, there are no existing customers or any revenue stream to help pay for fixed operating costs. You have to build the business to the break-even point and then profitability from scratch, which may take a substantial amount of time— weeks, months, or even years. If you do decide to start a business manufacturing products from scratch, you will find the best 202 things to make and sell for big profits featured in Chapter 6, along with numerous resources such as equipment suppliers, wholesale sources, industry associations, product specific publications, and construction plans to assist you in getting started.

Buying a Manufacturing Business

The second option is to purchase an existing manufacturing business, one that has a customer base and is generating revenue. If you want instant results and do not want to invest the time required to start a business from scratch, buying a currently operating business is probably a better choice. If you choose this route, remember that no less planning and research should go into finding the right business. Perhaps it will require even more research than starting a business from scratch because buying a business usually means a larger investment, which warrants careful research and planning to minimize risk. If you buy a business, you still need to research the marketplace, create a target customer profile, identify competitors, and develop business and marketing plans as you would for any business venture.

A big advantage of purchasing an operating business is that you can often negotiate terms, meaning you pay a portion of the purchase price upfront and the balance in installments or balloon payments. This gives you the ability to make the installments payments out of business revenues. In effect, you will actually be purchasing the business for no more than your down payment. Of course, before buying any business, make sure to hire a lawyer to examine the purchase agreement and an accountant to review financial statements and conduct a business valuation. Also, do your own investigative work. Talk to customers, employees, suppliers, and the local better business bureau. Make sure agreements and contracts with customers and suppliers are transferable, staying with the business and not the with the exiting owner. It is also a good idea to have the current owner stay on after the sale for a reasonable amount of time to train you in the manufacturing of the products, in operating the business, and in sales to make a smooth transition. Have a noncompetition clause built into the sale agreement to preclude the past owner from starting a business manufacturing similar products within a set geographic area for a fixed period of time.

If you decide to buy a manufacturing business, there are a number of options for finding the right one. You can contact commercial realtors, scan Business for Sale ads, or contact The International Business Brokers Association, ♂ www. ibba.org, which has links to more than 1,100 independent business brokers around the world. Another option is to go online and scan Business for Sale sites such as Biz Buy Sell, ♂ www.bizbuysell.com, which is billed as the internet's largest business-for-sale portal.

Buying a Franchise

You also have the option of purchasing a franchise involved in the manufacturing and sales of products. This is a great option for people who want a proven management system, initial and ongoing training and support, and the benefits associated with branding on a large-scale basis. With a franchise operation, you usually have the combined strength of many franchisees as opposed to the possible weaknesses of one independent small business. The combined strengths can help lower costs by purchasing goods and services in bulk and enable you to reach a broader audience through collective advertising.

Unfortunately, there are also disadvantages associated with purchasing a franchise. You typically have less control and independence in all areas of your business than you do when operating an independent business because one doctrine of the franchise model is conformity through consistent brand management. Also keep in mind that if you decide to buy a franchise, you still have to take the same precautions in terms of research and planning that you would when starting or purchasing any business. Make sure the franchise is engaged in something you want to do and believe you would enjoy. Become a customer to make sure that you like and believe in the products being made and sold. A good match is still a key requirement for success. Visit and talk to other franchisees to get firsthand feedback about the business, franchisor, and management systems. And always enlist the services of a lawyer to go over the franchisor's Uniform Franchise Offering Circular to decipher legalese for you.

If you decide that a buying and operating a franchise business is right for you, I have included a few franchise opportunities focused on the manufacturing and sale of products as resources in Chapter 6; they are highlighted with a star (★) icon. You can also contact the International Franchise Association, ✆ www.franchise. org, or the Canadian Franchise Association, ✆ www.cfa.ca. Both organizations can provide information to help you find the right franchise.

2

TAKING CARE OF LEGAL AND FINANCIAL ISSUES

Beginning a manufacturing products for sale business is like starting any business—there are legal and financial issues that must be considered, whether your business is making and selling doll houses from home or employing numerous people and shipping products worldwide. A few of the legal and financial issues that you will need to deal with are registering a business name and selecting a legal business structure, obtaining a business license and other related permits, obtaining a sales tax ID number, obtaining insurance coverage, and opening a commercial bank account.

Money spent on professional, legal, and financial advice is money well spent. Lawyers with small business experience will be able to advise you on which legal business structure best meets your specific needs, insurance and liability issues, legal documents, vendor agreements, and many other legal issues. In other words, they will decipher legalese for you and help make sense of complicated matters pertaining to business. Likewise, accountants will decipher the tough financial information you need to know in order to comply with state and federal tax issues, as well as help establish and maintain financial records.

Legal Business Structure Options

From a legal standpoint, the first order of business is to choose and register a business name for your new manufacturing venture, apply for and obtain the required licenses and permits, as well as select a business structure—sole proprietorship, partnership, limited liability corporation, or corporation. Issues such as start-up budget, business goals, and exposure to personal liability will be determining factors when selecting a business structure for most entrepreneurs. Many people choose a sole proprietorship if they are on a tight budget and comfortable with liability issues, whereas a partnership is the right choice if you will be operating your new manufacturing business with your spouse, a family member, or a friend. A limited liability corporation (LLC) or corporation is the right choice if you plan on substantially growing your business and if you want to minimize personal liability concerns.

Registering a Business Name and Permits

Registering a business name is very straightforward. You can name the business after your legal name, such as Steve's Patio Furniture Manufacturing, or you can choose a fictitious business name, such as East Coast Patio Furniture Manufacturing. Make sure that you have two or three alternate name options ready to go in case another business is already using your first choice. The cost to register a business name varies by state and province, but it is generally less than $200 to register a sole proprietorship, including name search and filing fees. Because you must show proof of business registration to establish a commercial bank account, buy products wholesale, and secure credit card merchant accounts, for instance, you have to register your business, there are no shortcuts. In the United States you can register your business name through the United States Small Business Administration, ♂ www.sba.gov to find an office near you. In Canada you can register your business through a provincial Canadian Business Service Center. Log on to ♂ www.cbsc.org to find an office near you.

Meeting licensing and permit regulations are also important issues to consider. It does not matter if you will be making and selling birdhouse part time or manufacturing products that are shipped worldwide; all businesses must meet various licensing and permit requirements, which vary widely depending on the product(s) you manufacture, operating location, how the products are sold, and how the products are shipped. In all probability, you will to need to obtain several licenses and permits. At a minimum, you will need a business license and a resale certificate or sales tax permit ID number to enable you to collect and remit sales tax on products sold. Almost all states and provinces now impose a sales tax on products sold directly to consumers. It is the business owner's responsibility to collect and remit sales tax. Sales tax permits are also needed when purchasing goods for resale from manufacturers and wholesalers so the goods can be bought tax-free.

Likewise, to legally operate a business in all municipalities in the United States and Canada, you will need to obtain a business license. Business license costs vary from $50 to $1,000 per year depending on your geographic location, expected sales, and the type of products you manufacture. Because they are issued at the municipal level, contact your city/county clerk or permit office for the full requirements. Additional permits and licenses that may be needed can include everything from a health permit if you manufacture food products to a home occupation permit if you are going to manufacture and sell products from home.

The U.S. Small Business Administration (SBA) provides an online directory indexed by state outlining where and how business licenses and sales tax permits and ID numbers can be obtained. This directory can be found at ♂ www. sba.gov/hotlist/license.html. In Canada, you can obtain a federal Goods and Services Sales/Harmonized Sales Tax (GST/HST) number by contacting the Canada Customs and Revenue Agency at ♂ www.ccra-adrc.gc.ca. Additionally, in the United States and Canada you can also contact your chamber of commerce to inquire about business license requirements and fees: United States, ♂ www. chamber.com; Canada, ♂ www.chamber.ca.

Sole Proprietorship

The sole proprietorship is the most common type of legal business structure, mainly because it is the simplest and least expensive to start and maintain. A sole proprietorship means your business entity and your personal affairs are merged together as one—a single tax return, personal liability for all accrued business debts and actions, and control of all revenues and profits. It is, however, still important to separate your business finances from your personal finances for record-keeping and income tax reasons.

The biggest advantage of a sole proprietorship is that it is very simple and inexpensive to form and can be started, altered, bought, sold, or closed at any time, quickly and inexpensively. Also, outside of routine business registrations, permits, and licenses, there are few government regulations. The biggest disadvantage of a sole proprietorship is that you are 100 percent liable for any number of business activities gone wrong, which can mean losing any and all personal assets, including investments and real estate, as a direct result of successful litigation or debts accrued by the business.

Partnership

A partnership allows two or more people to start, operate, and own a business. This is also a popular legal structure because like a sole proprietorship, a nonincorporated partnership is easy, quick, and cheap to form. However, if you do choose to start a business with a family member, friend, or business partner, make sure the partnership is based on a written agreement, not just a verbal agreement. The partnership agreement should address issues such as financial investment, profit distribution, duties of each partner, and an exit strategy should one partner want out of the agreement or die. Like a sole proprietorship, business profits are split amongst partners proportionate to their ownership and are treated as taxable personal income.

Perhaps the biggest advantage of a partnership is that financial risk and work are shared by more than one person, which allows each partner to specialize within the business for the benefit of the collective team. Record-keeping requirements are basic and on par with a sole proprietorship. Unfortunately, partnerships also have disadvantages. The most significant is that each partner is legally responsible and personally liable for the other partners' actions in the business because a nonincorporated partnership offers no legal protection from liability issues. All partners are equally responsible for the businesses debts, liabilities, and actions.

Limited Liability Corporation

A limited liability corporation combines many of the characteristics of a corporation with those of a partnership in that it provides protection from personal liabilities like a corporation, but has the tax advantages of a partnership. Limited liability corporations can be formed by one or more people, called LLC members, who alone or together organize a legal entity separate and distinct from the owners' personal affairs in most respects.

The advantages of a limited liability corporation over a corporation or partnership are that they are less expensive to form and maintain than a corporation, offer protection from personal liability that partnerships do not provide, and have simplified taxation and reporting rules in comparison to a corporation. Because of these advantages, limited liability corporations have become the fastest growing form of business structure in the United States. In the United States you can file online using a service such as Corp America, ♂ www.corpamerica.com, or contact the American Bar Association, ☎ (202) 662-1000, ♂ www.abanet.org, to find a lawyer who specializes in filing in your area. In Canada, you can file online using a service such as Canadian Corp, ♂ www.canadiancorp.com, or contact the Canadian Bar Association, ☎ (800) 267-8860, ♂ www.cba.org, to find a lawyer who specializes in filing in your area.

Corporation

The most complicated business structure is the corporation. When you form a corporation, you create a separate and distinct legal entity from the shareholders of the corporation. Because the corporation becomes its own entity, it pays taxes, assumes debt, can legally sue, can be legally sued, and, as a tax-paying entity, must pay taxes on its taxable income (profit) prior to paying any dividends to the shareholders. But the company's finances and financial records are completely separate from those of the shareholders.

The biggest advantage to incorporating your business is that you can greatly reduce your own personal liability. Because a corporation is its own entity, it can legally borrow money and be held accountable in a number of matters from a legal standpoint. In effect, this releases you from personal liability. The major disadvantage is double taxation. Corporation profits are taxed, and then the same profits are taxed again in the form of personal income tax when distributed to the shareholders as a dividend. Unfortunately, the same does not hold true if the corporation loses money. Financial losses cannot be used as a personal income tax deduction for shareholders. Again, in the United States you can file online using a service such as Corp America, ♂ www.corpamerica.com, or contact the American Bar Association, ☎ (202) 662-1000, ♂ www.abanet.org, to find a lawyer who specializes in filing in your area. In Canada you can file online using a service such as Canadian Corp, ♂ www.canadiancorp.com, or contact the Canadian Bar Association, ☎ (800) 267-8860, ♂ www.cba.org, to find a lawyer who specializes in filing in your area.

Insurance Coverage

Purchasing appropriate insurance is the only way that you can be 100 percent sure that in the event of a catastrophic event, your family, business, assets, and customers will be protected. Tracking down the right insurance for your specific needs depends on the products you will be manufacturing and can be a time-intensive endeavor because of the shear number of insurance companies and types of coverage available. It makes sense to enlist the services of a licensed insurance agent to do the research and legwork for you. Not only will the agent be able to decipher insurance legalese for you, but she will also be able to find the best coverage for your individual needs at the lowest cost. To find a suitable insurance agent in the United States, you can contact the Independent Insurance Agents and Brokers of America at ♂ www.iiaa.org. In Canada, you can contact the Insurance Brokers Association of Canada at ♂ www.ibac.ca. A few of the more important types of insurance coverage—property, liability, workers' compensation, and disability insurance—are discussed below.

Property Insurance

Property insurance generally covers buildings and structures on the property as well as the contents, whether you rent or own the location where you will be manufacturing your goods. Most property insurance policies provide protection in the form of cash settlement or paid repairs in the event of fire, theft, vandalism, flood, earthquake, wind damage, and other acts of God and malicious damage. Floods and earthquakes generally require a separate insurance rider. Property insurance is the starting point from which business owners should build, branching out to include specialized tools and equipment, office improvements, inventory, and various liability riders depending on the products you manufacture and sell.

Property insurance, at a minimum, should protect buildings, property, improvements to the business location, tools, equipment, furniture, cash on hand, accounts receivable and payable, as well as restricted liability which is discussed in greater detail below. Additionally, special riders will be needed if you install the products you manufacture at your client's locations, as well as tools, products, and equipment in transit to work sites. All insurance companies provide free quotes, but it is wise to obtain at least three so you can compare costs, coverage, deductibles, and reliability. If you are going to run your business from home, make sure to contact your current insurance agent, and ask questions specific to the products you will be making and selling. In nearly all cases, you will want to increase the value of the contents portion of the policy to cover equipment, inventory, and computers used for business.

Liability Insurance

No matter how diligent you are in terms of taking all necessary precautions to protect your customers and yourself by removing potential perils from your business and the products you make and sell, you could still be held legally responsible for events beyond your control. Product misuse and third-party damages have been grounds for successful litigation in the United States and Canada. So it is better to be safe than sorry. The best way to protect yourself is to get liability insurance that specifically provides protection for the type of manufacturing business you operate and the products you make. Extended liability insurance is often referred to as general business liability or umbrella business liability. It insures a business against accidents and injury that might occur at the business location, at clients' locations, or other perils related to the products and/or services sold. General liability insurance provides protection for the costs associated with successful litigation or claims against your business or you, and covers such things as medical expenses, recovery expenses, property damage, and other costs typically associated with liability situations.

Workers' Compensation Insurance

In the United States and Canada, workers' compensation insurance is mandatory for all the people your business employs—full-time, part-time, or seasonal. Workers' compensation insurance protects employees injured on the job by providing short- or long-term financial benefits as well as by covering medical and rehabilitation costs directly resulting from an on-the-job injury. If you have no employees and operate your business as a sole proprietorship or partnership, workers' compensation insurance is not mandatory unless your business is incorporated. Then officers and any employees must be covered. Rates are based on industry classification, which generally means the more dangerous the work, the higher your premiums will be. Likewise, the more claims for workers' compensation that your business files, the higher your rates will go. Workers' compensation classifications, forms, and guidelines can be especially confusing for first-time entrepreneurs. Fortunately, information about workers' compensation coverage can be found at U.S. Department of Labor Office of Workers' Compensation Programs online at ♂ www.dol.gov/esa/owcp_org.htm. This web page has links to workers' compensation rules and regulations in all states and the District of Columbia. In Canada, log on to ♂ www.awcbc.org, the Association of Workers' Compensation Boards of Canada, which provides links to all provincial and territorial worker compensation offices.

Disability Insurance

If you were sick or injured and could not work, would you have the ability to pay your business expenses and wages? If the answer is no, chances are you need to obtain disability insurance coverage. Disability insurance makes payments to you in the event that a physical illness, mental illness, or bodily injury prevents you from working. Policy benefits and costs vary, depending on coverage, but regardless of the policy you choose, be sure to have a cost of living clause built into the policy, which increases benefits proportionate to the consumer price index. Also tell your insurance agent that you want your disability coverage to include partial disabilities, which enables you to collect partial benefits while working part-time in your business if you cannot return to full-time active duty. And build in a clause that gives you the right to increase your disability insurance benefits as your business and income grows. Disability insurance can also be purchased to cover key employees, managers, and other business partners.

Financing Your New Manufacturing Business

How much money do you need to start your manufacturing business and where will the money come from? It depends on the type of products you will be making and selling, as well as your business location, equipment needs, and method of marketing. I have included a handy start-up costs worksheet (see Figure 2.1) designed to help you calculate how much money will be needed to start your business.

Start-Up Costs Worksheet

Use this worksheet (Figure 2.1) to calculate how much money you will need to start your new business. Ignore items not relevant to your specific business start-up and add items as required.

FIGURE 2.1: Start-Up Costs Worksheet

A. Business Setup

Business registration	$ _____
Business license	$ _____
Vendor's permits	$ _____
Other permits	$ _____
Insurance	$ _____
Professional fees	$ _____
Training and education	$ _____
Bank account	$ _____
Merchant accounts	$ _____

FIGURE 2.1: Start-Up Costs Worksheet, continued

Payment processing equipment $ _____

Association fees $ _____

Deposits $ _____

Other _____ $ _____

                Subtotal A   **$** _____

B. Business Identity

Business cards $ _____

Logo design $ _____

Letterhead $ _____

Envelopes $ _____

Other _____ $ _____

                Subtotal B   **$** _____

C. Office/Storefront/Workshop

Rent deposit $ _____

Damage deposit $ _____

Communication equipment/devices $ _____

Computer hardware $ _____

Software $ _____

Furniture $ _____

Other office equipment $ _____

Office supplies $ _____

Renovations and improvements $ _____

Fixed tools and equipment $ _____

Portable tools and equipment $ _____

Other _____ $ _____

                Subtotal C   **$** _____

D. Transportation

Upfront cost to buy/lease transportation $ _____

Registration $ _____

Insurance $ _____

FIGURE 2.1: Start-Up Costs Worksheet, continued

Special accessories	$ _____
Other _____	$ _____
Subtotal D	**$** _____

E. Web Site

Domain registration	$ _____
Site development fees	$ _____
Search engine and directory	$ _____
Equipment	$ _____
Software	$ _____
Content and web tools	$ _____
Hosting	$ _____
Other _____	$ _____
Subtotal E	**$** _____

F. Marketing

Research and planning costs	$ _____
Signs	$ _____
Brochures and fliers	$ _____
Catalogs	$ _____
Initial advertising budget	$ _____
Initial online promotion budget	$ _____
Product samples	$ _____
Other _____	$ _____
Subtotal F	**$** _____

G. Product Inventory

# 1 _____	$ _____
# 2 _____	$ _____
# 3 _____	$ _____
# 4 _____	$ _____
# 5 _____	$ _____
Subtotal G	**$** _____

FIGURE 2.1: Start-Up Costs Worksheet, continued

Adding Up the Costs

Business setup	$ _____
Business identity	$ _____
Office/storefront/workshop	$ _____
Transportation	$ _____
Web site	$ _____
Marketing	$ _____
Product inventory	$ _____
Total start-up costs	$ _____
Working capital	$ _____
Total investment needed	**$** _____

There are generally three types of capital needed when starting a business: start-up, working, and growth capital.

START-UP CAPITAL

Start-up capital is the money used to start the business and covers expenditures such as equipment purchases, business location rent, office furniture, legal costs, and training costs. There are ways of limiting the amount of start-up capital you need upfront, such as renting or leasing equipment as opposed to purchasing it; nonetheless, you will require some money to start a business.

WORKING CAPITAL

Working capital is critical because it is the money needed to pay all the bills and your wages until the business reaches a break-even point. More than a few entrepreneurs have failed because a lack of operating capital prevented their business from reaching positive cash flow. If your business is part time and you have other income sources, working capital is less critical, especially in terms of paying your wages.

GROWTH CAPITAL

Growth capital is the money needed should you decide to expand your business. Even if your plans are not to expand, lack of growth capital can become an issue if forces beyond your control, such as new competition or new government regulations, impact your business. You may not want to grow, but forces beyond your control may necessitate growth in your business, if only to survive and remain viable. It is not necessary to have growth capital sitting in the bank, but it is a good idea to have a plan in place to access it should the need arise.

Personal Savings

The first way to finance your business venture is by using your own personal savings. If you have the money, self-funding is a good option because it enables you to stay in control of how, when, and why funds are distributed. You do not have to satisfy a banker's or investor's requirements. You will not feel anxious about whether or not you can get the proper funding. You do not have to worry about debt accumulation. And there is no bank or investor loan and interest repayment to make each month. To fund your business start-up personally, the money can come from numerous sources—bank savings accounts, investment certificates, retirement funds, mutual funds and stocks, or insurance policies. In some instances, however, money that you remove from fixed certificates or retirement investments may be subject to additional personal income tax or penalties for early withdrawal or cancellation. It is always wise to consult with an accountant prior to cashing, selling, or redeeming any personal investment. Also keep in mind that, depending on the investment you want to liquidate, you might actually be earning a higher rate of return than the interest rate that you can secure for a business start-up loan. Additional self-funding options include borrowing against other personal assets, such as real estate, antiques, or a boat.

Love Loans

Another good way to fund your business start-up is to ask family members or friends for a loan, which is often referred to as a love loan. There is a potential downside to this method of financing: If your business venture were to fail, would you still be able to pay back the loan? If not, the relationship could be damaged beyond repair. But with that said, many successful business ventures have been built upon love loans. If you decide to borrow from friends or family to fund your business, treat the transaction as you would if you were borrowing from a bank. Have a promissory note drawn up and signed by all parties (see Figure 2.2), noting the full details of the agreement.

Bank Loans

If your credit is sound, you also have the option of applying for a secured or unsecured bank loan to finance your business enterprise. Secured loans are guaranteed

FIGURE 2.2: Sample Promissory Note

This loan agreement is by and between:

Borrower Information

Name _____

Address _____

City _____ State _____ Zip Code _____ Tel _____

Lender Information

Name _____

Address _____

City _____ State _____ Zip Code _____ Tel _____

I, (borrower's name here), promise to pay (lender's name here) the sum of $ _____,
bearing interest at the rate of _____% per annum, and payable in _____ equal
and consecutive monthly installments, commencing on the _____ day of each month
until paid, with a final installment of $ _____ on the _____ day of _____, 20_____,
upon which the loan shall be repaid in full with no further principal or interest amounts
owing.

_____ _____   _____ _____
  Borrower's Signature   Date   Lender's Signature   Date

_____ _____
     Witnessed by   Date

with some other type of investment, such as a guaranteed investment certificate. Unsecured loans are not secured with any investments or assets, and funds are advanced because of your credit worthiness. The advantage of a secured loan is that the interest rate is generally lower, by as much as 5 percent. The disadvantage of a secured loan is that many first-time entrepreneurs do not have investments to secure the loan; otherwise, they would be able to self-finance the start-up.

You can also talk to your bank or trust company about setting up a secured or unsecured line of credit. An advantage of a line of credit over a standard business loan is that you only have to repay interest based on the account balance and not the principal, which is exactly the type of funding flexibility new business start-ups need to get established and grow without the pressure of high debt repayment. If you decide to apply for a business loan or line of credit, go armed with a bulletproof business and marketing plan. Bankers want to know that they are investing in sound and well-researched ideas that have the potential to succeed. Many banks offer small business loan programs. Among them are Bank of America, ♂ www.bankofamerica.com, and Royal Bank, ♂ www.royalbank.com/sme/.

Government Business Loans

In the United States and Canada, there are also government programs in place to assist people in starting a new business. In the United States, these programs are administered through the Small Business Administration (SBA). The most significant of these programs is the SBA business loan program, which makes available start-up funding loaned from microlending institutions (participating banks and credit unions) and guaranteed in full or part by the SBA. There are various levels of qualification for the business loans program, so check with your local SBA office for more details and to see if you qualify. In Canada, most small business financial aid programs are administered through the Business Development Bank of Canada.

Even though these programs are in place in the United States and Canada to assist the funding needs for new and existing small business ventures, they are in no way a guarantee that you will secure financial assistance. Each application is based on the potential of the venture and the principals involved in the business. All the usual steps, such as a complete business and marketing plan, are required if you intend to pursue government small business funding.

United States	*Canada*
U.S. Small Business Administration (SBA) Financial Programs 409 Third Street SW Washington, DC 20416 ☎ (800) 827-5722 ♂ www.sba.gov/financing/	Business Development Canada BDC Building 5 Place Ville Marie, Suite 400 Montreal, Quebec H3B 5E7 ☎ (877) 232-2269 ♂ www.bdc.ca

Private Investors

Start-up funds can also come from private investors. But if you choose this route, be prepared to make compromises because they may want an equity position in the business, to work in the business, a high rate of interest, or a combination of any or all of these as a condition for funding. If you decide to take in a private investor who wants to remain silent in the business, then a good match between you is of less concern. However, if the investor will be taking a hands-on role in the business, effectively making him a partner, there are more issues to consider. For instance, you will need a formal partnership agreement. Likewise, all parties should share a similar excitement for the business and have similar future goals and ambitions. Also look for investors who have specific experience and resources that can be utilized for the benefit of the business, such as sales and marketing skills.

The most common way that people find investors to help finance a business start-up or expansion is by placing a classified advertisement in their local newspapers or an industry magazine, especially if the deal involves amounts less than $100,000. There is also a great number of venture capital web sites, such as Venture Directory Online, ♂ www.venturedirectory.com, or V Finance, ♂ www.vfinance.com, listing entrepreneurs or venture capitalists (also known as business angels) who are seeking to invest in new and existing businesses.

Bootstrapping Techniques

Financially challenged entrepreneurs also have the option of using bootstrapping techniques. The four main bootstrapping techniques are using credit cards, barter, leasing or renting, and supplier terms to help reduce the amount of money needed to get started.

CREDIT CARDS

The drawback to using credit cards to fund your business enterprise is that most have high annual interest rates, some as much as 20 percent. But if money is in short supply and you feel confidant that your manufacturing business will fly, using your credit cards may be your only option. If you are going to use credit cards to finance some or all of your business start-up, then plan early. Try to pay off your credit cards to a zero balance before starting, as doing so leaves you carrying less debt, with lower monthly obligations and the opportunity to borrow more money against the cards to start your business. Shop for credit cards with the lowest interest rate, no annual fees, and with air miles or redeemable shopping points. You should apply for credit cards that are specifically for small business use, such as the Visa Small Business Card, ♂ www.usa.visa.com/business, or American Express Small Business, ♂ www.americanexpress.com. Business credit cards generally charge a lower annual interest rate and include useful small business features such as online bookkeeping and access, business travel features, business insurance options, and no extra charges for cash advances.

BARTER

You can also barter for products, services, and equipment to help reduce the amount of money you need upfront to get your business started. Barter clubs for small business owners, such as National Trade Association, ♂ www.ntatrade.com, and First Canadian Barter Exchange, ♂ www.barterfirst.com, have become extremely popular. Online barter is especially popular because all it takes is a simple click of the mouse. The barter premise is very straightforward. Simply offer the goods that you manufacture in exchange for goods and services that you need to start, operate, or promote your business. For instance, if you manufacture furniture, offer to trade your goods to a local printer in exchange for business cards, stationery, and marketing brochures for your business. Bartering with other businesses will not supply all of the money that you need to start and operate your new business, but it can greatly reduce the amount of cash required.

LEASING AND RENTING

Leasing or renting equipment is another strategy. Although it will not completely fund your entire start-up, like barter it can greatly reduce the amount of cash that you need. Renting or leasing equipment, tools, or fixtures enables you to save your precious money for other business-building activities such as marketing. An added benefit of renting or leasing equipment is the fact that in most cases the total rental or lease payment is a 100 percent business expense for tax purposes, as opposed to a sliding scale of depreciation on owned equipment. When the lease or rental term is over, you can upgrade to a new model without having to worry about selling or trading in the old one, or simply turn it in and be done.

SUPPLIER TERMS

Another way to bootstrap your way into business is to ask your suppliers for a revolving credit account that gives you up to 90 days or more to pay for goods and services you need to start or operate your business or for materials that can be made into products and sold to customers for a profit. More othen than not, you have to demonstrate to suppliers that you are a worthy credit risk prior to their extending credit to your business. This is usually accomplished by the supplier conducting a credit check on you or through some sort of security guarantee that you provide. If your credit history is good, in some cases you can establish revolving credit accounts with suppliers that will give you up to 90 days to pay, which will enable you to make and sell products long before you have to pay for all or a portion of the raw materials used in the process.

Additional Money Issues

To keep your new business humming along, you will need to be paid in full and on time for the products you make. You also need a basic understanding of money management, even if you hire an accountant or bookkeeper to manage the books. Therefore, you will need to familiarize yourself with basic bookkeeping and money management principles and activities such as understanding credit, reading bank statements and tax forms, and making sense of accounts receivable and payable. Likewise, you also have to give careful consideration to the purchase payment options you offer customers, such as credit cards and revolving credit accounts for commercial customers. These topics and additional money issues are discussed in further detail below. Information about setting wholesale and retail prices for the products you make can be found in Chapter 4, Everything Else You Need to Know.

Opening a Bank Account

Once you have chosen a name and registered your business, the next step is to open a commercial bank account. Opening a business bank account is easy: Choose the bank you want to work with (think small business friendly), and set an appointment to open an account. When you go, make sure you take personal identification as well as your business name registration because proof of a legally formed business is generally required to open a commercial bank account. The next step will be to deposit funds into your new account (even $100 is okay). If your credit is sound, also ask the bank to attach a line of credit to your account, which can prove very useful when making purchases for the business or during slow sales periods to cover overhead until business increases. Likewise, while you are there, ask about credit card merchant accounts, debits accounts, and other services the bank offers to small business customers.

Bookkeeping

When you are ready to set up your financial books, there are two options—do it yourself or hire an accountant or bookkeeper. You might want to do both: Do your own books, but hire an accountant to prepare year-end financial statements and tax forms. If you choose the do-it-yourself option, invest in accounting software such as QuickBooks, ♂ www.quickbooks.com, or Quicken, ♂ www.quicken.com, mainly because the software is easy to use and makes bookkeeping almost enjoyable. Most accounting software also includes features that enable you to create invoices, track bank account balances and merchant account information, and keep track of accounts payable and receivable. If you are unsure about your bookkeeping abilities, you may want to hire a bookkeeper to do your books on a monthly basis and a chartered accountant to audit the books quarterly and prepare year-end business statements and tax returns. If you are only building picnic tables and selling them from home on weekends to earn a few extra bucks, there is little need for accounting software or accounting services. Simply invest in a basic ledger and record all business costs and sales. You have to use a common-sense approach when calculating how much to invest in your business versus expected revenues and profits.

Also remember to keep business and tax records for a minimum of seven years, as this is amount of time the IRS and Revenue Canada can request past business revenue and expense information. To find an accountant or bookkeeper in your area, you can contact the United States Association of Chartered Accountants, ☎ (212) 334-2078, ♂ www.acaus.org, or the American Institute of Professional Bookkeepers, ☎ (800) 622-0121, ♂ www.aipb.com. In Canada, you can contact the Chartered Accountants of Canada, ☎ (416) 977-3222, ♂ www.cica.ca, or the Canadian Bookkeepers Association, ☎ (604) 664-7576, ♂ www.c-b-a.ca.

Accepting Cash, Checks, and Debit Cards

In today's' supercompetitive selling environment, businesses must often provide customers with various payment methods, including cash, debit card, credit card, and electronic cash, especially businesses that mainly sell directly to consumers. In other words, you have to make it very easy and convenient for people to buy your products. Consumers expect choices when it comes time to pay for their purchases, and if you elect not to provide these choices, expect fewer sales. There is a cost to providing most of these purchase payment options—account fees, transaction fees, equipment rental, and merchant fees based on a percentage of the total sales value. But, these expenses must be viewed as a cost of doing business in the 21st century. You can, however, reduce fees by shopping for the best service with the best prices. Not all banks, merchant accounts, and payment processing services are the same, and fees vary widely.

Cash is the first way to get paid, which is great because it is liquid with no processing time required. As fast as cash comes in, you can use it to pay bills and invest in business-building activities to increase revenues and profits. The major downside to cash is risk. You could get robbed or lose it. In that instance, collecting from your insurance company could prove difficult if there is no paper transaction as proof. Even if you prefer not to receive cash, there are people who will pay in cash, so make daily bank deposits during daylight hours as required and also invest in a good quality safe for times when you cannot get to the bank.

Another popular way people pay is with a check, but not all businesses are comfortable with checks. You will have to determine if you will accept checks or not. If you do, take a few precautions to ensure you don't get left holding a rubber check. Ask to see a picture ID, and write the customer's driver's license number on the back of the check. If the amount of the check exceeds a few hundred dollars, ask the buyer to get the check certified or pay with a bank draft instead. Also get in the habit of checking dates and dollar amounts to make sure they are right. It can be time consuming to have to get a new check because of a simple error.

Debit cards are yet another option, but they require that you buy or rent a debit card terminal to accept these payments. Most banks and credit unions offer business clients debit card equipment and services. The processing equipment will set you back about $40 per month for a terminal connected to a conventional telephone line and about $100 per month for a cellular terminal, plus the cost of the telephone line or cellular service. There is also a transaction fee charged by the bank and payable by you every time there is a debit card transaction, which ranges from 10 cents to 50 cents per transaction, based on variables such as dollar value and frequency of use.

Credit Card Merchant Accounts

Many consumers have replaced paper money in favor of plastic when buying goods and services. This is true especially of people collecting shopping points and air miles offered by credit card companies. In fact, giving your customers the option to pay for purchases with a credit card is often crucial to success, especially if you plan to do business on the internet. Credit cards and electronic cash are used to complete nearly all web sales and financial transactions. Therefore, you will want to offer customers credit card payment options. To do this you will need to open a credit card merchant account. Get started by visiting your bank or credit union or by contacting a merchant account broker such as 1st American Card Service, ♂ www.1stamericancardservice.com; Cardservice International, ♂ www. cardservice.com; or Merchant Account Express, ♂ www.merchantexpress.com, to inquire about opening an account. Providing your credit is sound, you will run into few obstacles. If your credit is poor, you may have difficulties opening a merchant account or have to provide a substantial security deposit. If you are still unsuccessful, the next best option is to open an account with an online payment service provider, which is discussed in the next section.

The advantages of opening a credit card merchant account are numerous. Studies have proven that merchants who accept credit cards can increase sales by up to 50 percent. Not to mention that you can accept credit card payments online, over the telephone, by mail, or in person. You can also sell products on an installment basis by obtaining permission to charge your customer's credit card monthly, or as per agreement. Of course, these benefits come at a cost. You will have to pay an application fee and set-up fee, purchase or rent processing equipment and software, pay administration and statement fees, and pay processing and transaction fees ranging from 2 to 8 percent on total sales volumes. Once again, these fees must be viewed as the cost of doing business.

Online Payment Services

Online payment services allow people and businesses to exchange currency over the internet electronically. PayPal, ♂ www.paypal.com, offering personal and business account services, is one of the more popular online payment services with more than 40 million members in 45 countries. Both types of accounts allow funds to be transferred electronically amongst members, but only the business account enables merchants to accept credit card payments for goods and services. Another popular online payment service is Veri Sign Pay Flow, ♂ www.veri sign.com.

The advantages of online payment services are that they are quick, easy, and cheap to open, regardless of your credit rating or anticipated sales volumes, and you can receive payment from any customer with an e-mail account. You can also have the funds deposited directly into your account, have a check issued and mailed, or leave funds in your account to draw on using your debit card. The only real disadvantage is most services redirect your customers to their web site to complete the transaction. This can confuse people, who in some cases will abandon the purchase. Nonetheless, the advantages of online payment services far outweigh any disadvantages. If you plan on selling your products online, you will need to establish one or more ways for customers to pay for their purchases electronically.

Establishing Payment Terms and Debt Collection

In most cases there is no need to extend inhouse credit to consumers, but if you are going to sell your manufactured products to other businesses on a wholesale basis, you will need to establish a payment terms policy. Businesses generally want revolving credit accounts ranging from 30, 60, 90, or sometimes 120 days after delivery to pay. Ideally, you want to be paid as quickly as possible, so you might want to offer a 2 percent discount if invoices are paid within one week. It is important that you establish clear, written payment terms with each customer prior to delivering products. You also have to remember that credit is a privilege and not a right. New customers have to earn the right to buy on credit, meaning they should establish a history of buying and paying in full before you grant credit privileges.

If you do extend credit, make sure to conduct a credit check first, especially when larger sums of money are at stake and with new customers. There are three major credit reporting agencies serving the United States and Canada—Trans Union, ✆ www.tuc.com; Equifax, ✆ www.equifax.com; and Experian, ✆ www.experian.com. All three credit bureaus compile and maintain credit files on just about every person and business.

No matter how careful you are, once in a while you will not be paid on time—or at all. What can you do to get paid? The first rule is to keep the lines of communication open with your delinquent customer, and keep the pressure on to get paid by writing letters, calling, and personal visits. You cannot legally intimidate someone into paying you, but you can explain that you can hurt his credit rating or sue him in court if he does not pay. Another option is to hire a collection agency to collect the outstanding debt. The Association of Credit and Collection Professionals, ✆ www.acainternational.org, is a good starting point to find a collection agency to work with. The final option is to take the delinquent account to small claims court, but small claims courts have limits, ranging from $1,500 to $25,000 depending on your location, on how much you can sue for. Filing fees vary by state and province as well, and these must be paid upfront. But if you win, the fees are added to your award. You can learn more about the small claims court process and filing fees by contacting your local courthouse.

3

SETTING UP SHOP

To make products, you need a base of operations. In other words, you need to set up shop. Depending on the products you intend to make and sell, setting up shop can mean anything from converting a spare bedroom into a candle-making room to leasing an industrial factory so you can manufacture a full line of patio furniture on a mass scale. Ultimately, the products you make will dictate where you set up shop—at home, in a factory, or in a retail storefront.

Setting up shop goes far beyond a physical location and includes things such as equipment and tool needs, transportation, office furniture, technology, and communication devices. Further, setting up shop also means that you must build a business team, create a business image, and possibly take your business location online with a web site so you can sell your products to consumers around the globe. The purpose of this chapter is to cover some of the important issues related to locating your shop and business.

Making Products at Home

Can you legally operate a business and make products from your home? Chances are the answer is yes, but probably with restrictions. There is no across-the-board set of rules. Each community in the United States and Canada has its own home business zoning regulations and specific usage guidelines. Most municipalities allow residential home business operations, providing they do not have a negative impact on neighborhoods and there are no outstanding safety or hazard issues. From a zoning standpoint, potential issues include exterior signage, air pollution, parking, noise, fire, storage of hazardous substances, deliveries and shipping, employees working from your home, and customers visiting your home. Long before you decide to start and operate your business from home, you need to check zoning regulations and restrictions. I suggest a visit to your local municipal planning department or bylaws office for further information.

If you have the needed space and zoning permits, making products at home is a great idea because it keeps start-up costs low, minimizing financial risk. It is also very convenient to work where you live. A two-minute commute free of traffic is a great way to start the day. Information about merchandising and selling products from home can be found in Chapter 5, The Best Places to Sell the Things You Make. There is a lot to know about operating a business at home, more than space permits here. Consequently, you might want to check out 📖 *Entrepreneur Magazine's Ultimate Homebased Business Handbook* (Entrepreneur Press, 2004) from your local library or purchase a copy to keep as a constant reference. The book is an A to Z explanation about everything you need to know to start and operate a business at home.

Homebased Workspace Options

Depending on the products you make, homebased workspace options include a spare bedroom, converted garage, basement, renovated attic, new addition, or detached structure. Each option has advantages and disadvantages, and careful consideration must be given to the space needs of your family, as well as how space is currently being utilized for day-to-day living, special occasions, seasonal activities, and guests. Selecting the right workspace requires balancing the needs of your business, the needs of your family, and often the needs of your customers. As a rule of thumb, compromises will have to be made on all fronts.

When selecting your workspace, choose a room with a door so you can keep business in and family, friends, and pets out, as required. Try to work from one space because working out of two or three separate areas in the home is less productive. Make your workspace a single-use area, not a room that doubles as the children's playroom on weekends. If your home is small, single use space can be difficult to accommodate, but be creative and define a business-only workspace.

There are a multitude of points to consider when setting up business at home, such as:

- Do local zoning regulations allow manufacturing businesses to be operated from residential properties?
- Will you have to upgrade or install new mechanical services such as heat, cooling, electrical, and plumbing to accommodate your business?
- Do you have adequate space for manufacturing, parking, shipping, receiving, and storage?
- Do you need to install a ventilation system? If so, what about the air and odor pollution it expels? Will noise pollution bother your neighbors? If you will be operating a business that creates noise or generates byproducts (dust, mess, fumes), look to the garage or an outside structure as a possible solution.
- Do you have to upgrade your home to meet fire safety standards because of the business or the product you manufacture?
- Is the appearance of your home suitable for client visits? Peeling paint, threadbare carpets, and broken porch boards can send potential clients the wrong signals about your business.
- If applicable, do you have the space required to accommodate customer visits, and does your home have good access and visibility for customers?
- Can employees or outside contractors legally work from your home? And if so, do you have enough room, and can you provide them with the basic necessities, such as washroom facilities, space for breaks and lunch, and closet space for coats?

Planning and Renovating Your Workspace

You greatly maximize your chances of establishing the most productive workspace at the lowest possible cost if you take the time necessary to plan your workspace well in advance of actually setting it up. Planning enables you to carefully design your workspace, taking into account all of your needs, while avoiding potentially costly mistakes as a result of lack of planning. Assuming no renovations are needed, the first order of business is to empty and clean the workspace. This is also a good time to paint and take care of minor maintenance issues. The next step is to take measurements and make a scale drawing of the room on a large piece of paper or Bristol board, noting the location of windows, doors, electrical outlets, telephone jacks, cable outlets, and lights. Once you have an accurate, scaled floor plan, you can move on to purchasing tools, equipment, and furniture that fits your space and suits your business needs.

Ideally, you do not want to have to renovate if you do not need to. Sometimes, however, you will have to alter your workspace or other areas of your home to accommodate your new business. Renovating can be challenging for a number of reasons, but the main challenges are inconvenience, noise, mess, and cost. If renovating is unavoidable, you have to decide if you can do the work or an experienced contractor is necessary. If the job is straightforward, and if you have the time, tools, and talents necessary to do the work, by all means do the work. It can save you a substantial amount of money on labor costs. If the job is small but too complicated for you to tackle, consider hiring a local handyperson. Expect to pay about $25 to $35 per hour plus the costs of materials. If, however, your new workspace is a major renovation that includes upgrading mechanicals, removing walls, and installing new doors, you will be well advised to call in a professional contractor to carry out the required work.

If you decide to hire a contractor, the following are a few tips to ensure the job goes smoothly:

- Give the contractor all the details about your business, including the products that you will be making, selling space if needed, and the types of equipment you will be using. These details help the contractor understand the nature of the job, and he or she may have a few cost-saving suggestions to pass along.
- Obtain three quotes, and base your decision on value, quality, price, warranties, and reputation, not just the lowest price.
- Call the contractor's references to make sure past clients were satisfied, and request proof of liability insurance and workers' compensation insurance.
- Make sure that the scope of work and contracts are in writing, very detailed, all-inclusive, and signed by both parties.
- Set payment terms in four installments, 25 percent deposit, 25 percent progress installment, 25 percent on substantial completion, and the balance within 30 days after full competition.

- Find out which party is responsible for securing building permits and if the costs of these are included in the estimate. This is a very important point. If you decide to renovate without a permit and the required inspections from your local municipality, should there later be structural, electrical, or other mechanical problems with the work that has been done, your insurance company may not compensate you because the work was completed illegally.

- Make sure that all warranty information is included in the written agreement. The workmanship portion of the warranty should be a minimum of five years from the date of competition.

Making Products at an Alternate Location

If your home is not suitable as a manufacturing location, or if the products you are going to make are not suitable to be made at your home, you will need to rent or purchase a location. Best advice is to rent rather than purchase a location, at least until you have a proven and profitable business record. What location is right for your business venture—retail storefront or an industrial location such as a factory? This decision will largely be based on your marketing objectives as well as the types of products you are going to make. Some products such as designer fashions and specialty foods can be made and sold from a retail storefront, while others, such as furniture, that generate substantially more by-products are better suited to be manufactured in a industrial environment. Information about merchandising products from a retail storefront or factory can be found in Chapter 5.

Retail Storefront

As mentioned, not all products are suitable for retail storefront production, but many are, especially those such as specialty foods, designer fashions and accessories, awards and trophies, golf clubs, signs, stained-glass products, gift baskets, pottery, and pet treats. If your approach to marketing and sales is to mainly rely on walk-in traffic to generate new sales, you will need to rent a storefront location—in a mall, strip plaza, downtown location, or freestanding commercial building in a retail district.

Like any business that relies on walk-in traffic to generate the lion's share of sales, location, location, and location are the critical success factors. You have to choose your real estate wisely; without the right location the chance of failure and financial loss increases exponentially. Consequently, your storefront location needs to be in proximity to the largest percentage of your target audience, and it must also have excellent visibility. Choosing a less visible space to save $1,000 per month on rent is a waste of money, because you will spend an additional $2,000 a month on advertising to reach your target audience to inform them where your business is located. When selecting the right retail location there are also many additional points to consider, including:

- The rent must be within your budget, and the lease terms must be favorable.
- The location must meet your size requirements.
- The location must meet zoning, fire, and handicap accessibility regulations.
- Mechanicals such as electricity, heating, plumbing, and communications must meet your requirements.
- Renovations are costly. Look for a location that requires the least amount of alterations possible while still meeting your needs.
- The location should have adequate customer parking, preferably free, and also have good access to public transit.
- The store should have excellent visibility and meet your pedestrian foot and passing motorist traffic counts requirements.
- Regardless of location—mall, strip plaza, or free-standing building—the store should have great curb appeal and be consistent with the type of business image you want to project.

Additionally, make sure that there are no restrictive covenants in place that would prevent you from making your specific product, and be wary of rules that prevent you from marketing and promoting your business in the style that you want. Restrictive covenants could include things such as sign size, style, and placement, as well as store operating hours.

Factory

When renting an industrial location such as a factory to manufacture products, location is not as big a concern as it is with a retail location. But at the same time, the factory should still be central to suppliers, customers, transportation routes, and you and employees in terms of travel time and convenient access. Another area of consideration for manufacturing businesses are ever-increasing environmental rules and legislation such as energy consumption and hazardous and non-hazardous waste disposal. These rules have to be followed to the letter of the law, or offenders face steep fines. Therefore, it is in your best interest to find out about environmental rules specific to your business and the types of products you make, prior to setting up shop.

There are also additional issues to consider prior to signing a lease, including:

- Is the rent affordable, and are the lease terms favorable?
- Is the building large enough to meet your production, office, and storage needs?

- Is there adequate employee parking as well as adequate outdoor and indoor space to meet your shipping and receiving requirements?
- Is the building in good repair, or does it require substantial and costly alternations to meet your needs?
- Do the existing mechanical systems such as electricity, plumbing, heating, and communications meet your requirements, or are costly upgrades needed?
- Does the building meet zoning, fire, and safety regulations?

Equipping Your Office and Shop

Ultimately, the types of products you make and how these are sold will determine your needs in terms of office furniture, technology and communication devices, production tools and equipment, transportation and product delivery needs, and inventory management systems. But at the same time, every business needs the basics in these areas, and all are discussed in greater detail below.

Budget is the second issue when equipping your office and shop. Fortunately, there are a few ways to do this on a shoestring budget or at least substantially reduce the amount of money you need up front. The first is to barter or trade for what you need. For instance, if you make and sell patio furniture, contact the local sign shop and ask if they would be interested in trading signs for patio furniture items. Alternately, join a local barter club and trade the products you make with members that sell products and services you need for your business. You can also visit *Barter News*, ✄ www.barternews.com, which is an online magazine dedicated to the world of business barter clubs, organizations, and industry information, to track down a barter club in your area.

Another way to save money on office and shop equipment is to purchase secondhand, factory seconds, or floor models. Scan classified and auction listings in your local newspaper for secondhand office furniture and equipment. Generally you'll save as much as 75 percent by buying used. Also call around to office and equipment retailers and inquire about factory seconds or floor models available. Purchasing seconds or floor models with slight blemishes will often save you as much as 25 percent off the retail price. You can also take the no-money-down route and lease brand new office furniture, shop equipment, and computers for your business or rent these items—with the payments for both being 100 percent deductible as a business expenses.

Office Furniture

If customers will be visiting your manufacturing or showroom location, your office furniture and décor will need to reflect this. If not, it doesn't matter if your furniture is secondhand and mismatched; it just has to suit your needs. Office furniture needs vary from business to business. At minimum you will need a desk, chair, and file storage. Your desk should be large enough to accommodate a computer monitor with tower storage underneath, a printer, and a telephone/fax machine. If you can only splurge on one piece of office furniture, a comfortable and ergonomically correct chair should be that luxury item, especially if your business keeps you in front of the computer or on the telephone for long periods of time. Key features to look for in a good office chair are distance from the seat to floor, adjustable armrests, and seating positions.

Business and customer records are important. Consequently, an investment in a good quality locking file storage system is money well spent. Bookshelves and worktables are also indispensable items for the office. Bookshelves can be used to organize and store books, product catalogs, office supplies, and computer software and disks. Separate worktables are big time savers because they can be used for working on lower priority jobs, such as opening and sorting mail and bookkeeping duties.

Technology

Like office furniture, there are basic technology needs for every business, including computer, operating system, software, monitor, modem, and printer. Depending on the products you make and how these are sold, you might not need the latest technology, but your equipment must be reliable.

- *Computer.* The main considerations are processing speed and data storage capabilities. Because both change on a daily basis, it's best to buy as much speed and memory as you can afford. Desktop computers range in price from a low of $600 to as much as $3,000 for a top-of-the-line system. If your business takes you on the road a lot, consider purchasing a notebook computer, again with as much speed and memory capacity as you can afford. Expect to pay in the range of $1,500 to $4,000.
- *Monitor.* Monitor options are a standard monitor, a flat screen monitor, or a flat panel LCD monitor. LCD monitors are the best choice if desk space is limited. New 17-inch monitors start at about $150, and can go as high as $1,500 for a 21-inch LCD model.
- *Keyboard and mouse.* A basic keyboard and mouse cost about $50, but if you dislike wires cluttering your desktop, consider spending an extra $100 to upgrade to a wireless keyboard and mouse set.
- *Modem.* The majority of computers come with a standard 56K modem, which is needed to connect to the internet. You can opt for a more expensive

modem, giving you the ability to connect to high-speed cable internet (if available in your area), which allows you to download files up to 20 times faster than a standard dial-up internet connection.

- *Printer.* An ink jet printer starts at about $50, while a laser printer costs in the range of $200 to $1,000 depending on features, color options, and print speeds. I suggest you buy a laser printer if you are going to be doing a lot of printing because on average each printed page will cost half as much as what it costs to print a page with a ink jet printer.
- *Digital camera.* A digital camera is an indispensable piece of equipment for business owners. You can take pictures of products and, because the images (photographs) use digital technology, transfer them to your web site, e-mails, or desktop publishing programs. Desktop publishing then enables you to easily create brochures, presentations, catalogs, and fliers in-house and for a fraction of what it costs to have these items created at a printer.

Communications

The proliferation of high-tech communication devices in the last few years makes it very easy to spend a lot of money, but if you can get by with the basics to get started, you can upgrade to new and better equipment from future profits.

- *Telephone.* The first communication device you need is a desktop telephone. Ideally, it will have business features and functions such as on-hold, conferencing, redial, speakerphone, broadcast, and message storage capabilities.
- *Fax machine.* Although fax transmissions have greatly declined in the last few years because of the increased use of e-mail use, a fax machine will still be needed to operate your business. If you do not want to purchase a separate fax machine, you might consider purchasing an all-in-one office document center, which usually includes a telephone, fax, scanner, and copier in one machine. Expect to spend in the range of $250 to $600 for an all-in-one model.
- *Cellular telephone.* A cellular telephone is now a must for all business people. Not only do they enable you to take incoming calls from almost anywhere, but they also enable you to stay in constant contact with your best customers and hottest prospects. Cellular telephone service plans are now very inexpensive, less than $50 per month will give you nearly unlimited access to as many minutes as you need. Consider purchasing a cell phone with internet features so you have the ability to check e-mail when you are away from your computer.

- *Internet connection.* You will also need an internet connection that enables you to access the internet and send and receive e-mails. Unlimited dial-up access generally costs in the range of $15 per month; high-speed access generally runs in the range of $20 to $50 per month, but you will also need to upgrade your modem at additional cost if you choose high speed.

Tools and Equipment

Tool and equipment requirements will be determined by the types of products you manufacture. Entrepreneurs engaged in manufacturing garden sheds will need much different tools and equipment than those engaged in making seashell crafts, for instance. Because requirements vary widely, I have included specific tool and equipment information for many of the products listed in Chapter 6. There are options in terms of how you acquire tools and equipment for your business. You can purchase new tools and equipment, lease them, or rent them on an as-needed basis to get started on a shoestring budget.

The advantage of purchasing new tools and equipment is obvious—no need to worry about equipment breakdowns. At the same time, purchasing new tools and equipment can be a very costly endeavor. Purchasing tools and equipment secondhand is a viable option because with a bit of legwork, it is possible to buy good quality items in excellent working condition at a fraction of the cost of new. Scan classified ads for the equipment you need, check out business closeout sales, and bid for tools and equipment at auction sales and flea markets. The benefit of leasing or renting tools and equipment is lease and rent payments are 100 percent tax deductible, unlike a sliding scale of depreciation for new or used equipment. Ultimately, your tool and equipment requirements, as well as your budget, will determine if you buy, lease, or rent.

Product Delivery

Product delivery is an important aspect of every manufacturing business when selling direct to consumers or direct to business. There are numerous options for getting your products from point A to point B. You can deliver products, hire a delivery service, contract with a courier, use airfreight, or if your products are small, rely on the postal system. Decisions are typically based on factors such as quantity, cost, schedule, and type of product(s) being delivered. Whatever the delivery method, costs vary depending on product weight, overall dimensions, schedule, geography, and insurable value.

You will also need to consider how you will pack items for transportation and the costs of packing and shipping materials. Will you require boxes, wooden containers or pallets, bubble wrap, envelopes, tape, Styrofoam® pellets, and plastic bags? Most courier and freight companies sell packing and shipping materials, but shop around because in small quantities these are very expensive. Office supply stores like Office Depot, ♂ www.officedepot.com, generally have lower costs on packing and shipping supplies, and the lowest costs are found at packaging wholesalers.

Delivery costs and related supplies will have to be calculated and added to product pricing. All of the major courier and freight companies such as Fed Ex, ♂ www.fedex.com, and UPS, ♂ www.ups.com, as well as the U.S. Postal Service, ♂ www.usps.com, and Canada Post, ♂ www.canadapost.ca, have software that automatically calculates shipping charges based on the information you enter. A few other benefits of this software are that it allows you to print customer labels, track packages, and automatically arrange for pick-ups and deliveries.

Inventory Management

You also have to give thought to how you will manage your inventory, both completed products as well as raw materials. If you are making and selling products one at a time or in very small quantities, inventory management is important but very easy to manage: Simply invest in a spiral notebook, create a few columns for product description and units, and you are pretty much set. Likewise, you can also create your own basic inventory management system using your computer and a spreadsheet program such as Excel.

However, if you are a mid- to large-volume manufacturer with numerous distribution channels, you will need a much more sophisticated inventory management system. Chances are you will need to invest in inventory management software with features such as customer database options, invoice creation, label making, inventory tracking, bar code scanning, tax codes, and automatic inventory reordering. Prices for inventory management software vary depending on features and peripherals such as fixed and wireless scanners. You can search online business software directories such as Soft Scout, ♂ www.softscout.com, and The Software Network, ♂ www.thesoftwarenetwork.com, to find appropriate inventory management software.

The second aspect of inventory managements is physical. You need a place to put your inventory, one that is easily accessed, dry, and secure, as well as apparatus such as shelving or bins to hold both raw materials and the completed product. If you do not have space at home, you will need to rent space. Security, cost, size, and proximity to your home must be considered for off-site storage. Public mini storage services are one of the best storage alternatives because you are not tied to long-term leases and need not worry about utilities and maintenance because that is included in the rent.

Building Your Business Team

Not even a small sole proprietorship business can be built and operated by one person; it requires a team effort in order to start, grow, and succeed in business. Depending on the products you make and how these are sold, your business team could include family members, employees, suppliers, and professional service providers.

Family

Family members working in the business, and even those not working directly in the business, make up the first part of your business team. All family members will to some degree have an affect on your business, and the business will have an affect on your family. It is inevitable. Consequently, the goal is to gain the support of the family for your new venture and for them to understand the reason why you want to start or buy a business. Don't be upset if your family members do not share your level of enthusiasm for your business plans. Remember, in most cases the new business is your dream, not theirs. As is the case with any business venture, there are inherent financial risks, whether you buy or start a business manufacturing products. In turn, this may make some family members nervous, so you want to make sure all issues are resolved prior to getting started. Most importantly, do not view family members as a pool of temporary help when you get busy or argue that you are building a legacy for the next generation. The decision to work in the family business must be left up to each person.

Employees

Depending on the products you make and your business goals, you may or may not need employees. Hiring employees is a big decision—costs increase, extra administrative paperwork develops, and employees must be managed. But if you want to significantly grow your business, at some point you will have to hire employees. The trick is to hire the right people from the start, which is often easier said than done. What are the characteristics of a good employee? Good employees are productive, project a professional image, are honest, loyal, confident, and punctual, and can work with minimal supervision. Hiring good employees is only part of the equation. To attract good employees, you need to be able to provide them with a fair salary, opportunities for advancement, job security, new challenges, benefits, and, above all, recognition if you want to attract and retain top talent.

If you hire people to work in your business, you have to comply with labor laws and regulations governing employment practices, including but not limited to minimum wages, workplace health and safety issues, hours, and workers' compensation insurance coverage. As an employer, you will need to obtain an Employer Identification Number (EIN). You are also required to withhold and remit employee income tax and Social Security Insurance. More about labor laws in the United States can be learned by contacting the Department of Labor, ☎ (877) 889-5627, ✆ www.dol.gov. To obtain an Employer Identification Number in the United States, visit your local Internal Revenue Service office or download the EIN form from the IRS web site, ✆ www.irs.gov. More about labor laws in Canada can be learned by contacting Human Resources Development Canada, ☎ (800) 567-6866, ✆ www.hrdc-drhc.gc.ca. To obtain an Employer Identification Number in Canada, visit your local Canada Customs and Revenue Agency office or download the EIN forms at the CCRA web site, ✆ www.ccra-adrc.gc.ca.

Suppliers

A business can only be as strong as each supporting partner, and because of this, product and service suppliers are important members of your business team. Decisions to pick one supplier over another cannot be based only on the lowest price. You have to factor in additional considerations such as payment terms, guarantees, and reliability. Remember, the promises your suppliers make to you are the promises you make to your customers. Payment terms are often more important than price. With the right terms, you have the opportunity to make and sell products and get paid before having to pay your suppliers. Ideally, you want 90-day payment terms on a revolving account basis, but you will find that most suppliers will offer 30 days and discounts for cash orders or early settlement. Also think about the tools, equipment, or marketing materials that you need to start or grow your business. Can any of your suppliers provide these for free or at greatly reduced costs? Many have assistance and support programs in place offering vendors valuable equipment, marketing materials, and cooperative advertising opportunities that will enable your business to be more efficient, productive, and profitable. Items that you might be able to tap your suppliers for include:

- ongoing specialized training
- advertising specialties such as pens, notepads, and hats
- contest prizes, management, and support
- special event signs, posters, banners, and table tents
- technical support and customer service assistance

- computer hardware and software
- specialized tools and equipment

Professional Services

When selecting professional service providers such as lawyers, accountants, and consultants, it is imperative to keep in mind that it is the professional's experience, knowledge, and advice that you will be leveraging to start your business, grow your business, and ultimately help guide you to success. Ground zero is finding and working with a good lawyer, because anyone who has ever been in business knows that operating a business and having access to good legal advice go hand in hand. Competent lawyers with small business experience will be able to advise on the best legal business structure for you, insurance and liability issues, drafting of legal documents, money collection and small claims courts matters, estate planning and continuation of your business, and other contracts. Contact the American Bar Association, ☎ (202) 662-1000, ♂ www.abanet.org, to find a lawyer in the United States, and The Canadian Bar Association, ☎ (800) 267-8860, ♂ www. cba.org, to track down a lawyer in Canada. Both associations can help you locate a lawyer in your area that specializes in legal matters pertinent to small business.

Even with the proliferation of accounting and bookkeeping software, hiring an accountant to take care of more complicated money matters is wise. Accountants pride themselves on the fact that they do not cost you money, but rather make you money by discovering items overlooked on tax returns, by identifying business deductions you never knew existed, and by creating solid equity-building financial plans. To find a small business CPA in your area, contact the Association of Chartered Accountants in the United States, ☎ (212) 334-2078, ♂ www.acaus.org. In Canada, contact the Chartered Accountants of Canada, ☎ (416) 977-3222, ♂ www.cica.ca.

Professional consultants have long played a role in helping small business owners meet and exceed their business and marketing objectives through coaching, planning, new business development, and training strategies. Consulting experts are available in just about every business discipline imaginable, including small business, logistics, marketing, sales, employee and management training, product development and packaging, import and export, computer and internet technologies, franchising, advertising, and public relations. The first step in hiring a business consultant is to define your objective. What do you want to fix, improve, or venture into? Once you know your objective(s), then you can select and interview a few potential candidates for the job. There are a number of online consultant directories such as The Training Registry, ↗ www.training registry.com, which lists consultants by specialty and indexed geographically. Elance Online, ↗ www.elanceonline.com, and Guru Online, ↗ www.guru.com, are also great places to find expert consulting services.

Creating a Business Image

When setting up your enterprise, you will also need to create a business image to help brand your products and project a positive and appropriate image for your business. This is especially important for small business owners because most do not have the advantage of elegant storefronts or far reaching advertising campaigns to wow customers. Instead, they must rely on imagination, creativity, and paying attention to the smallest detail when creating and maintaining a professional business image. Information below covers simple and inexpensive ways that you can create a positive business image using logos, slogans, a professional print identity package, uniforms, and attention-grabbing product packaging.

Logos and Slogans

Business logos and promotional slogans play a major role in building consumer awareness of your business and products, which is referred to as branding. Logos are especially effective here because of their visual recognition qualities, that is, they can tell consumers instantly that this is a brand they know, like, and trust. A great logo can be tricky to create, unless, of course, you happen to be a graphic designer or artist. In the event that you are neither, don't worry. There are many logo design services, such as The Logo Company, ↗ www.thelogocompany.com, and Logo Bee, ↗ www.logobee.com, that can help you create a professional logo for your business. Basic logo design costs start at about $100.

To develop a slogan, start by thinking about and recording the number one benefit people receive from buying and owning your product and create a brief, yet powerful slogan incorporating the number one benefit. The retailing powerhouse Home Depot slogan, "You can do it. We can help," is a perfect example of a slogan aimed directly at their primary target audience—homeowners who want to fix and improve their properties themselves.

Once you have decided on a logo design and a promotional slogan, you must consistently incorporate these into every area of your business, including stationery, signage, promotional materials, uniforms, packaging, and advertising. The more often consumers are exposed to your brand through the consistent use of logos and slogans, the more they will remember your product and the stronger you brand will become.

Print Identity Package

Business cards, stationery, receipts, envelopes, presentation folders, marketing brochures, catalogs, fliers, newsletters, and account statements are all business identification items that should be incorporated into one package. Key to a great print identity package is consistency throughout the entire package and marketing program. You want to develop a standard color scheme and font, combine these with your logo and slogan, and use them consistently so that consumers begin to visually link your business with your identity program.

Remember to obtain three quotes for all of your printing needs, and do not necessarily buy based only on price. Instead, base your purchasing decision on quality, value, reputation, and turnaround time. In addition to your community printer, there are also many printers doing business online, such as Print USA, ♂ www.print usa.com, which offers free quotes on a wide variety of printed business products.

Uniforms

Top businesspeople have long understood the benefits associated with uniforms emblazoned with their business names and logos. These benefits include branding the business name and products, projecting a professional image, helping to identify employees from customers, and providing a terrific advertising and promotional tool. Even small businesses can capitalize on the benefits of getting everyone uniformed without having to break the budget because great looking uniforms do not have to be expensive. As little as $20 will purchase golf shirts silk-screened or embroidered with your business name and logo, hats start a $10 each, jackets for about $50, and T-shirts to give away to customers and at special promotions cost about $10 each. All is money wisely spent to project a professional image and advertise your business and products.

Product Packaging

Great packaging is like a great advertisement; it grabs attention, builds interest, creates desire, and motivates consumers to buy. Mediocre packaging can kill a great product, whereas incredible packaging will sell a mediocre product. You have to think of your product packaging as the silent salesperson. It doesn't talk, but it speaks volumes about your product and, more importantly, why people should buy it. What would you tell people face to face if you were trying to persuade them to buy your product? Your answer should be on your packaging. The importance of product packaging cannot be overlooked. In fact, if you can afford to hire just one professional in terms of everything having to do with your business, that professional should be a packaging expert. This expert can design and create a package that will get the desired results, which means an avalanche of sales. If you intend to wholesale, consign, or sell your products through an online retailer or from a retail storefront, you will also need to obtain a Universal Product Code, otherwise known as a bar code, and have this printed on your packaging or accompanying tag. Subdivisions Inc., ☎ (310) 927-1644, ♂ www.buy abarcode.com, sells and registers bar codes. At time of writing, the cost of each bar code is $35, plus a one-time registration fee of $75.

Taking Your Venture Online

How big is online shopping? Really big. American consumers alone spent more than $95 billion buying products and services online in 2003, and according to Forrester Research, online business-to-consumer sales are expect to top $133 billion in 2005 and $230 billion by 2008! Needless to say, there is good reason to be excited about selling your products to a global audience of online consumers.

E-commerce is very involved, and you need to know more about setting up an online business than space provides for here. But the information featured in this section is a good starting point and covers the basics such as building a web site, choosing a domain name, registering with search engines, keyword optimization, and permission-based marketing. Additional information about selling your products online via eBay, e-auctions, and internet malls can be found in Chapter 5.

Building a Web Site

The advantages of selling the products you make online are very obvious—low cost for a 24-hour-a-day store, communication with customers in moments, access to consumers around the globe, and the ability to update marketing messages quickly. But the first question you have to ask is, "Do I need a web site?" If you plan on selling your products online, it would be wise, although not totally necessary, to build your own web site. You do have the option of utilizing other online venues such as eBay to sell products. However, if your goal is to make online sales a major part of your marketing strategy, you should learn as much as you can about e-commerce and make the necessary investments to get your business online. Alternately, if you plan to sell mainly from home and other offline venues, having your own web site is of lesser importance. Ultimately, your decision will depend on your marketing objectives and future plans.

Once you have made the decision to build a web site and make internet marketing an active part of your business, there are many plans to be made and questions to answer.

- How much is your budget to build your web site?

- Who will build it?
- Who will maintain it, and how much will it cost?
- Who will host your web site, and how much will it cost?
- What shopping cart system will you use, and what purchase payment options will you offer customers?

The first option is to design, build, and maintain your own web site. There are a plethora of web site building programs available to enable novice webmasters to build and maintain their own sites. You will still need to be familiar with computers and the internet if you choose this option, regardless of the "no experience required" advertisements. The cost to maintain your site will vary by content needs, maintenance needs, and your sales and marketing objectives. Hosting costs vary depending on the services you select—e-commerce shopping carts, payments systems, order tracking, web site statistics, and database systems options. Expect to pay a minimum of $50 per month for basic business web hosting and about $250 per month for premium services.

The second option is to hire a professional to design and build your site. Fortunately, costs for this have dramatically decreased in the past few years. It is not uncommon to spend less $1,000 to have a fully functional web site built with e-commerce, visitor interaction, and database marketing options. Regardless of who builds it and how your site is built, all successful web sites share qualities that make them popular with visitors and customers. They include products and information that appeal to the target audience, tools and information that create a sense of online community, and ease of use and navigation.

Domain Name

Selecting a domain name for your web site requires much thought because the domain name you select must be suited to the products you make and sell, which unfortunately is often easier said than done because good dot.com designations are becoming increasingly difficult to acquire. The domain name you choose should also be short, easily remembered, and easily spelled. Start the process of choosing a domain name right away, and register a few variations as soon as you have compiled a short list. Domain name registration fees vary depending on the designation and the registration service you choose, but expect to pay from a low of $5 per year for a budget registrar to as much as $50 per year with a full-service registration company. Most registrars also offer discounts if you register a name for a longer period—you can for up to ten years. The majority of domain registration services also provide additional internet and e-commerce services and packages, ranging from web site design to shopping carts, hosting and maintenance services, and web site promotional services. A few of the more popular domain name registration services are Go Daddy, ♂ www.godaddy.com, Register, ♂ www.register.com, and Network Solutions, ♂ www.networksolutions.com.

Search Engine Registration

The number-one way people find products online is by using keyword submissions via search engines and directories. In fact, some studies suggest as many as 90 percent of internet users search for the products and information they want with keyword submissions. There are hundreds of search engines and search directories on the internet, and because you don't know which one people will use, your web site and web pages need to be registered with many search engines and directories, especially the big guns like Google, ♂ www.google.com, and Yahoo!, ♂ www.yahoo.com.

Search engines like Google are indexed by bots, or spiders, which extract specific information and keywords from web site pages and use this information for indexing. Search directories like Yahoo! have people called directory editors who compile the information by hand, and index and group based on relevancy to the submitted search. These days the line between a search engine and a search directory is increasingly blurred. Most major search engines and directories use both mechanical and human power to build and index information or supplement each other's services, so you need to register with both.

Many entrepreneurs find registering their web site and web pages a frustrating task because most search engines and directories have individual submission policies, which means no standard regulations or guidelines to streamline the registration process across the board. If you do not want to register yourself, you can use search engine and directory submission services such as, Add Me, ♂ www .addme.com, Submit It, ♂ www.submit-it.com, and Submit Express, ♂ www.sub mitexpress.com, that will automatically submit or register your web site to all major search engines and directories, as well as periodically update your submissions. Often you only have to complete one relativity basic form. Some submission services are free, but the majority charge fees if you want quick listings, regular maintenance, and other premium listing services. These services offer small business owners with limited time to optimize their web sites for the best search rank results great value for a relatively small fee.

Keyword Optimizing

Keyword optimizing is important because, as mentioned above, an estimated 90 percent of internet shoppers use keywords and keyword phrase submissions to find the products and information they want online. You should aim for a keyword density of about 5 percent. This means that keywords will comprise 5 out of every 100 words of content in your site, including keywords in your page titles, headers, meta tags, and hyperlinks. At the same time, keep in mind that each web page is unique in terms of the products and information featured as well as your marketing objectives. Therefore, you want to make sure that you select keywords and phrases that best represent the products and marketing objectives for each page. When selecting keywords and phrases, be descriptive and remember few people type in single search words. Consequently, combining keywords into short descriptive phrases is wise and will help improve overall search rankings.

One way of creating good keywords for your site is to create lists of words that describe your products and conduct search engine and directory submissions using these words. The top ten results from other web sites selling similar products will help you pinpoint the best and most descriptive keywords to use when optimizing keywords throughout your own site. Also, always include the maximum number of keywords each search engines will allow. Search directories partly base ranking on the quality and relevance of the content rather than just on the density of keywords, so concentrate on quality and relevant content as well to improve search results. If you think optimizing your keyword selection is outside your comfort zone, there are many keyword creation services that will optimize your keyword selection for a fee; a couple of these services are Keyword Handbook, ♂ www.keywordhandbook.com, and Word Tracker, ♂ www.word tracker.com.

Permission-Based Marketing

What is permission-based marketing, and why is it important to your online business? Permission-based marketing means exactly that; people give you their permission to send them information about your business or products via e-mail. This information can include everything from your monthly e-newsletter to electronic product catalogs, to a special promotional offer, to a quick note saying thanks for being a great customer. Gaining permission to send marketing and other information can be very important and beneficial to your online business. First, if people ask to be included in your electronic mailings, in all likelihood they are very interested in the products you make and sell. Second, when you have a person's permission to send her information electronically, you won't be spamming, that is, sending e-mail messages to people without their permission. You should know that there are laws in the works that will make spamming illegal in the future, and those caught spamming will face hefty fines. Third, you have the opportunity to build a very valuable in-house electronic mailing list, which can be used for any number of research, marketing, and selling activities. To take advantage of an electronic mailing list, you will need to purchase customer database software, so you can compile, store, and manage your subscriber database, or contract with a remote database management systems provider.

Your final question should be, "How do I get people to give me their permission to send them information electronically?" It's easy. Via your web site, collect information from your visitors, and while you do, ask for their permission to send them periodic information electronically. Do this by staging—staging contests, giving away freebies, granting access to a private section of your site with a code, or asking visitors to sign an e-guestbook.

4

EVERYTHING ELSE YOU NEED TO KNOW

The information in this chapter is everything else you need to know to get started and operate your business. You will learn how to create a business (and marketing) plan, price your products, provide great customer service, effectively advertise your business and products, and a host of additional helpful information, ideas, and tips that have been specifically developed to put you on the path to long-term success and profitability.

Your Business Plan

All business ventures need a business plan, whether you plan to build a global manufacturing empire or just make wind chimes at home to sell at weekend flea markets. Why? So you can minimize financial risks while maximizing the potential for profitability. All successful businesses are built upon a solid research and planning foundation. Do not feel intimidated by the research and planning process. It is nothing more than collecting, analyzing, and recording information you need to know to start, operate, and prosper in business. Your business plan does not have to be complicated. A few well-researched and documented pages covering the basics are sufficient to reveal the information you need to describe your business and products, identify your customers, build competitive advantages, and develop your marketing strategies. Remember, in writing a thorough business plan, you also develop your marketing plan, a vital component of business success.

Your business plan should be divided into three main sections—company, marketing, and financial—with subsections in each covering critical information and details. You can use the information that follows as a road map leading you through the process of creating your own business plan in step-by-step format. If you need more specific information, there are many business books available at your local library, book retailers, or online at Barnes and Noble, ♂ www. barnesandnoble.com, or Amazon, ♂ www.amazon.com. Equally, there are also many business plan software programs and templates available to assist you in writing, formatting, and preparing a business plan. A few are at Palo Alto, ♂ www. paloalto.com, My Business Kit, ♂ www.mybusinesskit.com, and Plan Magic, ♂ www. planmagic.com. Further, most word processing software programs include basic business plan templates and tutorials to help novice entrepreneurs create and write a business plan.

The Company Section of Your Business Plan

The company section of your business plan is where you describe your business in detail. This information is categorized in four subsections—business description, management team, legal issues, and risks and contingencies.

Business Description

In the business description area, you want to provide a general overview of your business and the product(s) you will make. Include information such as the business name, location, and the legal structure—sole proprietorship, partnership, limited liability corporation, or corporation. Also note the business start date, or expected start date, and if the business is already operational, briefly describe the current stage of development, successes to date, as well as challenges to date. Finally, briefly describe the products you make and how these will be sold.

Management Team

Next, you want to describe the management team, the type of people your business needs to hire or contract with in order to manufacture the product(s), operate the business on a day-to-day basis, and drive sales to meet sales objectives. Start by listing the owners of the business and describe their experience, training, and expected duties. Also list key employees, and describe their experience, training, remuneration, and the duties each will perform. If you plan to contract with independent sales agents to sell your products, describe their experience, the duties they will perform, and how they will be remunerated. Finally, list professional service providers (lawyers, consultants, accountants), and describe the services they will provide to the business.

Legal Issues

In this section, you want to describe any legal issues in terms of setting up and operating your business, including legal issues that are specific to the products you intend to produce. Further, record all licenses, permits, or registrations that are needed, or have been obtained, as well as the cost of each. These might include business license, vendors permit, employer identification number, sales tax permits, import/export certificates, zoning/building permits, and fire safety/hazardous materials permits. In this section, list your insurance requirements, such as fire insurance, general liability insurance, automotive, health, or business interruption insurance, along with the date each is needed and the costs of each. Finally, list and describe any intellectual properties such as trademarks, patents, or copyrights that the business owns, has applied for, or will be using under license from the property owner. Include the nature of these intellectual properties, and the advantages associated with ownership or right of use.

Risks and Contingencies

It is also important to identify and discuss the risks associated with your products, marketing environment, and other aspects of your business, as well as contingency plans that can be activated in the event that Plan A does not come to fruition. For instance, one risk might be that a major supplier providing a key ingredient needed to manufacture your product goes out of business. This loss would have a negative impact on your business. A contingency would be to identify in advance two or three alternate suppliers where this key ingredient could be purchased. In other words, in business you also have to plan for the unexpected.

The Marketing Section of Your Business Plan

Why is marketing research and planning important to small business owners? Based on your research and the information revealed, you will be able to prove that there is sufficient demand for your product, that you can compete in the marketplace, and that the market is large enough to support your sales and marketing goals. Think of it this way: Before spending a bundle of cash to set up and equip a factory capable of producing 10,000 birdhouses per month, you first need to know that there is sufficient consumer demand for birdhouses to support your manufacturing capabilities.

In the marketing section of your business plan, you want to describe the marketplace, identify you target customer, discuss competition, set sales goals, cover the marketing 4 Ps, and record your marketing budget and action plan. This information can then be used to market your products and guide your marketing decisions from where you are now to where you want to be in the future.

Marketplace Description

The biggest benefit of researching and recording marketplace information is that it enables you to greatly reduce your exposure to financial risk, increase your chances of capitalizing on marketplace opportunities, and prove that there is a big enough marketplace to support your anticipated sales. The main information you will need to research and include in this section of your marketing plan is a description of the geographic trading area that your business will serve, the current size of the marketplace, the potential size of the marketplace, and the current economic status of the marketplace.

Target Customer Description

Of course, you have to know who the people are who are most likely to buy your product(s), that is, your target customer. Researching, collecting, and recording this data enables you to create a target customer profile so you can aim your advertising, marketing, and sales activities directly at your target customers. This focus saves you money and time by not targeting advertising and marketing activities where they will be ineffective. What do you need to know about your target customers? You need to know

- where they are located geographically.

- the percentage of male versus female.
- their age range, level of education, marital status, and what they do to earn a living.
- what is most important to them when making purchasing decisions—price, value, service, warranty, or quality.
- the publications they read, radio stations and programs they listen to, and television stations and programs they watch.
- the recreational and social activities they participate in.

Competition Analysis

You also need to know your competitors, the other businesses making the same products as you and selling to the same target audience. You can use the information you gather and record about your competition to develop strategies to turn their weaknesses into your strengths as well as to capitalize on marketplace opportunities. Get started by listing your main competitors, describing their strengths and weaknesses, as well as noting what they do well that you should also be doing.

Strengths are the skills and resources you have that can be capitalized upon and used to your advantage to help you reach business and marketing objectives. Therefore, describe what strengths and resources your business has and how your products will be positioned in the marketplace, all relative to competitors—low price leader, quality above all, or high-end.

Sales Goals

Your sales goals should be projected in easily measured and quantifiable financial terms. If you are planning on utilizing more than one sales method, such as trade shows, internet, or salespeople, you will want to separate and list goals for each sale method individually. You want to identify and record your first month and six-month sales goals, as well as your first year and five-year sales goals. Support your sales goals information and figures by including the marketing and promotional activities that will be utilized to reach them.

Four Ps of Marketing

Developing your marketing strategy revolves around the four marketing Ps— product, price, place (distribution), and promotion. It is the combination of the four Ps that creates your marketing mix, which is, in effect, the entire marketing process. Essentially, the four Ps are about finding the right combination of each, enabling you to create the perfect marketing mix comprised of the marketing strategies that will allow you to meet and exceed your marketing objectives.

- *Product.* Describe in detail the product(s) you make, including special features, how customers benefit from using the product, competitive advantages, guarantees, and any key product research and development programs planned.
- *Price.* Describe how much you will charge for your product(s), how you arrive at your selling price, and your pricing strategy. Also list competitors' prices and how your customers can pay for their purchases, e.g., credit cards, debit cards, and electronic transfers, as well as the benefits to your business and costs associated with of providing these payment options.
- *Place (distribution).* Describe the primary method you will utilize to sell your products—retail storefront, homebased, wholesale, or factory direct, as well as secondary methods—eBay, trade shows, flea markets, consignment, craft shows, or other special events. Describe the operations system you will utilize to manage sales from initial order to delivery and after sale customer service and follow-up.
- *Promotion.* Describe how you will advertise and promote your products—newspaper, television, radio, Yellow Pages, and signs, as well as marketing materials such as fliers and business cards. Also detail any direct sales tactics you will employ, including personal contact selling, mail, telephone, and electronic. Finally, describe how you will utilize public relations and the internet to promote your products.

Marketing Budget and Action Plan

When developing your marketing budget, use a ground-up approach to calculate the cost of each marketing activity you intend to use to advertise, market, and sell your products. Break down each by individual cost, and add them together to estimate your overall marketing budget. The simplest way to do this is to list all of your main marketing activities, the time period each covers, and the cost to implement each.

In terms of your action plan, it is really nothing more than a big do-to list broken into categories and timetables outlining when each marketing activity will be implemented and managed, as well as how and when you will measure the progress, success, or failure of each. By measuring results incrementally, you can make sure that marketing activities are working and keeping you on track to meet your sales objectives. Also restate contingency marketing plans that will be activated should any of your original marketing strategies fail to meet sales goals and objectives.

The Financial Section of Your Business Plan

Most people feel intimidated by financial planning because of lack of experience, but remember, it only has to be as difficult as you want to make it. For a small business venture operated by a sole proprietor, you only have to cover the basics, which are funding requirements, sources of funding, and a break-even analysis. All are discussed in greater detail below. For larger ventures, there are additional financial data that should be included, such as a balance sheet, income projections, and capital equipment and inventory lists. Business plan and accounting software programs through Palo Alto, ♂ www.paloalto.com, and QuickBooks, ♂ www.quick books.com, include customizable templates for financial forecasting and statements.

Funding Requirements

Describe how much money is needed to start or grow your business, what the money will be used for, and any future funding requirements. Start by describing your current funding requirements—purchasing tools, equipment, and inventory, leasing a business location, and obtaining business permits, for example. Next, describe any future funding requirements and what the money will be used for—business expansion, equipment upgrades, or a web site, for example. Equipment and inventory lists should include what you currently have, what is needed in the short-term (less than 12 months), and what is needed for the long-term (more than 12 months). Additionally, you should include the number of units required, the cost of each, and the date when the required items will be purchased.

Funding Sources

The next step is to identify and describe where the money will come from to meet your funding requirements—bank loan, private investors, or partnerships—how the money will be repaid (cash or equity), and where the money will come from to meet repayment schedules, which is generally from anticipated business revenues. If you are going to obtain money from more than one source, describe each, and if this includes borrowing money to start your business or meet any funding needs, describe the terms and conditions, including interest rates and how the money will be repaid and the repayment schedule.

Break-Even Analysis

A break-even analysis is used to determine how much product you must sell for total incoming revenues to match total outgoing expenses, thereby achieving a break-even point. To calculate your break-even point, you will need to calculate your fixed and variable costs, as well as the desired gross margin for each sale. For example, if you make and sell garden arbors and your fixed costs were $10,000 per annum, and you sold each arbor for $500, which includes variable costs and a profit margin of 25 percent, you are left with a gross profit of $125 per sale. Therefore, you would need to sell 80 garden arbors per year to break-even—$10,000 in fixed costs divided by $125 gross profit equals 80 sales per year, or about seven sales per month.

Pricing Your Products

Product pricing is a very important element of the marketing mix and your marketing strategy. If your prices are too high or to low, you will run into trouble because of perceived value and quality issues. Factors influencing pricing formulas and strategies include costs associated with the manufacturing of products, fixed operating overheads, marketplace economic conditions, primary and secondary competition in the marketplace, consumer demand, seasonal pressures, political pressures, psychological factors, and how you want to position your products in the marketplace. Consumers see prices in clearly defined terms—the price that you charge for your product versus how the product will fill their needs and give value. When your pricing is correct, consumers don't think twice because they feel the price is fair in comparison to the value and benefits derived from the product. However, as soon as your price goes below or above the threshold of what consumers feel is in the fair range for your product, you will meet resistance to the sale.

Setting prices and determining your pricing strategy has much to do with positioning your products in the marketplace and with external factors that can potentially influence the prices you charge. You can position your products and become known for low prices, moderate prices, or prestige prices. Your positioning strategy answers two vital questions: Where do your products fit into the market? How does your target audience view your products in relationship to competing products?

Low-Price Strategy

A low-price strategy means that you sell the products you make at the lowest or near-lowest price for similar products in the marketplace. A low-price strategy generally means you have to sell a greater volume of products than you would at a higher price to produce an equivalent profit margin. The majority of small business owners wisely choose not to compete or position their products in the marketplace based on low prices. Many national and international retailers have already adopted a low-price strategy, making it difficult for the small independent business to compete at this level.

Moderate-Price Strategy

A moderate-price strategy means that you produce a good quality product delivered to consumers at a fair price. This is the pricing strategy that the majority of small business owners wisely choose to adopt. It leaves you enough financial leeway for competitive advantages to be developed and introduced to separate your products from competitors' products, advantages such as a stronger warranty or more value-added features. The moderate-price strategy gives small business owners the most flexibility in terms of combining value and good service at a fair price, which is difficult to achieve if you adopt a low-price strategy.

Prestige-Price Strategy

A prestige-price strategy is generally used to deliver very high-quality products in an upscale or exclusive environment. The quality or delivery of the product is not necessarily always superior; sometimes it is only perceived to be better by consumers. Prestige pricing can be a deliberate pricing tactic in which you set your prices higher to separate your products from competitors by projecting an image of quality and exclusivity. If you are selling a niche product to a very small target audience, a prestige-price strategy can work extremely well. But if you are making and selling common and widely available products, it can be very difficult to create a persuasive enough argument that compels consumers to spend more than they ordinarily would spend on similar quality products.

Competition Price

Competition pricing simply means you find out how much your competitors are charging for their products, and charge more or less depending on how you want to position your products in the marketplace. The downside to a competitive pricing is that it is not very scientific. Your costs to produce and deliver products may be more or less than your competitors', and what may be a profitable price point for one business may not be for another charging the same price. It is easy to find out how much competitors charge for their products—mystery shop their businesses, buy their products, and scan their advertisements, web sites, and catalogs. If you decide to price your products based on competitor pricing, make sure that you create unique competitive advantages that motivate consumers to buy your products and not your competitors' products.

Cost Plus Price

Regardless of the pricing strategy you adopt, you need to cover all costs associated with producing your products and operating your business, as well as generate a profit after all expenses are paid. To get to that point, you have to calculate your variable costs associated with manufacturing the product, your fixed operating costs, plus a profit. The formula is:

$$\text{Variable costs} + \text{Fixed costs} + \text{Profit} = \text{Selling price}$$

The first step is to determine how much money you need and want to earn per hour. The second step is to calculate your fixed costs, which are business expenses such as the telephone, rent, and insurance, costs that do not fluctuate regardless of the number of sales you make. The third step is to determine the costs incurred manufacturing products and the costs associated with selling these products. The final step is to calculate and add a profit. Every business needs to generate a profit in order to stay in business and stay competitive in the marketplace. Most small business owners use a percentage to calculate a profit, such as total costs plus 20 percent.

Making Happy Customers

When you stop to consider that it costs ten times more to find a new customer than it does to keep a customer you already have, it makes perfect sense to keep all of your customers happy and buying. How do you make happy customers? It is a combination of many things, including a quality product, service with a smile, customer appreciation, and a strong warranty program.

Providing Great Customer Service

One of the easiest customer service concepts to grasp is the simple fact that people like to do business with people they like. Consequently, it stands to reason that you should go out of your way to be likeable—smile, take an interest in your customers, treat them fairly, and thank them for their business. That's about all it takes to provide great customer service. Another easy customer service concept to master is always fix the customer first. When you have an unhappy customer, look for ways to fix your customer first and without hesitation. Once this has been achieved, turn your attention to the source of the problem or complaint. Chances are whatever caused the problem is not putting money in the bank, your customers are, and that is why they get fixed before anything else. Also keep in mind the vast majority of customer service complaints arise from mismatched expectations. It makes sense to reduce the potential for mismatched expectations between you and customers by reviewing all details of the sale prior to product delivery and by asking customers their expectations. You need to know your customers' expectations are in line with the product they are purchasing.

Another large part of what makes up great customer service is how you show your customers that you appreciate their business. When your customers feel appreciated, they go out of their way to continue supporting your business, and equally important, they go out of their way to refer your business and products to other people. There are lots of ways to thank your customers. Send greeting cards on holidays, birthdays, and other milestones. Host an annual customer appreciation party, and invite your best customers to a local restaurant. Or if the budget is tight, host the party at your home. Give customers key chains, pens, notepads, calendars, coffee mugs, travel mugs, clocks, mouse pads, or T-shirts emblazoned with your business name and logo. It doesn't matter how you thank them, just as long as you do.

At the end of the day, the best way to provide great customer service is to treat your customers the way that you like to be treated when you trade your hard-earned money for goods or services. Besides, going the extra mile for customers almost always means price is less of a factor in buying decisions. When you treat people in an appreciative way, you no longer have to work as hard to persuade them to your way of thinking. When was the last time that you stopped shopping at a particular business because you received exceptional service?

Product Warranties

Another important element of providing great customer service is to put your money where your mouth is and back up your claims of a high-quality product by providing an ironclad warranty. Not only can an ironclad warranty be used to support your marketing claims, but you can also use your warranty to separate your products from competing products in the marketplace. For instance, if a competing product is warranteed for five years, make yours ten. If competitors' product warranties are loaded with small print that voids the warranty for almost any reason, zap the small print from yours and make it unconditional. Consumers have become very savvy and want to know that if a product malfunctions or breaks down for any reason, they have recourse to get the problem fixed. Yes, depending on the products you make, there have to be warranty terms and conditions to protect your business. But at the same time, every business making and selling products should strive to develop the strongest warranty possible. After all, you know the quality of the product you make, and if you are not prepared to back it up with an ironclad warranty, then don't be surprised if consumers are skeptical when it comes time to buy it.

Returns and Refunds

At some point you will have customers that want to return products, request a refund, or cancel a product order. It is inevitable; all businesses making and selling products face return, refund, and cancel order issues. Consequently, it is best to establish return, refund, and product order cancellation policies before opening for business. The following are a few points you will need to consider:

- Will you allow customers to return products they have purchased from your business, or will all sales be final?
- In what condition will you allow products to be returned?
- How long will your product return or refund policy be—7, 14, 30 days, or longer?
- Will you offer customers the option of exchanging products for similar products, a credit against future purchases, or an outright cash refund?

If you are going to provide refunds, make sure your policy corresponds with the payment method. If the customer paid in cash, offer a cash refund. If the customer paid with a credit card, you will need to credit his or her charge account. And, if a customer paid by check, make sure the check has cleared your bank before refunding any money.

The final consideration is product order cancellations. Most U.S. states and Canadian provinces have consumer protection mechanisms in place that enable consumers to cancel orders within a prescribed time, which is generally referred to as a *cooling off period*. However, there is not a single standard time limit to this law. You will need to contact the SBA or your lawyer to inquire about your specific area and how the law is applied. At the same time, when customers buy made-to-order products from your business, make sure that you get a deposit before making the product(s). The deposit should be at least equal to the costs of materials that will be needed to make the product, but preferably you will want to secure a 50 percent deposit.

Advertising Your Products

Advertising is a tool that can drive consumers in mass numbers to your business to buy products. Advertising can also be a complete waste of time and money, reaping little, if any, sales or long-term branding benefits. Consequently, small business owners with limited advertising budgets have to make well-researched and informed decisions when it comes to allocating precious money to advertising activities.

Always remember that you do not need to spend a bundle advertising the products you make, but you do have to make sure the money you spend on advertising reaches your target audience: the people that need and want to buy the products you make. There are numerous ways small businesses can utilize advertising mediums to reach their target audience in a cost-efficient and effective way. The best are advertising in newspapers, magazines, promotional fliers, signage, online, and free publicity, all of which are discussed in greater detail below.

Great Advertising

Great advertising is composed of many elements—attention-grabbing headlines, powerful images, an incredible offer, and a call to action. It is the combination of these that goes into creating a great advertisement, one that gets the results that you want. This combination is referred to as the AIDA advertising formula—attention, interest, desire, and action. Even if you plan on doing little in the way of traditional advertising in newspapers or magazines, you still need the ability to create great advertising and copy for use in packaging, sales letters, catalogs, fliers, newsletters, signage, or web site content.

You only have a brief moment to grab the attention of your target audience and pull them into your message, so start with a powerful headline. For example, a wedding gown designer might use, "Do you want to wear the world's most beautiful gown on your wedding day?" Clever advertising also appeals to people on an emotional level, utilizing emotional triggers to spark basic human feelings such as the need for friendship, the need for security, and the desire to achieve. The best way to appeal to emotional triggers is through the use of powerful images in your ads. When used properly, emotional triggers can double and even triple ad response rates.

To stand out in a sea of advertising, you also have to provide an incredible offer, something that your target audience cannot get elsewhere. Your incredible offer can be a deeply discounted price, a value-added bonus, limited product quantity, or some other type of offer to motivate your target audience to take action and buy. Always remember your advertising must ask people to buy and give them compelling reasons to do so, as well as provide the contact information they need to take action. Unlike multinational corporations with a bottomless money pit for brand-building advertising, small business owners have to ask for the sale every time, regardless of the advertising or communication medium.

Newspaper Advertising

Never get lured in by huge circulation numbers, critical placement promises, and frequency discounts. Instead, always purchase newspaper advertising based on your marketing plan, advertising budget, and the publication's ability to reach your target audience. There are basically two types of newspaper advertising options—display advertising and classified advertising. For the majority of small businesses manufacturing products, classified advertising offers much greater value than display advertising. First, display advertising is very expensive and placing only the occasional ad because of a limited budget does not work (special sales or promotional events excluded). You need repetition in order to build long-term beneficial awareness of your business and products. Further, most newspapers are jammed cover-to-cover with display advertisements, leaving your ad fighting with hundreds of other ads to capture the readers' attention. If you opt to buy display advertising space in newspapers, first ask for the media kit or card, which tells you about the newspaper's readership base, who they are, where they come from, what they do for a living, their level of education, and how much money they make. This data will enable you to determine if the newspaper's target audience is your target audience.

On the other hand, classified advertising is unquestionably one of the best advertising options for product makers. Not only are classified ads easy to create and cheap to run, but they also almost always have a higher response rate than display advertisements because people generally read the classifieds looking for a specific product to buy, not for entertainment as in other sections of the newspaper. Because classified advertisements are cheap to run and quick to post, continually look for ways to improve your results by testing new ads in various publications. Test your headline, your main sales message, and your special offers on a regular basis. Classified advertising rates vary by publication, number of words, number of insertions, and other factors such as the use of icons, borders, and photographs, which, by the way, almost always increase response rates, making the extra cost a very wise expenditure.

There is a huge variety of newspapers—national, regional, daily, community weeklies, commuter, buy-and-sell, school, association and club, and electronic—so it is easy to be overwhelmed when choosing one to advertise your products. Fortunately, online directories such as News Link, ♂ www.newslink.org, and News Directory, ♂ www.newsdirectory.com, can help you narrow down the options as both list thousands of publications indexed by type, audience, and location served.

Magazine Advertising

If you manufacture a niche or specialty product that is not common or widely available, advertising in magazines offers a great opportunity to reach a very select target audience in a relativity cost efficient manner. This is because many magazines cater to one specific portion of the population with a specific interest, such as cars, home decorating, sports, entertainment, pets, hobbies, gardening, and so on. Advertising in these magazines enables you to reach people with interests relevant to your product. The main downside to magazine advertising is that unlike classified advertisements you cannot expect immediate results. It takes continuous and consistent exposure to your target audience before the effort equals increased sales.

The first place to find out more about a magazine's particular target audience is through the publisher's media kit or fact sheet. In the kit, you will find information about who reads the magazine, number of subscribers, their average incomes, hobbies, and educations. Media kits give you the opportunity to carefully research the publication's readers to determine if they meet your target audience requirements before you jump in and sign up for a 12-month, full-page advertising contract. To locate magazines and other publications that cater to a specific audience, visit Pub List, ☞ www.publist.com, which is a free directory listing in excess of 150,000 print and electronic publications.

There is also much debate about which size advertisement is the best, a full page, half page, third page, quarter page, and so forth. All have their pros and cons. Full-page advertisements can be costly, but you get great exposure. Quarter-page ads are much cheaper, but are often placed near the back of the magazine with other advertisements on the same page. You also have to consider frequency, the number of times that your target audience is exposed to your advertisement in the same magazine. Most advertising experts agree there should be a minimum of three times, but preferably six to twelve times concurrently for an ad to have real impact on sales.

Promotional Fliers

Promotional fliers represent one of the best advertising vehicles and values available to small business owners because they are a fast and frugal, yet highly effective way to promote your products. You should take the time needed to learn basic desktop publishing skills and purchase computer hardware and desktop publishing software programs, such as those offered by Adobe, ☞ www.adobe.com, and Corel, ☞ www.corel.com, so you have the ability to design and produce your fliers in-house. In addition to saving money, having the ability to create your own fliers also saves time because you can create promotional materials and be ready to use them within a day, instead of waiting days or weeks working around a print shop's schedule. Once your fliers been have been created and printed, they can be copied in bulk for as little as two cents each at your local copy center, or you can invest in a high-speed laser printer for about $350 and also keep printing in-house.

The great benefit of printed promotional fliers is that they can be used everywhere and for everything, often as a replacement for your business cards. Hand them out at flea markets, trade shows, and networking meetings. Hire students to canvas busy parking lots tucking fliers underneath windshield wipers, and leave them in public spaces and on transit for riders to read and take home. You can also stock a supply of promotional fliers and thumbtacks in your car and make a weekly run posting your new fliers on every community bulletin board in your area—at supermarkets, libraries, schools, community centers, laundries, fitness clubs, churches, and gas stations.

Signs

Signs are one of the lowest cost, yet highest impact, forms of advertising because they work to promote your products 24 hours a day, 365 days a year, for free. But with that said, don't go cheap when having signs made for your business. Signs must be professionally designed and constructed because you always want to make a positive first impression and project an appropriate image. Faded signs, peeling paint, torn banners, or signs that require any sort of maintenance or look homemade send out negative messages about your business and the products you sell. The majority of signs today are designed on a computer, printed, and cut on large sheets of vinyl, easily installed, long lasting, and very inexpensive. Basically, there are no reasons to go cheap or make your own.

Installing signs at home can be tricky business because of local laws. These laws typically stipulate the size, placement, and style of sign permitted. Often commercial signage is not even permitted in residential neighborhoods. There is no one set of regulations in terms of home business signage. Each municipality has its own regulations. A call to the city planning department will usually answer any questions in terms of homebased business signs. Keep in mind that if you are not going to have customers coming to your home to view and buy products, you will be better off not having signs there.

Chances are you also need to obtain event signage and banners to use at flea markets, consumer shows, and community events. Portable promotional signage should also be professionally designed and include attention-grabbing design elements such as vivid colors and images of the products you sell to perfectly describe your products at a glance. If you are going to use your vehicle for business even occasionally, sign it using magnetic signs or stick-on vinyl signs. Not only sign the vehicle, also park in high-traffic locations when not in use, even if this means feeding parking meters. Always think about maximizing the marketing value of these rolling billboards.

Online Advertising

There are a number of ways that you can promote your products using the internet. In fact, there are so many online promotional methods that many books have been written solely on the topic, but space here limits us to discussing the basics—banner advertising, e-publications, and pay-per-click programs.

Advertising banners are very popular way to promote products and drive traffic to your web site or online location where your products can be purchased. Depending on the target audience you want to reach, banner advertising costs range from a few dollars per thousand impressions to a few hundred dollars per thousand impressions. The lure of low-cost banner advertising might be tempting, but results can suffer dramatically by not presenting your advertising message to your primary target audience. Bigger is not always better. Mega web sites may attract thousands, if not millions, of visitors, but that does not necessarily mean they are comprised of your target audience.

Many product manufacturers have found advertising in electronic publications to be a highly effective way to reach their target audience at a very modest cost, and with an estimated 100,000 electronic publications distributed monthly to choose from, you can definitely find one that reaches your target audience. Before committing to advertising, find out audience size, demographics, and advertising costs. Again, bigger is not necessarily better because these publications often contain more advertisements. Your main consideration should always be to reach your target audience. Ezine Listings, ♂ www.ezinelistings.com, lists thousands of electronic publications indexed by subject.

Pay-per-click programs are another highly effective form of online advertising. They involve bidding on priority keywords you believe your target audience uses to search for the products you sell. The big players are Google's AdWords, ♂ www.adwords.google.com, and Overture's Pay-for-Performance, ♂ www.overture.com. Each program has different requirements and rules for keyword selection, but both programs are similar in the way you bid for keywords. For instance, you can bid one dollar for a specific keyword and if you are the highest bid, you win and get top search results rankings. On the other hand, if you bid 20 cents and someone else bids more for the same keywords, your ranking will be greatly reduced.

Public Relations

Few advertising or marketing activities can match the effectiveness and credibility of good PR. After all, our daily lives revolve around news distributed in all formats—broadcast, print, and internet. We read newspapers, watch television, surf the internet, and listen to the radio, and do so to be entertained and informed. That is why it is important to develop a public relations strategy for your business. Most small business owners don't realize they could easily create publicity buzz around the products they make and sell. All that is required is to think creatively, identify the unique user benefits and competitive advantages associated with your products, and use these as the basis for creating publicity buzz. Once you have done that, put it on paper in the form of a press release and send it to appropriate media outlets. If you are new to writing press releases, read a few first to get an idea about how to angle your story, how to benefit the media's audience, the type of information to include, and formatting tips. A good place to read actual press releases is at PR Web, ♂ www.prweb.com. There you can surf through thousands of press releases for free, which can help you write your own.

You can also use a grassroots approach to get valuable publicity simply by getting involved with the community where you live and do business and informing people about the products you make. It's proven that people like to do business with people they know and like, and they refer friends, family, and associates to these businesses. So it makes sense to get active in your community—clubs, churches, charities, and business and social functions are all great places to meet new people, help out, pass out business cards, and talk about your business and your products. Sponsorships are also a fantastic way to help out the community and publicize your business at the same time. You can sponsor a little league team, a charity event, or any number of community events. Or, for the really ambitious, develop, sponsor, and manage a special event for the benefit of the entire community, such as "(your business name here) beach clean up day."

5

THE BEST PLACES TO SELL THE THINGS YOU MAKE

Making a fantastic, high-quality product is only half the job. Selling it represents the other half. This chapter is devoted to helping you learn basic selling techniques as well as the best places to sell the products you make—home, retail storefront, wholesale to retailers, online, or at events. As you read, keep in mind that many of the sales and marketing ideas in this chapter are portable, that is, most merchandising and selling techniques that work for homebased showrooms for example, will also produce sales results at trade and consumer shows.

Selling Basics

Whether your intentions are to make craft products part time and sell them at weekend flea markets or to manufacture a full line of home décor products and sell them worldwide, you still need to know how best to sell your products so that you maximize the potential for success. Don't feel intimidated if "selling" is not your strongest business skill. The vast majority of people who start businesses are not professional salespeople. You don't have to be. Selling success is a combination of education, practice, persistence, building on your strengths, and duplicating what gets the best results in terms of location, promotion, price, and technique.

So what are the basic selling skills that you should learn? You need to get ready to sell, learn how to qualify buyers, brush up on your negotiating skills, ask for the sale, and ask for referrals, all of which are discussed below.

Getting Ready to Sell

Preparation is the starting point for all selling. You have to know what you are selling inside out and upside down and how customers benefit by purchasing and using your products. Product knowledge can be acquired from research, specialized training, suppliers, and published information, as well as feedback from customers and hands-on experience. You must also know your target audience, the people who need and want the products you make inside out. Where does your target audience live? How can you gain access to them? How often do they buy? And, on what do they base their buying decisions—price, quality, convenience, or features?

Being prepared to sell means you also know your competition thoroughly— what people like and dislike about their products, prices, and guarantees. The final aspect of getting ready to sell is having a toolbox packed with great sales tools. Think of your sales tools as the instruments you will use to grab your prospects' attention, create buying desire, and, most importantly, motivate them to take action and buy. Depending on the products you make, sales tools can include promotional literature, product samples, attention-grabbing signage, customer testimonials, ironclad guarantees, value-added promotions, and numerous purchase payment options such as credit cards, debit cards, and consumer financing for big-ticket items.

Qualifying Buyers

Qualifying buyers is the process of asking potential customers questions and using their responses to determine if they really want to buy what you are selling.

The importance of qualifying your buyers is obvious. The better qualified a prospect is, the greater the chance you will close the sale. Qualifying buyers basically revolves around three issues—needs, decision making, and money. First off, you have to determine right away through questioning if the person needs or wants what you have to sell. It makes no sense to waste your time trying to sell a doghouse to someone who doesn't have a dog and has no plans on getting a dog anytime soon.

You must also make sure you are dealing with the person who has the authority to make the buying decision. The best way to find out is to simply ask, "Who will be making the purchasing decision? Will you be making the decision on your own, or will there be other people involved in the purchasing decision?" Again, you do not want to waste time trying to sell to people who do not have the authority to make the buying decision.

Finally, you also have to be able to determine if the person has the money or access to the money needed to make the purchase. Ask, "What is your budget?" or "Can you afford it?" However you phrase the question, you have to know they can afford to buy what you are selling. This is not to say all hope is lost if they cannot afford to buy, but you will have to explore other options, such as a cheaper model or financing.

Becoming a Power Negotiator

In business you never stop negotiating. You negotiate with customers to buy more and at higher prices. You negotiate with suppliers for lower prices and better terms. You negotiate with your bank for lower merchant account fees. Consequently, learning how to become a power negotiator generally results in selling your products at higher prices and in greater quantities while paying less for the products and services needed to operate your business.

In negotiations, the more information you have about your prospect in terms of their wants, needs, and budget, the stronger your position becomes for getting what you want out of the selling and negotiating process. This means you have to find out as much as you can about what your potential customer's wants and needs and how these are prioritized—by benefits, budget, quality, or schedule. Having this information lets you know what the other person wants to achieve through negotiations—for example, lower price, longer warranty, or more features.

Also, remember if someone really needs the product you are selling, price often becomes a secondary issue to user benefits, such as an improved lifestyle or solving a problem. Therefore, before negotiations start, you must first position the value of your product in relationship to the benefits the person will receive by buying and owning it. This is a critical step because if what you have to sell is properly positioned in terms of customer perceived value, it gives you increased leverage and power to get what you want in the negotiating process without having to accept less money or other unfavorable conditions.

Asking for the Sale

The golden rule of closing sales is very simple but often overlooked: Always ask for the sale. Few people will take it upon themselves to offer you the sale unless they are asked to do so. If you do not ask for the sale every time you present your products, all you will have accomplished is to educate your prospect, which makes them a very easy closing target for competitors that ask for the sale.

Closing is an essential selling skill, but at the same time it is nothing more than the natural progression in the sales cycle. You qualify, present, overcome objections, and you close. Therefore, asking for the sale should be nothing more than a formality. In fact, you can go one step further and assume that all prospects will buy. Do this by making statements like, "We can deliver this for you next week." "I just need your signature on this agreement so we can get started." Or, "How would you like to pay for this?" You can also phrase the closing question in the form of an alternate choice question such as, "So which one do you prefer, the basic patio set or the premium patio set?" The alternate choice pulls your prospect into making a buying decision and selecting one of the options you present. Not buying is no longer an available option, based on the alternate choice closing question.

At the end of the day, volumes can and have been written about closing sales. The most successful salespeople, however, are the ones who take the time to qualify buyers, identify and understand their customers' needs, meet these needs, and always ask for the sale.

Asking for Referrals

One of the fastest and most effective ways to increase sales and profits, while reducing sales cycle time and the costs associated with finding new customers, is to get more referrals. It is safe to say that referrals are often the defining mechanism between business success or failure for many of small business owners. This is especially true when you consider that it is much easier to sell a warm prospect, someone familiar with your products and business, than a cold prospect who doesn't know your business or products.

How do you get more referrals? There are a number of ways, but the easiest is simply to ask. That's right, getting more referrals often requires nothing more than asking for one. People seldom offer you referrals unless asked to do so. Therefore, much like always asking for the sale, you must also always ask for referrals. Wording the question doesn't have to be difficult or particularly clever, "Mrs. Jones, do you know anyone who would benefit from the products we make?" Or, "We take pride in providing the best products at fair prices. Do you know anyone, like you, who needs our products and that wants to be treated fairly?" But don't stop with just your customers. Also enlist your family members, friends, suppliers, and business associates to refer your business and your products to their friends, families, co-workers, and customers. The idea is to build an army of people that can refer your business to others. You will quickly discover that when other people believe in your business and the products you make and sell, they will be more than happy to spread the word by telling others.

Selling from Home

Now that you have the basic selling skills down, this section focuses on selling the products you make directly from home by utilizing interior showrooms, exterior display, and in-home sales parties, as well as simple and cost-effective advertising methods such as classified ads and fliers to promote homebased sales. One of the advantages of selling from home is it can be combined with many other sales strategies, including online sales, craft shows, and flea markets. There are also a great number of benefits to selling from home, including no commute, tax advantages, and making the most out of existing resources.

Not every home is suitable for product sales, and some communities do not allow homebased businesses at all. But for entrepreneurs who have suitable homes and products, selling from home has the potential to generate enormous revenues and profits, and it is also very convenient. In addition to the information discussed below, additional information about operating a business from home is featured in Chapter 3, Setting Up Shop.

Interior Showrooms

Homebased entrepreneurs have lots of options in terms of establishing an interior showroom to showcase and sell products. You can convert your garage, basement, den, or just about any room of your home into a well-stocked showroom to peddle your wares. Ideally, the space you choose will have a separate entrance to provide privacy for your family and customers alike. You will also need to decide if your showroom will be open every day, weekends only, or only occasionally and to post the appropriate operating hours.

What are the best products to sell from a homebased interior showroom? Some products are better suited than others, but at the same time, just about any product can be showcased and sold from an interior showroom. A few of the better-suited products include costume jewelry, refurbished antiques, pottery, clothing, custom-made furniture, craft products, food products, art, fashion accessories, and toys. Regardless of the products, be sure to display and merchandise your products just like a traditional storefront retailer. Take advantage of proper display cases, racks, lighting, mirrors, and signage, and renovate and decorate the showroom to project the appropriate image for your business and products.

Exterior Display

Displaying products for sale outside your home is the second option, and a good one because potentially you get increased interest from passing motorists and pedestrians that can see the products you make and sell. Perfect products to display outdoors include patio furniture, greenhouses, sheds, whirligigs, arbors, utility trailers, refurbished power equipment, birdhouses, mailboxes, and weathervanes. Ultimately, the products you make and sell will determine the best places around the home to display them—patio furniture right on your own sundeck, greenhouses in the garden, and weathervanes adorning your roof line.

Theft can become problematic when displaying products outdoors, so be sure to install motion lights, fencing, and gates as required. Like in an interior showroom, you also have to consider the image you want to project for your business. Things such as peeling paint, overgrown gardens, and broken windows will have a negative impact on business. Consequently, before displaying products for sale, make sure you first spruce up the exterior of your home and property, make repairs as necessary, and keep on top of on-going maintenance.

In-Home Sales Parties

In-home sales parties are an excellent selling option for the right products. You simply enlist people interested in making extra money to organize and host parties right in their own homes to sell your products. Your new sales force can be paid in three ways. One, they earn a commission based on their total sales. Two, they can buy product from you wholesale and resell at retail, keeping the profit. Three, they can receive free products instead of money; the amount is based on their total sales. Perfect candidates to recruit to your sales team include stay-at-home parents, students, retired folks, and anyone else looking to make extra money working from home.

The biggest advantage of home party sales is zero competition. Salespeople have the undivided attention of party guests. In a few short hours, sales agents can earn hundreds in profits, and so can you from their hard work. The best products to sell at home sale parties are clothing, specialty foods, cosmetics, bath and body products, soaps, candles, costume jewelry, gift baskets, children's toys and products, lawn and garden products, and aromatherapy products. Your sales agents can take orders for products, which you can later ship from your central location. Or, they can have product on hand for customers to take home. You will need to supply each with product samples, sales brochures, and a sales and operations manual that includes how they can organize and host the event. The following tips are guaranteed to boost sales and profits at in-home sales parties.

- *Offer free gift-wrapping for smaller items.* Doing so motivates people to buy extra product as gifts for others not in attendance.
- *Design and print $10-off gift certificates.* Distribute one to each guest in attendance, but mark void if not used that night. People will feel compelled to buy rather than risk losing the $10.
- *Offer additional savings at various purchase levels.* For example, buy $50 worth of product and receive a $5 credit, $100 to receive a $12 credit, and $200 to receive a $30 credit toward the purchase of more product.
- *Offer a discount.* In advance of the party, tell guests that if they bring a friend, both will receive a 10 percent discount on all purchases.
- *Stage a contest, and give away a prize at each party.* Have guests complete an entry form, including full contact information, and draw for the prize. The entry forms can be later used to build a database of potential customers, which can be routinely contacted with special offers via e-mail, mail, and telephone.

Promoting Homebased Sales

Retail storefront or selling from home, consumers have to know what you sell, where you are located, and how they can contact you. Consequently, you need to advertise. For budget-minded entrepreneurs, the best and least expensive ways to promote homebased sales are with attention-grabbing signage, classified advertisements, fliers, and word-of-mouth advertising.

Providing local laws permit, exterior signs are one of the best promotional tools for homebased sales. You can advertise what you sell, business hours, and regular specials for zero cost outside of routine sign maintenance. Buy two types of exterior signs. One, a stationary backlit sign installed as per local ordinance, and two, a portable backlit sign with interchangeable letters, giving you the ability to alter your marketing message to promote new products, sales, and special events as needed.

Next, use cheap and free classified advertisements in your local newspaper to promote your business and products. People seldom search classified ads for entertainment; they are always looking to buy a specific product. In your ads, include a product description, contact information, price, and an attention-grabbing device such as a border, bold headline, or icon.

Fliers are a fast and frugal promotional tool for advertising your homebased business and products. Providing you have a computer and basic design savvy, you can create your own fliers at home and have them copied for pennies each at your local copy center. Use the fliers to promote your business, products, and specials, and pin the fliers to community bulletin boards, tuck them under parked-cars' windshield wipers, or have students deliver them door-to-door throughout the community.

Finally, word-of-mouth advertising is the ultimate cheap source of highly effective advertising because it costs nothing. But how do you get it? Get out in the community, and talk to people. Tell them about your high-quality products that you sell at fair prices. Provide incredible customer service when people do buy, and never stop thanking them for supporting your business. Combined, these simple practices will increase word-of-mouth advertising for your business exponentially.

Selling from a Retail Location

If selling the products you make from home is not an option, perhaps you will need to rent retail space such as a storefront or mall kiosk to sell your products directly to consumers. Alternately, you might choose to rent industrial space as a location to manufacture as well as sell products. This option is known as selling factory direct to consumers. Selling products from a commercial retail location as opposed to selling from home has advantages. First, customers may perceive your business as more professional. Second, retail locations generally have much better visibility than a primarily residential district, thereby greatly increasing the potential for walk-in business and higher sales revenues. There are also disadvantages, namely the additional cost of rent, utilities, and building maintenance and the need to hire employees to keep the store staffed during normal retail business hours. If you sell from a retail storefront, a mall kiosk, or factory direct, many of the merchandising ideas featured in this section are portable and can be employed to display and sell products regardless of the selling location.

Retail Storefront

In Chapter 3, Setting Up Shop, it was mentioned that not all products are suitable to be made and sold from a retail storefront. Perhaps the best suited are specialty foods, designer fashions and accessories, awards and trophies, golf clubs, signs, stained glass products, gift baskets, pottery, and pet treats. Retailing is a very broad subject and continually evolving. What worked in the 1950s does not work in today's highly competitive retail environment. In fact, what worked as recently as last month might not work today.

Space limitations in this chapter do not permit discussing everything you need to know to sell products from a retail storefront. Information featured here covers only the tip of the retailing iceberg. You need to carefully research and plan every aspect of a retail venture in order to maximize the potential for success. You have to invest the time and financial resources needed to educate yourself about retailing—buy and read books on retail businesses, hire retail sales consultants, join retailers' associations, and talk to a whole bunch of retailers before taking the leap of faith and opening up shop. But with that said, the following information will give you the basics and a starting point from which to branch out.

The objective when designing a retail store and merchandising products is to appeal to the largest segment of your target audience so that they will feel comfortable in the store and will want to return and shop often. This is one area in which it pays to hire a professional retail store designer. When arranging product displays, think profit zones—the areas around the sales checkout, around the entrance, and areas on a direct path to the sales counter. These areas account for the largest percentage of impulse buying. Consumers also go shopping for pure entertainment value, and you have to keep this in mind when creating in-store merchandise displays. Make product displays exciting, attention grabbing, and memorable by using props, signage, and live demonstrations. Also group products together that compliment each and make a logical sales package. Designer clothing should be displayed with fashion accessories such as handbags, costume jewelry, and shoes, for instance. Complimentary product grouping helps to increase sales and the value of each sale.

Window space is one of the best and least expensive marketing tools available to most retailers; think of your window space as a 24-hour silent salesperson that never sleeps. Windows can be used to display new products, demonstrate products, and motivate impulse buying. In short, well-planned and executed window displays can increase revenues and profits. If you are new to designing window displays, buy books on the topic, and armed with a camera get out and look at what other retailers are doing with their windows. Take pictures and make notes about window displays that work, so you can get your creative juices flowing. The best window displays are lean and mean with one central focal point; you do not need your entire inventory on display. You might also want to occasionally create window displays around popular entertainment, sports, or musical events, and use props and movement to make your displays come alive. Remember, the goal is to grab attention and pull people into your shop to buy.

Mall Kiosks

Kiosks and pushcarts also represent great selling opportunities for vendors with the right products. I am sure that many of you think hot dogs, ice cream, and popcorn when you think of pushcarts or kiosks, but they are also use for selling any number of products, including costume jewelry, clothing, crafts, gift baskets, wind chimes, birdhouses, candles, cosmetics, soaps, and specialty foods. There are both interior and exterior styles, though the focus here is on interior kiosks and pushcarts that you find in malls, office buildings, government buildings, airports, and train stations. Many of these carts and kiosks are available to rent on a short- and long-term basis, from a day to a year. Generally speaking, it is the building or property management company that rents vending space, so these are the people that you want to contact. In addition to a vendor's permit, most locations also require you to have liability insurance. The locations mentioned above can be lucrative in terms of revenues, but vendors who specialize in selling from mall kiosks tend to fare the best and produce the highest sales, especially during the Christmas shopping season.

Factory Direct

There are advantages and disadvantages associated with selling factory direct. On the plus side, consumers, rightly or wrongly, perceive buying factory direct as getting good value because they believe they are paying less than retail by cutting out all middlemen. Depending on your approach to marketing and your pricing philosophy, you may indeed elect to sell at a discount. You may choose not to. Regardless, the consumer's perspective is she is getting a deal by buying products directly from the factory. Another advantage of factory-direct sales is you have the opportunity to complement other sales and distribution methods, such as wholesales sales, online sales, and selling via events such as trade shows. Likewise, you can also use the factory direct sales approach to move slow moving inventory, dated products, seconds, and product returns in a cost-efficient manner. This can be achieved by hosting a monthly, quarterly, semi-annually, or annual scratch-and-dent sale.

The biggest disadvantage to selling products directly from your factory is interruption. Will you be throwing a wrench into the gears? If your sales and marketing efforts are aimed mainly at wholesale sales and mass production, trying to sell from your manufacturing location could prove to hinder sales rather than bolster them, especially for businesses with few, if any, support staff. When you sell in a retail environment, you have to wait on customers, answer the telephone, have a clean and organized business interior and exterior, and to keep regular store hours. There are also safety concerns because you do not want customers wandering around the production area, with the potential to be injured.

Additional issues to consider and address if you choose to sell directly from your manufacturing location include establishing a product showroom space separate from production space, advertising and promoting factory-direct sales, providing customer conveniences such as parking and washrooms, and concerns involving zoning, fire, safety, and handicap access. Ultimately, you will have to weigh the advantages and disadvantages associated with factory-direct sales to determine if the opportunity enhances or distracts from your sales and marketing objectives.

Selling to Retailers

Truly ambitious entrepreneurs may choose to skip selling their products directly to consumers altogether and instead go after the big market opportunities, wholesaling their products in mass quantities to independent retailers and chain retailers or to middlemen wholesalers, distributors, or import/export specialists. If so, information about how to go about selling wholesale is featured in this section. Yet another option is to sell the products you make directly to other businesses. Products such as gift baskets, advertising novelties, art, and furniture are examples of products that businesses buy to give to customers as gifts or to use in their businesses. One of the best and least costly ways to get started selling your products to other businesses is to join business and nonbusiness clubs and associations so you can network with members. This is a grassroots approach to building your business through personal contacts and word-of-mouth.

Wholesale

If you are a big thinker and want to wholesale the products you make in mass quantities, there are basically three avenues available to you—the grassroots approach, the established wholesale channel approach, and the business-to-business trade show approach. All three have advantages and disadvantages and are discussed in greater detail below. Depending on your products, price point, and business and sales objectives, you may elect to combine one or more of these approaches to wholesale the products you make.

THE GRASSROOTS APPROACH

The grassroots approach is nothing more than setting appointments with independent and chain retailers, and armed with product samples and catalogs, you present and pitch your products. Of course, this is often easier said than done. Securing appointments with independent retailers is not difficult and generally only requires a telephone call or introduction letter to get the ball rolling. However, chain retailers are an entirely different ball game. All buying decisions are made at the head office level. First, it can be very difficult to get past the gatekeepers and to the people who make buying decisions. Second, if you do get five minutes of their time, you better have something very impressive to pitch, otherwise, get use to rejection. Chain retailers want to know why they should buy your products, what are the competitive advantages and special features, and how their customers benefit by purchasing them? In addition, they'll want to know, how you are going to promote and support the product in terms of guarantees and advertising to motivate consumers to go to the retailer's store and buy. It is possible to land vendor accounts with major chain retailers, but be prepared to work hard and smart to accomplish this goal.

THE ESTABLISHED WHOLESALE CHANNEL APPROACH

This approach is much like the grassroots approach, but instead of setting appointments with retailers, you set appointments with businesses that already have established channels of distribution in place, namely wholesalers, distributors, and exporters. You sell your product to the wholesaler, who in turns sells it to the retailer, who in turn sells it to the consumer. The major downside associated with this option is price point. You have to have the ability to sell your product for drastically less than retail, often by as much as 60 percent off retail in order for the wholesaler to be able to sell to retailers at a profitable price point. Having said that, you can make up lower profits per unit by selling in larger quantities. Contact the National Association of Wholesale Distributors, ☎ (202) 872-0885, ♂ www. naw.org, to find a wholesaler that sells the types of products you make.

THE BUSINESS-TO-BUSINESS TRADE SHOW APPROACH

The third, and arguably best, approach is to exhibit your products at business-to-business trade shows, which are basically the same as consumer trade shows with one big exception: Wholesale buyers representing national and international retailers of all sizes attend, and they are there to buy in quantity. There are industry trade shows for just about every type of product imaginable—craft products, fashions and accessories, furniture, garden products, food products, recreational products, and more. Best of all, unlike consumer shows, buyers do not want to purchase products and take immediate delivery; they are there to scout products, negotiate prices, and place orders for future delivery. Therefore, all you have to bring are product samples and a catalog listing your products, accompanied by order forms indicating unit pricing, bulk pricing, payment terms and methods, delivery schedules, minimum order amounts, warranty information, and return policy. The National Mail Order Association, ☎ (612) 788-4197, ✆ www.nmoa. org, publishes an annual *Industry Trade Show, Importer, and Wholesale Marketplace Directory*, which includes listing information on more than 150 product trade shows, as well as wholesale publications, trade magazines, and manufacturer directories.

Consignment

Should you place your products on consignment with retailers? Yes and no. Yes, consigning products can be a viable way to get your products in retail stores and ultimately purchased by consumers. No, consignment is not suited to all products, and there are additional drawbacks such as high sales commission fees, loss of control over merchandising, and having to wait weeks, sometimes months, before being paid on sales. Suitable products for consignment include items such as craft products, art, gift products, woodcrafts, and designer fashions. If you decide to go the consignment route, there are four main points to consider: types of retailers and location, consignment agreement, merchandising and pricing, and inventory management and product delivery.

TYPES OF RETAILERS AND LOCATION

Not all retailers accept consignment products, although many do, especially those selling gift and craft products. You have to choose wisely and make sure your products are compatible with the types of products the retailer sells. Likewise, you also have to decide if you will consign with local retailers and/or out-of-town retailers. Both have advantages and disadvantages. Consigning locally is very convenient, easy to deliver, and simple to monitor inventory, whereas out of town consignments add travel time and shipping costs. On the other hand, consigning out of your local area opens the possibility of selling more products to a broader audience of consumers. Overall, when selecting retailers to consign with, consider the types of products they sell, their current sales, their reputations, and if they have established consignment programs in place.

CONSIGNMENT AGREEMENT

The devil is always in the details. Closely scrutinize the retailer's consignment agreement before signing on the dotted line. Here is what you need to know in advance of shipping or delivering products:

- How much is the retailer's sales commission on products sold? Depending on the value of the product, expect the retailer to retain a commission in the range of 25 to 50 percent.
- Does the retailer generate a consignment sales report, how often do you get paid on products sold, and how is the payment made—check, direct deposit, or cash?
- What are the retailer's policies in terms of consignment product returns, refunds, and theft, and does the retailer's insurance cover your products in the event of fire, flood, or other causes of damage?

MERCHANDISING AND PRICING

Ideally, you want the ability to merchandise and price your products. Unfortunately, this is not always the case. Many retailers that accept consigned products reserve the right to decide how the products will be merchandised inside the store as well as the retail selling price. The right to merchandise and price your products is the key to successful and profitable consigning. Consequently, fight for this right, but at the same time go armed with the tools needed to persuade the retailer to your way of thinking. These tools include but are not limited to:

- a high-quality, in-demand product.
- if applicable, a strong product guarantee or warranty.
- competitive pricing.
- attention-grabbing packaging and merchandise displays.

Likewise, also fight for the best real estate inside the store—close to the checkout, around the entrance, and good window visibility. Ultimately, the retailer is in the business of selling goods, not simply displaying goods. You have to develop products and merchandising strategies that will motivate people to buy.

INVENTORY MANAGEMENT AND PRODUCT DELIVERY

You will also need to develop an inventory management system, which will have to be standardized and centralized if you consign products with more than one retailer. The simplest way of doing this is to create a consignment form listing initial inventory stocked, removing items as they are sold or removed from the store, as well as listing new products stocked. It is crucial to keep a very accurate record of all inventory and to obtain signatures every time products are restocked or removed from the store. Not only will this protect against inventory shrinkage, but also over time you will be able to determine what products sell best at each of the retailers and at what times of year, enabling you to develop marketing strategies to maximize sales at each location. Additionally, you will also have to think about product delivery. Will you hand deliver to all consignment accounts or have products shipped? If your accounts are close, you can deliver to each. If not, it will probably be cheaper to have products shipped. In this latter case, you have to find out how much this will add to the unit cost of each product.

Manufacturers' Agents

Many manufacturers enlist the services of manufacturers' sales agents to find new customers for their product(s) locally, nationally, and internationally. This is especially true of manufacturers who do not have the financial or people resources to undertake establishing distributorships and vendor accounts in far-flung locations, as well as manufacturers that have a limited product line, too small to grab the interest of major wholesalers or distributors. The job of the agent is to represent the manufacturer's products, prospect for new business, and establish and service vendor accounts on behalf of the manufacturer. Thus, sales agents will help you grow your business by selling your product lines to wholesalers, distributors, corporations, retailers, other small businesses, institutions, or whomever meets your target audience.

Contracting with one or more sales agents is a great alternative to hiring salespeople to sell your products. First, most manufacturers' agents prefer to work on a contract basis for tax reasons and to maintain the ability to represent more than one manufacturer at a time. This means less paper work for you and no need to provide employee benefits. Second, sales agents come armed with the tools they need to sell—transportation, computer hardware and software, and cellular telephones, saving you money by not having to purchase and maintain these items. Third, and perhaps the biggest benefit of contracting with sales agents, is the fact that they bring two big assets to the table—the ability to prospect effectively for new business and in most instances, an existing customer and contact base that can be capitalized upon immediately for the benefit of your business.

Almost all sales agents prefer to work on a performance-based fee system, retaining a commission of total sales. Depending on the product(s) sold, the extent of services provided, and the hard costs associated with providing these services, commissions range from 5 to 30 percent of total sales value. To find a suitable sales agent, you can contact The Manufacturers' Agents National Association at ☎ (949) 859-4040, or log on to ✆ www.manaonline.org. Likewise, you can also log on to Find A Sales Agent, ✆ www.findasalesagent.com, which is an online sales agent directory.

Selling Online

There are literally thousands of ways to promote and sell products online, but this section will focus on three—eBay, e-auctions, and internet malls. Of course, you can and should also develop your own e-commerce web site so you can sell your products to an audience of worldwide consumers. The advantages of internet e-tailing are obvious—open 24-hours a day, trade information to customers in minutes, and ability to update your marketing message and strategy quickly, conveniently, and very inexpensively. However, it is not suggested that you use a web site as your sole means of selling products online. Instead, use your site in combination with other online sales methods such as eBay as well as offline venues such as homebased sales and trade and consumer shows. Further considerations are who will build, maintain, and host your site and how much will all this cost? Also, you will need shopping carts, online payment systems, content, web tools, and a strategy for promoting the site and your products. More information about building and promoting a web site can be found in Chapter 3, Setting Up Shop.

eBay

Online auction and retail marketplace giant, eBay, ✆ www.ebay.com, has more than 100 million registered users around the globe, has set up camp in more than 20 countries worldwide, and even more amazing, has 450,000 registered users claiming to sell products through eBay for their sole source of income! Volumes can, have, and will continue to be written on the subject of profiting from doing business on eBay. But this book is not about eBay, and space does not permit a detailed explanation about how it works. eBay is as wide as it is deep, so you should spend lots of time on its sites, take advantage of its sponsored workshops, and read books about eBay selling to further your knowledge before you get started.

The most popular and common type of eBay auction is the traditional, or classic, auction. In this type of auction, there is no reserve price set, and at the end of the one-, three-, five-, seven-, or ten-day auction, the highest bid wins. The theory of a short auction is it enables you to generate more heat and bidding excitement whereas a longer auction might eventually lead to diminished interest as time passes. On the opposite side of the coin, a longer auction means your product(s) will be exposed to more potential buyers and might fetch a higher price. Ultimately, you will have to play around with auction lengths a bit to find what works best for what you sell. eBay also offers a *Buy it Now* option, which means you can set a price for your product and a buyer can purchase it for the set price without having to wait for the auction to end. But once you receive a bid, the *Buy It Now* icon disappears and the sale reverts back to a traditional auction.

Sellers also have the option to set a reserve price for the item. A reserve price is the lowest possible price a seller is prepared to take for the item, but buyers do not know how much the reserve price is, only that there is a reserve. Once a bid exceeds the reserve price, the item sells to the highest bidder. If the reserve price is not met before the auction expires, the item does not sell and the seller can choose to relist the product for sale or not. Many sellers like to set a reserve price matching their cost as a way to protect against selling for less than cost.

A third option is a Dutch auction, which is a good choice for product manufacturers that have multiple units of the same products for sale, such as 25 birdhouses, 500 candles, or 10 Adirondack patio chairs. There is no upper limit to how many of the same products you can list using a Dutch auction—10 or 10,000, it's up to you. Bidders have the option of selecting how many they want to purchase—one, some, or all. Sellers start by listing the number of items for sale along with the starting bid. Bidders enter the amount they are willing to pay along with the number of units they want to purchase. The winning price is determined by the lowest successful bid at the time the auction closes, and all winning bidders receive this price even if their bid was higher. The concept is that if you receive bids for more items than you have for sale, then the lowest bids drop off, raising the price. Bidders can rebid a higher amount to stay in the game if they choose. A Dutch auction is a great way to move large quantities of products quickly and efficiently, especially high-demand products.

eBay also offers sellers who qualify an opportunity to open their own eBay storefront. At present it offers three packages—basic, featured, and anchor store. Depending on the package, features could include 24-hour customer service, 5 to 15 customizable web pages to feature products for sale, traffic reporting and administration, in-site advertising, and keyword promotion programs. There are many benefits to having your own store, including the opportunity to build repeat business with customers, longer listings so you can spend more time selling and less time listing products, your own web address and linking programs, listing in the eBay store directory, and an internal in-store search engine enabling customers to conveniently browse through your products.

Some useful eBay information sites are:

- eBay Learning Center, ♂ http://pages.ebay.com/education/index.html
- eBay Promotional Tools, ♂ http://pages.ebay.com/sellercentral/tools.html
- eBay Seller's Guide, ♂ http://pages.ebay.com/help/sell/index.html
- eBay Selling Internationally, ♂ http://pages.ebay.com/help/sell/ia/selling _internationally.html
- eBay Shipping Center, ♂ http://pages.ebay.com/services/buyandsell/ship ping.html
- eBay Stores, ♂ http://pages.ebay.com/storefronts/start.html

Some helpful books on eBay are:

- 📖 *Building Your eBay Traffic the Smart Way: Use Froogle, Datafeeds, Cross-Selling, Advanced Listing Strategies, and More to Boost Your Sales on the Web's #1 Auction Site*, Joseph T. Sinclair (American Management Association, 2005)
- 📖 *eBay for Dummies*, Marsha Collier (For Dummies, 2004)
- 📖 *eBay Powerseller Secrets*, Debra Schepp and Brad Schepp (McGraw-Hill Osborne Media, 2004)
- 📖 *eBay Strategies: 10 Proven Methods to Maximize your eBay Business*, Scot Wingo (Prentice Hall, 2004)
- 📖 *Make Big Profits on eBay: Start Your Own Million Dollar Business*, Jacquelyn Lynn and Charlene Davis (Entrepreneur Press, 2005)

Other e-Auctions

Although eBay is the undisputed king of online auctions, at the same time it is not the only game in town. You do not want to limit your selling options to a single venue, especially if you can combine other online auction options to complement eBay sales. There are hundreds of other online auction sites, such as Auction Fire, ♂ www.auctionfire.com, and Yahoo Auctions, ♂ www.auctions.yahoo.com. While some are good, most are not worth the time or effort to bother listing products. Consequently, spend some time to research and select the ones best suited to your products and marketing objectives. Some are general auction sites with numerous categories ranging from clothing to furniture to toys, while others are more product or industry specific, such as fine art, books, antiques, and sports memorabilia. Some operate on a highest bid, reserve bid, and/or Dutch auction format depending on the site and products offered for sale.

Many of the same marketing and promotional techniques used on eBay to attract and secure top bids are portable and can be applied to other online auction sites. People making and selling very specific items are encouraged to explore alternate auction services because they do attract targeted buyers searching for specific products. To find more specific online auction sites, visit online auction directories such as Net Auctions, ♂ www.net-auctions.com, and The Internet Auction List, ♂ www.internetauctionlist.com; both list hundreds of online auction web sites.

Internet Malls

Just like bricks and mortar shopping malls, internet malls offer consumers a one-stop shopping opportunity for a wide range of products and services. There are a number of companies and services offering internet mall and e-storefront programs. The big players in this arena are eBay, ♂ www.ebay.com, Amazon, ♂ www.amazon.com, and the Internet Mall, ♂ www.internetmall.com; but there are also hundreds of smaller outfits offering numerous online selling opportunities for the small e-tailer. A few of these include outfits such as American Internet Mall, ♂ www.aimone.com, Canadian Internet Mall, ♂ www.cdn-mall.com, and Mall Park, ♂ www.mallpark.com.

Most internet malls or e-storefront programs offer two basic types of services. One, they operate as a directory service listing product and/or service categories, and for a fee your business can be listed under one or more appropriate categories. To take advantage of this option means you already have or are building a web site so you can link to the mall's directory. Two, the internet malls and e-storefront services offer a more complete package, which can include one or more of the following: domain name registration, web site building, hosting, e-commerce tools, back-end administration tools, and promotion. There are also programs that blend the two types according to your needs and budget. Fees vary widely depending on your level of participation and the services you need, but generally they start at a few hundred dollars in development fees along with ongoing monthly fees ranging from $20 to $500.

Again, before signing on the dotted line, do your homework to ensure the mall has a good reputation with vendors and shoppers, offers the services you need, attracts your target audience, and has a strong marketing campaign in place to promote the mall and participating vendors.

Selling at Events

In addition to the numerous places to sell your products already discussed in this chapter, there are also many special events that provide fantastic selling opportunities—trade and consumer shows, arts and crafts shows, flea markets, and community events.

Trade and Consumer Shows

For small business owners, few marketing activities in the bricks and mortar world can match the effectiveness of trade and consumer shows as a way to showcase and sell your products to a large audience at one time, in one place, and in a very cost-effective manner. Depending on the show and duration, you have the potential to come in contact with hundreds, if not thousands, of qualified prospects. The difference between trade shows and consumer shows is trade shows are generally businesses exhibiting for, and selling to, other businesses, whereas consumer shows are for the general public to attend, browse, gain information, and shop.

At present, there is a trade or consumer show for every imaginable type of product, service, activity, or industry. In fact, at the time of writing there are in excess of 10,000 trade and consumer shows hosted annually in North America, for home and garden, food, sports and recreation, gifts, photography, and baby shows. Fortunately, surfing the numerous trade show directories on the internet such as Trade Shows Online, ♂ www.tradeshows.com, makes it very easy to research shows and to gain valuable insights into location, costs, attendance statistics, and competition. You should, however, attend shows in person first to get a feel for the vendors, management, and audience before making the commitment to exhibit, especially for more expensive and out-of-town shows.

The show pace can be fast and furious, and time is a commodity that is always in short supply. So it is important to have a well-rehearsed sales plan ready to put into action. Your sales plan should revolve around four key elements—engage prospects, qualify prospects, present your products, and close the sale. Also, when designing your booth and displays, keep in mind that booths alive with exciting product demonstrations draw considerably more interest and larger crowds than do static booths. Consequently, arrange your booth and display so that you can make products, while demonstrating user benefits and features in front of a live audience.

Arts and Craft Shows

Arts and crafts shows are an excellent forum for selling high-quality handmade products such as folk art, fine art, woodturnings, sewing and needlecraft specialties, soaps, candles, and costume jewelry. Shows range in size from small church-organized shows with a handful of vendors to international fine arts and crafts shows lasting for a week and drawing hundreds of vendors and thousands of consumers from around the globe. But most are small events over a weekend and take place in community centers, exhibition buildings, hotels, convention centers, and school gymnasiums. Booth rent varies widely from $5 to $500 per day, depending on the size of the show, expected audience, and marketing push to promote the event. Visit the large and more expensive shows before signing on to make sure the show and audience meet your exhibiting criteria, and talk to other vendors to get firsthand feedback about the show. Additional points to consider include admission fees, parking, competition, rent, operating history, and attendance statistics. Crafts Shows USA, ♂ www.craftshowsusa.com, provides a free online directory service listing information on hundreds of craft shows.

Once you have decided to show and sell your products, be sure to create a checklist a week before the event, and check off each item or task as completed so you are 100 percent ready to sell come show time. Likewise, in-booth demonstrations of your art or craft always draw crowds and grab more attention than exhibits without demonstrations, and a busy booth equals more selling opportunities. On the topic of booths, displays, and products, keep them clean, organized, and use mirrors and lighting to brighten your sales space. Because shows can be very busy, price all items to save time repeating prices to everyone who asks. Also, create a couple worthwhile *show specials* to pull shoppers into your booth. A 50-percent-off show special may seem excessive, but revenues and profits can be made up in volume sales and through up-selling opportunities.

Ideally, you will want to accept credit cards and debit cards because it increases impulse buying by as much as 50 percent. You will also need a receipt book, credit card slips, calculator, pens, price gun or blank price tags, and a cash lockbox. Also bring along a basic toolbox for last-minute changes or emergencies. Stock the toolbox with a hammer, screwdrivers, flashlight, wrench, extra light bulbs, cleaner, rags, stapler, and garbage bags. Finally, stock lots of packing materials, including newspaper, plastic bags, boxes, tape, string, and scissors, and offer free gift wrapping. Associations such as the Arts and Crafts Association of America, ☎ (616) 874-1721, ♂ www.artsandcraftsassoc.com, and the Canadian Crafts & Hobby Association, ☎ (403) 291-0559, ♂ www.cdncraft.org, are also excellent sources of information about making and selling crafts.

Flea Markets

There are an estimated 750,000 flea market vendors peddling products in the United States and Canada at more than 10,000 flea markets, bazaars, and swap meets; some attract crowds in excess of 25,000 a day. Even more impressive: Many vendors are earning as much as $50,000 a year working only a two days a week. Good flea markets are everywhere, but visit a few first to get a feel for the venue, vendors, and visitors before deciding where to set up shop. Check out the venue—do they charge admission, is there adequate parking, and do they heavily promote the event? Check out the vendors—what do they sell, how much are they charging, how much are they selling, and how many are selling the same things as you? Check out the visitors—are they buying or browsing, how many are there, and do they meet your target customer profile? To find flea markets, visit online directories like Flea Market Guide, ✄ www.fleamarketguide.com, Flea USA, ✄ www.flea markets.com, and Keys Flea Market, ✄ www.keysfleamarket.com. All list hundreds of flea markets indexed geographically.

There are also many types of flea markets—weekends only, everyday, summer only, outside under tents, open air, and inside swanky buildings resembling mall retailing more than flea market vending. All have advantages and disadvantages. For instance, outside flea markets are subject to weather: wind, rain, sun, heat, and cold. Booth rents also widely vary from a low of $5 per day to as much as $100 for single-day events. Other considerations include customer and vendor parking, electricity, phone lines for credit card and debit card terminals, on-site ATM machine, washrooms, food services, and overall organization.

You will also need to supply your own transportation and equipment such as dollies to load and unload merchandise and displays. Some flea markets provide merchandising tables, canopies, and displays, whereas others rent these items separately. Still others do not supply anything except for the booth. Here are more tips to get you started on your way to earning huge profits selling your products at flea markets.

- *Take a box stocked with items.* Bring along tape, string, receipt books, calculator, pens, fliers, business cards, credit card slips, magic markers, price gun or label marker, scissors, cleaning products and rags, and packing supplies like newspaper, plastic bags, and cardboard boxes.
- *Get a merchant account and wireless terminal for debit cards and credit cards.* Many people bring cash to flea markets, but it is proven that accepting plastic can increase impulse buying by as much as 50 percent. Accepting checks, even with proper identification, is not recommended. Also, make sure you have an ample cash float and supply of small bills for change.
- *Invest in professional displays and sales aids to help boost revenues and profits.* Have bold and colorful professional signs and banners made, purchase high quality and attractive displays on wheels for easy loading and transportation, keep your merchandise clean and organized, and even consider uniforms, such as T-shirts, hats, or golf shirts with an identifier like Pete's Patio Furniture emblazoned across them.

- *Hand out fliers to everyone passing, even if they do not buy.* The fliers should describe your products and contact info—web site, telephone number, and business address. To increase the effectiveness of this simple marketing trick, print tips on the back of the flier so people have reason to hang onto it rather than toss it in the trash once home. For instance, if you make and sell canoe paddles, list 20 paddling tips on the back or 20 great places to canoe.
- *Develop a system for capturing names and addresses.* You can utilize this information for direct marketing purposes—mail, e-mail, and telemarketing. Hold a contest and use the information on the entry ballot to build a database, or ask people to subscribe to your product catalog.
- *Be ready to haggle.* Everyone shopping at flea markets expects to bargain and wants to flex his or her negotiation muscle. Price items 10 to 20 percent higher so you have room to negotiate yet still get your price.
- *Use all types of attention-grabbing devices.* Stand out by using colorful banners, balloons, lights, music, and flags. Large markets have hundreds, sometimes thousands of vendors all vying for the attention of shoppers, so you need to be creative and stand out in the crowd.
- *Develop ways to engage people and get them into your booth.* Flea market vendors cannot afford to be wallflowers; there are far too many competitors chasing the same consumers. You have to be creative. One method is to use product demonstrations to pull them in.

Community Events

Parades, fairs, holiday celebrations, farmers' markets, public markets, street vending, rodeos, music festivals, and swap meets, every community has numerous events and celebrations throughout the year. Many of these events provide excellent opportunities to sell the products you make—costume jewelry, clothing, candles, soaps, silk-screened T-shirts, handbags, craft items, and specialty foods, to mention a few. Local associations, such as the chamber of commerce, a charity, sports group, social club, church, school, or local government departments, usually organize community events. Therefore, you will need to contact event organizers to inquire about available vending opportunities. Rent or booth fees and permit costs vary depending on the type of event, anticipated crowd, and duration of the event. Some are free, but most charge. The most expensive are usually fairs and exhibitions, which can cost as much as $500 a day.

Selling at community events is like any other retailing opportunity—think booth location within the event, signage, professional displays, quality merchandise, fair pricing, quick service, and a smile. Combine these with an outgoing personality, and you cannot help but sell and make lots of profits in the process. This is to say, never assume your products will sell itself. Get involved, chat with people, show and tell them about the benefits and features of your products, and have fun. Also, be sure to print fliers describing your business and products and how people can contact you after the event by including web address, e-mail, telephone numbers, and showroom address, if applicable. The fliers should be given to both people who purchased products and people just looking or passing by.

6

THE BEST 202 THINGS YOU CAN MAKE AND SELL FOR BIG PROFITS

Now the real fun begins. In this chapter, you will discover the best 202 things to make and sell for big profits. Of course, not every person has the skills or finances needed to make each of the products listed. Some people will be better equipped than others to make and sell certain products. But don't worry, there is a product suited for everyone here, as you will soon discover. Ultimately, once you have considered all of the important issues such as your current skills, investment criteria, objectives, and interests, you will be the judge of what product(s) you are best suited to make.

The criteria used to select the best products to make and sell is based on a number of factors, including:

- proven demand
- minimal to moderate investment levels
- excellent profit potential
- appeal to different personalities, experiences, and skills levels

The information presented in this chapter is in brief synopsis format. The product is explained, along with marketing information, and often equipment and training requirements. For people who would prefer to own and operate a franchise, instead of starting their own business from scratch, I have also listed franchise business opportunity resources as available. These are flagged with a star icon ✯.

At a Glance

At the end of each product listing featured in this chapter, you will find capsulated information covering the amount of investment needed to start the business, skill level requirements, and helpful resources. This information provides a helpful overview of the business and product featured, so that at a glance you will have general information answering the questions: "How much money must I have to get started? Are there any special skills needed to make the product? And, what do I do next?"

🖐 Investment

Business start-up investment information provided should only be used as a guideline. Actual start-up costs may be higher or lower than indicated. The investment figures shown are for new businesses started from scratch and are not reflective of the costs associated with purchasing a business or a franchise. Investment figures also do not take into account the need to purchase transportation, specialized tools and equipment, and working capital reserve or to buy or rent and substantially renovate a business location, but these figures do cover the basics, such as business registration, basic tools and equipment, a computer, business cards, fliers, minimal materials inventory, and a small initial advertising and marketing budget.

BUSINESS START-UP INVESTMENT CATEGORIES

Investment: Under $2K   = Start-up investment less than $2,000
Investment: Under $10K = Start-up investment $2,001 to $10,000

Investment: Under $25K = Start-up investment $10,001 to $25,000

Investment: Over $25K   = Start-up investment greater than $25,000

Skill Level

Information is also provided about the skills needed or, in many instances, not needed make and sell the product. This information is based on a scale of one to three. Level 1 represents the lowest skill requirement. There is no experience or training needed; you can learn how to make the product mainly through trial and error and practice. Skill level 2 means general knowledge and previous experience is recommended. Skill level 3 means training is recommended. This information should only be used for general purposes. It is the responsibility of all entrepreneurs to make sure that you have the skills needed to make and sell any product before getting started.

SKILL LEVEL CATEGORIES

Skill Level: 1 = No previous experience needed

Skill Level: 2 = Experience recommended

Skill Level: 3 = Training recommended

Resources

Each product featured includes helpful resources to get you to the next level should you decide to pursue any of these product manufacturing and business ideas. Resources include associations, tool and equipment suppliers, products, publications, and franchise or business opportunities, although no recommendation is an endorsement of any company, association, product, or service. You may elect to contact and even do business with sources listed, or you may choose not to. The decision is entirely up to you. However, every effort was made to select only reputable companies, associations, products, and services to list as resources.

At the end of the day, you must be comfortable in the knowledge that you are doing business with reliable and honest sources. This can only be accomplished with research. Learn everything you can about any company or organization you intend to do business with. All should be happy to answer questions and supply references. If not, look for companies that will. It is your time, money, and energy, all very valuable assets. Do your homework to protect these assets!

RESOURCE ICONS

☎ Contact telephone number

ℐ Web address

📖 Book, magazine, or publication
★ Franchise or business opportunity

202 Things You Can Make and Sell

Garden Arbors

Building beautiful wooden garden and walkway arbors is easy, even if you are a novice woodworker. All you need is a small workshop space, arbor design plans, and equipment such as table and miter saws. In total, an investment of only a few thousand dollars will put you on your way to earning big profits making and selling garden arbors. Utilize your own garden and yard as an outdoor arbor showroom displaying your best designs. To get the telephone ringing and potential customers dropping by your home to view arbors, advertise in your community newspaper in the classifieds, by posting fliers on bulletin boards, and by joining gardening clubs in your area to network and spread the word about your arbors. Additionally, display your best designs at home and garden shows, and sell to a worldwide audience by listing your arbors for sale on eBay, in internet malls, and through e-commerce sites specializing in home and garden products.

AT A GLANCE

 INVESTMENT: Under $2K

 SKILL LEVEL: 1–2

 RESOURCES
—Garden Plans, arbor plans, ♂ www.gardenplans.com
—📖 *Trellises, Arbors & Pergolas: Ideas and Plans for Garden Structures*, Larry Johnston (Better Homes and Gardens Books, 2004)
—Woodworkers Workshop, arbor plans, ♂ www.woodworkerswork shop.com

---

Hobby Greenhouses

Hobby greenhouses have become a very popular addition to any backyard or patio space, especially for the baby boomer generation as they look for ways to keep active and enjoy life as they slip into retirement. Manufacturing hobby greenhouses is not difficult, even if you have little construction experience. You will need a well-equipped workspace, along with design and construction plans, or you can build and sell hobby greenhouses from your own or your customers' designs. Construction materials can include a wood, steel, aluminum, or plastic frames with soft plastic, hard plastic, tempered or laminated glass panels, or a combination of these materials depending on your construction preference and retail price point. Hobby greenhouse prices range from a few hundred dollars for basic models to $5,000 for models with all the bells and whistles. Hobby greenhouses are generally sold in a kit, making them easy to ship to your customers, and they require little more than basic hand tools to assemble once on site. The best way to sell hobby greenhouses is to erect a display model right at your own home, advertise locally in the classifieds, attend gardening clubs, exhibit at home and garden shows, and make sales via online marketplaces such as gardening web sites and eBay.

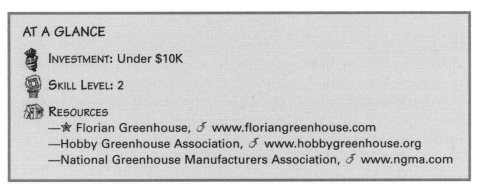

AT A GLANCE

INVESTMENT: Under $10K

SKILL LEVEL: 2

RESOURCES
—☆ Florian Greenhouse, ♂ www.floriangreenhouse.com
—Hobby Greenhouse Association, ♂ www.hobbygreenhouse.org
—National Greenhouse Manufacturers Association, ♂ www.ngma.com

Awnings

Retractable shade and rain awnings are a welcome addition to any patio space. Homeowners seeking protection from the sun and rain will be your number-one target audience. But at the same time, don't discount recreational vehicle owners and business owners with outdoor patio space, especially restaurants and cafes. Purchasing metal fabrication equipment and a commercial sewing machine, coupled with experience or training, will enable you to manufacture awnings in any size and in any fabric color to meet your customer's specifications. Offer hand crank awnings or fully motorized ones that open and close with the push of a button. Depending on size, model, and fabric selection, retail prices range from a few hundred dollars for a small basic awning to $5,000 for large motorized awnings. Awnings can be sold direct from home with the aid of awning displays supported by local advertising. Awnings can also be sold through online marketplaces like eBay and by exhibiting at home and garden and RV shows.

AT A GLANCE

 INVESTMENT: Over $25K

 SKILL LEVEL: 2–3

 RESOURCES
—Astrup, awning-making equipment and supplies, ☞ www.astrup.com
—☆ Awesome Awnings, ☎ (919) 468-1611, ☞ www.awesomeawn ings.com
—Ontario Sewing Automation, awning-making equipment and sup- plies, ☎ (905) 850-3537, ☞ www.ontariosewingautomation.ca
—Professional Awning Manufacturers Association, ☎ (651) 222-2508, ☞ www.awninginfo.com

Gazebos

Garden, hot tub, deck, and patio gazebos have become a very popular purchase for many homeowners, and you can cash in on the demand by starting a business man-ufacturing and selling gazebos. There are a couple of options in terms of how you manufacture gazebos. The first is to design and preassemble gazebos at your shop and then disassemble them so they can be sold and easily shipped to customers in a ready-to-assemble kit format. The second option is to build the gazebo at your cus-tomer's location. Both options have advantages and disadvantages, so you will need to decide which method is best for you. Gazebo construction requires a bit more carpentry skills than many of the other products listed in this chapter. There-fore, you should have some construction experience to start this manufacturing business. You can build from your own designs, purchase standard gazebo design plans, or build from your customers' specific designs. Selling methods will depend on the manufacturing method you choose, kit format or full assembly, and include direct from homebased gazebo displays, online sales, exhibiting at home and gar-den shows, and wholesale sales to building and garden centers.

AT A GLANCE

 INVESTMENT: Under $10K

 SKILL LEVEL: 3

 RESOURCES
—Backyard Spaces Gazebo Plans, ☞ www.backyardspaces.com/gazebo.html

— *Gazebos & Other Outdoor Structures*, Joseph F. Wajszczuk (Creative Homeowner Press, 1995)

—Handyman Plans, ✆ www.handymanplans.com

Garden Sheds

Garden sheds are very versatile and can be used as an affordable way to add workshop space, an art studio, guest accommodation, a backyard playhouse for the kids' garden and, of course, to store garden tools and patio furniture. These are all reasons why garden sheds have become a popular purchase for many homeowners, making them an excellent product for you to manufacture and sell. So what skills and equipment do you need to start manufacturing garden sheds? You need basic construction experience so that you have the ability to design and build a quality shed. On that note, you can develop your own designs to meet customers' specific needs or purchase standard garden shed design plans and, if needed, slightly tweak each to customer specifications. In terms of tools and equipment, you will need a well-equipped workshop with items such as a table saw, air compressor, and hand tools. Depending on the sheds you design, they can be prebuilt and shipped to customers in a ready-to-assemble kit format. Or, you can custom build sheds at each customer's location. Garden sheds can be sold online and by exhibiting at home and garden shows, but perhaps the easiest way to get started is to sell them right from a display at your own home supported by local advertising, signs, and word-of-mouth advertising.

AT A GLANCE

 INVESTMENT: Under $10K

 SKILL LEVEL: 3

 RESOURCES
—Better Designs Shed Plans ✆ www.abetterdesigns.net
— *Building a Shed: Expert Advice from Start to Finish*, Joseph Turini (Taunton Press, 2003)
—Mammoth Tools, ☎ (516) 942-0905, ✆ www.mammothtools.com
—Shed Plans, ✆ www.shedplans.com

Fence Panels

Almost all new wooden fences being installed today are constructed from prebuilt fence panels in three-, four-, five-, and six-foot heights by standard eight-foot widths. Typically these fence panels are constructed from pressure-treated wood or natural cedar and are available in a wide range of design styles. To get started building and selling fence panels you will need a workshop at home or in rented space equipped with basic hand tools, air tools, jigs, and design plans. In total, expect to invest in the range of $5,000 to $10,000 into equipment. Make sure to purchase lumber directly from mills or wholesale in bulk to keep your materials costs to a minimum. Along with building and selling standard fence panels, you can also construct custom fences panels from architect's drawings or from your customers' designs. Finished fence panels can be sold on a retail basis directly to homeowners by advertising locally in the newspaper and exhibiting at garden shows, as well as on a wholesale basis to building supply centers, nurseries, general contractors, landscape contractors, and property developers. Extra income can also be earned by installing the fence panels you construct.

> **AT A GLANCE**
>
> **INVESTMENT:** Under $10K
>
> **SKILL LEVEL:** 2
>
> **RESOURCES**
> —North American Wholesale Lumber Association, ☝ www.lumber.org
> —Mammoth Tools, ☎ (516) 942-0905, ☝ www.mammothtools.com
> —Western Red Cedar Lumber Association, ☝ www.cedar-outdoor.org

Custom Wood Gates

Custom wooden gates are the latest craze to take the home improvement industry by storm, with homeowners lining up to purchase them and paying as much as $1,500 for each one. Providing you have carpentry experience and a creative flair, you can cash in on the demand by making and selling your own line of custom wooden gates. The absolute keys to success in this business are quality products and unique one-of-a-kind gate designs. Use an assortment of number-one grade hardwood and softwood lumber in the construction of the gates, combine this with appealing details such as glass, iron, copper, or mosaic tile inserts and antique hardware. Solicit business by calling on designers, architects, and landscape and fencing contractors, as well as by renting display space at home and garden shows to exhibit you custom gates and by advertising online and in specialty gardening and home improvement publications.

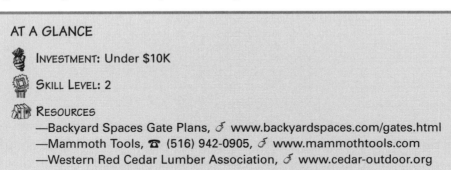

AT A GLANCE

INVESTMENT: Under $10K

SKILL LEVEL: 2

RESOURCES
—Backyard Spaces Gate Plans, ✆ www.backyardspaces.com/gates.html
—Mammoth Tools, ☎ (516) 942-0905, ✆ www.mammothtools.com
—Western Red Cedar Lumber Association, ✆ www.cedar-outdoor.org

Concrete Lawn Ornaments

Not only are concrete lawn ornaments easy to make, they are also very easy to sell for top dollar, which makes this a fantastic homebased manufacturing opportunity that anyone can tackle. As mentioned, making concrete lawn ornaments is easy. All you need are an assortment of molds, concrete, dyes, and paints, and the rest is simply following instructions to complete the product. The first step is to make or purchase molds for the types of concrete lawn ornaments you want to make—animals, people, objects, birdbaths, sundials, and more. The sky is the limit, especially if you build your own molds. Ornaments can be left natural concrete colors; dyes can be added to the concrete during the mixing process; or ornaments can be painted once they have cured. Sales options include selling from home by displaying the ornaments in your front yard along with approximate signage, exhibiting at garden shows, selling at flea markets and craft shows, selling online through venues such as eBay and internet malls, and selling to garden centers, building supply centers, gift retailers, and flower shops on a wholesale basis.

AT A GLANCE

INVESTMENT: Under $10K

SKILL LEVEL: 1

RESOURCES
—Concrete Success, concrete molds and supplies, ✆ www.concrete-success.com
—The Cement Mould Company, concrete molds and supplies, ✆ www.cementmoulds.com
—The Ornamental Concrete Directory, industry information and resources, ✆ www.ornamentalconcrete.net

Garden Ponds

Garden ponds alive with fish, and plants are a welcome addition to any home, mainly because they are a natural, relaxing, and a scenic addition that can provide enjoyment for the entire family. Garden ponds can be small, three to four feet in diameter, or large enough to accommodate swimming. However, this manufacturing opportunity is focused on building and selling small garden ponds. There is little that you need to know in order to start manufacturing and selling these ponds. You should probably concentrate your efforts on building the ponds at your customer's location. Garden ponds can be built from any type of small water container such as a barrel or a rigid pond liner, which are available in a wide variety of shapes. They can also be built by digging a hole to the desired depth and shaping and lining the pond area with a PVC or EMPD liner or cement. The best garden ponds include features such as waterfalls, fountains, underwater lighting, water plants, and fish, as well as a decorative stonework border. The best way to market garden ponds is to construct both fixed and portable samples so potential customers can see them. Fixed sample ponds can be built at your home, whereas portable ponds can be exhibited at home and garden shows.

AT A GLANCE

 INVESTMENT: Under $10K

 SKILL LEVEL: 1–2

 RESOURCES
—Garden Ponds 101, industry information portal, ✆ www.gardenponds101.com
—Pond Market, pond products and information, ✆ www.pondmarket.com
—Pond Tips, industry information portal, ✆ www.pond-tips.com

Potting Benches

The gardening craze is red hot in North America and you can carve yourself a portion of this profitable pie by starting a business manufacturing and selling garden potting benches. Every serious gardener needs a stationary or portable potting bench outfitted with useful features such as easy-to-clean work surfaces, water connections, built-in storage cabinets, drawers, and bins. Portable models have wheels on two legs for ease of moving around the garden and patio. Potting benches are not difficult to make, especially designs that are mainly constructed of wood. Ones that also incorporate metal are somewhat more difficult to make because welding skills and equipment as well as sheet metal bending skills and equipment will be required. Therefore, you will need to design and build to your skill level, at least to get started. Sales can take place through a number of venues including online via gardening-related web sites, at garden shows, homebased sales supported by local advertising and word-of-mouth referrals, and garden and building supply centers on a wholesale basis. Also, be sure to join internet groups and clubs focused on gardening, as well as local gardening clubs in your area, to network with members for business.

AT A GLANCE

 INVESTMENT: Under $10K

 SKILL LEVEL: 1–2

 RESOURCES
—Garden Plans, potting bench plans, ♂ www.gardenplans.com
—Mammoth Tools, ☎ (516) 942-0905, ♂ www.mammothtools.com
—U-Bild, potting bench plans, ♂ www.u-bild.com

Patio Furniture

In terms of an easy business to start and operate, lawn and garden patio furniture manufacturing has the potential to be one of the most profitable. Because consumer demand is proven, there is no need to reinvent the wheel. Just design and build a good quality product, and sales will follow. Patio furniture can be constructed from various materials—wood, plastic, iron, pre-cast cement, marble, and fiberglass—or a combination of these materials. However, wood is the easiest to work with and also requires the least amount of specialized equipment and construction materials to get started. Regardless of the type of patio furniture you decide to manufacture and sell, great selling methods include a homebased showroom (your patio), direct to businesses such as restaurants, home and garden shows, exhibits, and online marketplaces. You might want to consider concentrating on the high-end market, supplying only the best custom patio furniture and catering to those with substantial enough budgets to make the purchase. If you choose this route, be sure to establish working relationships with designers, architects, and deck builders, as all can refer business to you.

AT A GLANCE

 INVESTMENT: Under $10K

 SKILL LEVEL: 1–2

 RESOURCES
—Mammoth Tools, ☎ (516) 942-0905, ♂ www.mammothtools.com
—U-Bild, patio furniture plans, ♂ www.u-bild.com
—Wood Projects, patio furniture plans, ♂ www.woodprojects.com

---

Picnic Tables

Building and selling picnic tables is about as easy as a manufacturing business can get, but at the same time, do not underestimate the profit potential of this simple venture. To get started, you need only basic carpentry skills and tools, as well as a bit of workshop space for cutting lumber. Assembly can be conducted outside. There are a number of ways that you can make your picnic tables unique and different from competitors, such as using only recycled building materials, incorporating useful features like slide-out barbeque tables or serving trays, or adding decorative features like tile mosaics and built-in flower vases for elegant outside dining. Also offer items like bench cushions and umbrellas to increase per unit sales value and profit. On a large scale, picnic tables can be mass produced and sold wholesale to retailers or directly to high-volume users like campgrounds and RV parks. On a small scale, focus your marketing efforts on direct-to-consumer sales by selling picnic tables from home and at gardening and outdoor enthusiast consumer shows.

AT A GLANCE

 INVESTMENT: Under $2K

 SKILL LEVEL: 1

RESOURCES
—Mammoth Tools, ☎ (516) 942-0905, ♂ www.mammothtools.com
—U-Bild, picnic table plans, ♂ www.u-bild.com
—Woodworkers Workshop, picnic table plans, ♂ www.woodworkers
    workshop.com

Garden Stepping-Stones

Making and selling garden stepping-stones is a little known, yet simple manufacturing opportunity that can generate excellent profits. And creating stepping-stones is a lot of fun. The main supplies you need to make garden steppingstones are molds, cement, reinforcement mesh, and items such as tiles, glass, colored stones, or embossed designs to decorate the surface. Molds, as well as the rest of the supplies needed, are widely available, including through the sources listed below. You can also make your own molds out of wood, plastic, or metal. There is not much involved in making stepping-stones—fill the mold one-half full with concrete, lay in the reinforcing mesh, pour in the balance of the concrete, wait about 30 minutes to add decorations on top, and let dry for a couple days. Presto, a completed stepping-stone ready to sell. In total, each costs approximately $2 to $3 to make and retails in the range of $15 to $25 each, depending on size and complexity of design. Expect to sell wholesale to garden centers for about one-half the retail sale price. In addition to wholesale sales, stepping-stones can be sold at gift shows, home and garden shows, craft fairs, online, and at flea markets. Selling from home supported by signage and local advertising is a good idea because you can create elaborate stepping-stone walkways to show customers and really showcase the beauty and functionality of the product.

 AT A GLANCE

 INVESTMENT: Under $2K

 SKILL LEVEL: 1

Outdoor Brick Barbeques

An outdoor barbeque is a useful and attractive addition to any backyard or patio space, which is why so many homeowners are shelling out big bucks to have one installed. If you have masonry experience and tools, designing and building brick barbeques is a snap and very profitable. Start by picking a barbeque specialization—wood, charcoal, natural gas, or propane grill. Additional popular outdoor kitchens features include built-in refrigeration, sinks, food preparation areas, and lighting elements, which can all be incorporated into the design. Outdoor barbeques are built upon a concrete slab or concrete footing, and there are many choices available in terms of construction materials, including new bricks, used bricks, rustic cobblestones, or cultured stone veneers. You should also offer clients all brick and stone options so you do not narrow your target market. Design and built two elaborate brick or stone barbeque display models, one in your own backyard to as a sales display and the second on a platform outfitted on wheels or a trailer bed for easy transportation to home and garden shows. Also contact designers, architects, and custom homebuilders to inform them about your business, as all can become customers or refer their clients to your business.

AT A GLANCE

 INVESTMENT: Under $10K

 SKILL LEVEL: 2

 RESOURCES
—Barbeques and Grills, ✂ www.barbequesandgrills.com
—Entrepreneur, small business portal, ✂ www.entrepreneur.com
—The Outdoor Cooker, ✂ www.theoutdoorcooker.com

Wooden Planters

Decks, patios, balconies, gardens, and lawns are not complete until they are adorned with decorative wooden planters overflowing with flowers, ivy, herbs, and specialty shrubs to turn every outdoor space into a private oasis. Designing and building wooden planters is easy and a very inexpensive business to get started. You don't have to be an experienced woodworker to build professional-looking planters. All you need are basic tools, a workshop, and easy-to-follow, step-by-step construction plans, which are widely available from a number of sources, including the ones listed below. Build standard box planters, hanging wooden planters, or decorative planters made to resemble windmills, wheelbarrows, animals, buildings, people, cars, or just about anything imaginable. Sell the planter at garden shows, flea markets, and craft shows, by renting kiosk space at malls; and directly from your own front yard supported by local advertising, drive-past traffic, and word-of-mouth referrals.

AT A GLANCE

INVESTMENT: Under $2K

SKILL LEVEL: 1–2

RESOURCES
—Mammoth Tools, ☎ (516) 942-0905, ♂ www.mammothtools.com
—Scrollsaw, wood planter plans, ♂ www.scrollsaw.com
—U-Bild, wood planter plans, ♂ www.u-bild.com

Adirondack Chairs

At the cottage, on the deck, or under a shade tree in the backyard, lounging in an Adirondack chair has been a favorite way to relax for millions of people for more than a century. Adirondack chairs are not difficult to make and require only a small amount of production space and basic woodworking tools and equipment. You can build from your own designs or purchase plans from the sources listed below. Adirondack chairs are generally constructed from cedar wood and can be left untreated to age naturally, painted in bright colors, or stained to meet your customer's specifications. Selling is easy because the chairs basically sell themselves. Your options include online sales through eBay, internet malls, or your own web site and by exhibiting at home and garden shows.

Wholesale sales to building centers, pool and patio retailers, nurseries, and chain retailers are also options, providing you have the space and equipment to mass produce the chairs. Another sales option is to display the chairs in your front yard and use appropriate signage to grab the attention of passing motorists.

 AT A GLANCE

 INVESTMENT: Under $2K

 SKILL LEVEL: 1–2

 RESOURCES
— 📖 *Easy-to-Build Adirondack Furniture*, Mary Twitchell (Storey Books, 1999)
—U-Bild, Adirondack furniture plans, ♂ www.u-bild.com
—Wood Zone, Adirondack furniture plans, ♂ www.woodzone.com

Hammocks

Few people can resist the temptation of spending a sunny summer afternoon napping in a hammock under a shady tree, which is one reason hammocks are hot sellers. You will need to decide which types of hammocks you are going to manufacture—camping, chair, swinging, stand, or portable hammocks, mainly because each type has a specific target market. Fortunately, with practice, hammocks are not difficult to design and produce, especially if you purchase hammock components and concentrate on assembly and sales. A sewing machine will be required, as well as carpentry and possibly welding equipment if making stationary hammock frames are in the plans. Material choice—cotton, canvas, or rip-stop nylon—will depend on the types of hammocks you will be manufacturing. Additional income can be earned by making and selling hammock accessories such as sun shades, pillows, cushions, frames, carrying bags, rain covers, and blanket liners for camping hammocks. Sell hammocks online, at recreations shows, at public markets, and by advertising in publications catering to camping, leisure activities, and gardening.

AT A GLANCE

INVESTMENT: Under $2K

SKILL LEVEL: 1

RESOURCES
—Earth Guild, hammock-making supplies, ☎ (800) 327-8448, ♂ www.
  earthguild.com
—King Cord, hammock-making supplies, ☎ (877) 474-8864, ♂ www.
  kingcord.com
—U-Bild, hammock plans, ♂ www.u-bild.com

Birdhouses

Millions of birdhouses are sold annually in North America. So why not capitalize on the demand and start a part-time enterprise building and selling birdhouses? Birdhouses are very easy to build. Basically, all you need to get started are design plans, a small workshop, and an assortment of basic power and hand tools. Keep in mind, however, that there are different types of birdhouses for the various species, so a bit of research will be needed to pinpoint the types of birdhouse you will build. You might also want to consider using only recycled materials in the construction of the birdhouses. Doing so will give you a very powerful marketing tool (environmentally friendly) as well as keep costs to a minimum; in most cases, used wood can be acquired for free. Displaying samples of all of the birdhouses you make and sell at your home with bold, attention-grabbing signage ensures people and motorists passing by will stop in and browse through your selection. In addition to selling from home, birdhouses can also be sold on eBay and at flea markets, home and garden shows, and crafts shows.

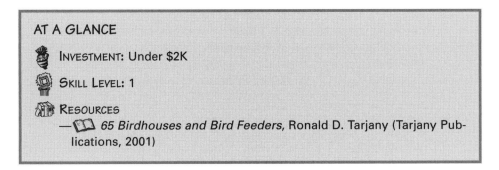

AT A GLANCE

INVESTMENT: Under $2K

SKILL LEVEL: 1

RESOURCES
— 65 Birdhouses and Bird Feeders, Ronald D. Tarjany (Tarjany Publications, 2001)

—Scrollsaw, birdhouse plans, ✂ www.scrollsaw.com
—📖 *Sunset Building Birdhouses*, Don Vandervort (Sunset Publishing, 2002)
—U-Bild, birdhouse plans, ✂ www.u-bild.com

Mailboxes

Don't be fooled into thinking that the profit potential of this seemingly simple enterprise must be low. Elaborate mailboxes made from specialty materials such as exotic hardwoods, copper, iron, and cultured stone can sell for $1,000 and more, and at this kind of retail sales value, you can easily pocket $250 to $350 on each sale. Design, build, and sell just one custom mailbox a week and you'll earn upwards of $25,000 per year, with only a part-time effort and from just a small, homebased workshop. The key to success is, of course, marketing. So what are your marketing and sales options? First, you can market your mailbox design and construction services to custom homebuilders and renovators. Second, you can advertise in specialty publications that reach your target audience. Third, you can sell through online marketplaces that reach your target audience as well as directly from homebased displays. The final option is to exhibit your products at home and garden shows.

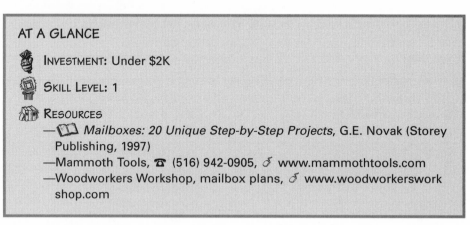

AT A GLANCE

INVESTMENT: Under $2K

SKILL LEVEL: 1

RESOURCES
—📖 *Mailboxes: 20 Unique Step-by-Step Projects*, G.E. Novak (Storey Publishing, 1997)
—Mammoth Tools, ☎ (516) 942-0905, ✂ www.mammothtools.com
—Woodworkers Workshop, mailbox plans, ✂ www.woodworkerswork shop.com

Weather Vanes

Making and selling custom-built weather vanes could put you down the path to financial prosperity. These architectural features hearken back to simpler times and add charm to any home. Weather vanes can be constructed from a variety of materials, including fiberglass, injection-molded plastic, steel, and wood, in any style such as a rooster or sailboat. The best weather vanes are made from copper for a truly authentic appearance. These require the pattern to be cut from a sheet of copper, each piece to be soldered together, and often parts are textured using a mallet or similar tools to shape and create detailing. Needless to say, if you choose copper as your construction material, practice and time will be needed to master the craft. Weather vanes can be sold in a number of ways utilizing a number of selling venues. You can display them at your own home along with signage to encourage inquiries from passing motorists, advertise in specialty publications geared to the home restoration and improvement market, sell online through eBay and internet malls, and exhibit them at home, garden, and art shows.

AT A GLANCE

 INVESTMENT: Under $10K

 SKILL LEVEL: 1–2

 RESOURCES
—Traditional Building, weather vane manufacturers' directory, ☎ www.traditional-building.com/3-weathr.htm
— 📖 *Folk Art Weather Vanes: Authentic American Patterns for Wood and Metal*, John A. Nelson (Stackpole Books, 1990)

Lawn Characters

There are two primary groups of target customers for lawn characters—homeowners and entrepreneurs. Many homeowners purchase fun and attractive character cutouts to display on their lawns and in their gardens. Character cutouts such as gardeners bending over tending their gardens with their knickers visible or colorfully painted butterflies mounted on a stick stuck in the flower garden are popular. Entrepreneurs on the other hand purchase character cutouts for an entirely different reason, which is to profit. They do this by renting character cutouts to people that want to announce a special milestone or occasion, such as a stork to announce the birth of a baby or oversize wedding bells to announce an engagement. Character cutouts are very easy to make and require nothing more than tracing the desired character pattern on plywood, cutting it out with a jig saw, sanding the edges and surface, and applying paint or vinyl decals to resemble the desired character. Lawn characters are also very easy to sell. To sell to homeowners, display the cutouts on your own lawn accompanied by appropriate signage. Sell at flea markets, garden shows, crafts shows, and online through eBay and internet malls. To sell to entrepreneurs, create a bundled "business opportunity package" inclusive of various characters accompanied by a business manual explaining how to operate and market the business. The character cutout business opportunity package can be advertised for sale online, in small business magazines, and by running classified advertisements.

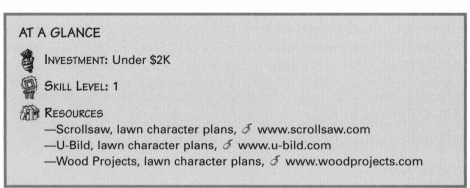

AT A GLANCE

INVESTMENT: Under $2K

SKILL LEVEL: 1

RESOURCES
—Scrollsaw, lawn character plans, ♂ www.scrollsaw.com
—U-Bild, lawn character plans, ♂ www.u-bild.com
—Wood Projects, lawn character plans, ♂ www.woodprojects.com

Wind Chimes

Beautiful sounding and aesthetically pleasing wind chimes can be constructed from a wide range of materials, including bamboo, anodized aluminum, copper, stone, cast iron, glass, seashells, and ceramic tiles. And you can design and build them in just about every size, style, and price point imaginable to suit any individual's taste and budget. Now the best news: No special skills are needed to design, make, and sell wind chimes. Likewise, tool and equipment requirements to make wind chimes are almost nonexistent. Depending on the construction materials you choose, expect to use nothing more than basic hand tools. Sell your wind chimes through online marketplaces such as eBay or internet malls, by displaying your products at craft shows, home and garden shows, and weekend flea markets, by renting kiosks space at malls and public markets, and by establishing wholesale accounts with gift retailers. Also, don't overlook salespeople and business owners as potential clients. You may be surprised by how many would be willing to buy wind chimes to give to their best customers as appreciation gifts. And of course, if you have a few hundred displayed in your yard with for-sale signs posted, there is no doubt you will attract the attention passing motorists.

AT A GLANCE

INVESTMENT: Under $2K

SKILL LEVEL: 1

RESOURCES
—The Crafters Mall, craft products marketplace, ♂ www.procrafter.com
—Entrepreneur, small business portal, ♂ www.entrepreneur.com
—Mammoth Tools, ☎ (516) 942-0905, ♂ www.mammothtools.com
—National Craft Association, ♂ www.craftassoc.com

Whirligigs

You may be wondering what exactly a whirligig is and how it works. By definition, it is the action of an object that spins on an axis when driven by the wind. The simplest whirligigs have wings or blades that catch the wind, causing them to spin. More sophisticated whirligigs have a mechanical mechanism that converts the rotational motion of the propeller into an action such as duck wings flapping or a person waving. Most are made of wood and stand about 12 to 24 inches tall, although some metal ones are the size of a car and sit atop 20-foot high poles. But big ones are the exception and not the rule. Whirligigs can be mounted on mailboxes, roofs, poles, or stuck in the lawn with a stake. They are built and painted to resemble people, buildings, planes, or just about anything you can imagine. More important than how they work is the fact that millions are sold every year, and cashing in on the demand is easy because whirligigs are very simple to make and sell. All you need are basic woodworking tools and skills, a workshop space, and design plans. Whirligigs can be sold at craft shows, toy shows, garden shows, online through eBay and internet malls, or directly from your front lawn alongside attention-grabbing signage.

AT A GLANCE

INVESTMENT: Under $2K

SKILL LEVEL: 1

RESOURCES
—Scrollsaw, whirligig plans, ♂ www.scrollsaw.com
—U-Bild, whirligig plans, ♂ www.u-bild.com
—📖 *Action Whirligigs: 25 Easy-to-do Projects*, Anders S. Lunde (Dover Publications, 2003)

Party-in-a-Box Business

With everyone leading such busy lives, who has the time to buy all of the paper products and novelty items needed to throw one heck of a party? Not many, and this reason alone is a strong argument for starting a party-in-a-box business. Prepare all of the products people would need to throw a party, but all conveniently packaged in one box. Customers simply open the box, decorate, and handout the party favors to guests, and that's it, it is party time! Depending on the theme of the party—children's birthday, adult birthday, retirement, anniversary, special achievement, bachelor, bachlorette, engagement, wedding, Christmas, New Years, or Fourth of July, each box can contain hats, flowers, banners, ribbons, balloons, piñatas, invitations, streamers, glow sticks, noisemakers, games, confetti, and other party supplies specific to the theme. All of these party products can be purchase in bulk at deeply discounted wholesale prices from any number of party product distributors, such as the ones listed below. Advertise in your local newspaper and by pinning promotional fliers to bulletin boards, and also be sure to build working relationships with event and party planners, restaurants, and daycare centers, as all can become a good source for referral and repeat business. Let customers order by phone, fax, and e-mail, and offer free local delivery.

AT A GLANCE

 INVESTMENT: Under $2K

 SKILL LEVEL: 1

 RESOURCES
—American Party Company, wholesale party supplies, ♂ www.eparty site.com
—Party and Paper Warehouse, wholesale party supplies, ♂ www.partyand paperwarehouse.com
—Shindigz, wholesale party supplies, ♂ www.shindigz.com

Specialty Trees and Shrubs

Growing and selling trees and shrubs right from home is a fantastic way to earn an extra few thousand dollars every year, or even every month—if you're not looking for income tomorrow. Surprisingly, not much yard space is required. You can purchase Japanese maple seedlings for about 75 cents each wholesale, pot or plant in burlaps, wait a season or two while they grow, and resell them right from home for $25 to $50 each. A 20-foot-square garden area is large enough to support 300 seedlings, which in turn can produces approximately 100 saleable trees annually when planting is alternated. Wow, that is as much as $5,000 every year from just a small patch of ground in your backyard. Imagine what you can earn by planting a 50-, 60-, or 100-foot square seedling tree garden. In addition to selling directly to consumers from home and through garden shows, you can sell the trees and shrubs to garden centers and landscape contractors wholesale.

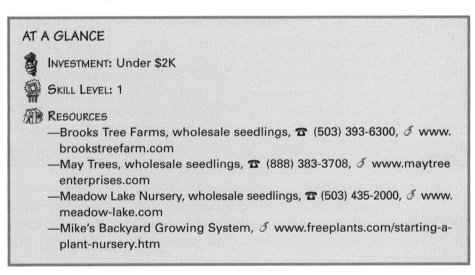

AT A GLANCE

INVESTMENT: Under $2K

SKILL LEVEL: 1

RESOURCES
—Brooks Tree Farms, wholesale seedlings, ☎ (503) 393-6300, ♂ www.brookstreefarm.com
—May Trees, wholesale seedlings, ☎ (888) 383-3708, ♂ www.maytree enterprises.com
—Meadow Lake Nursery, wholesale seedlings, ☎ (503) 435-2000, ♂ www.meadow-lake.com
—Mike's Backyard Growing System, ♂ www.freeplants.com/starting-a-plant-nursery.htm

Christmas Trees

North American consumers spend more than $1 billion annually buying real Christmas trees, and you can slice yourself a piece of this very lucrative pie by starting your own Christmas tree farm. Owned or rented, the number-one requirement for starting a Christmas tree farm is land, and plenty of it. Other requirements include equipment such as a tractor, a green thumb, and some marketing savvy. Purchasing seedlings in bulk will be needed for starting stock, and you will also need to plant new seedlings every year to ensure a harvestable inventory. Sales can be approached in a number of ways, including a you-cut-it operation enabling customers to visit the farm, select, cut, and take their tree home. Alternately, you can rent parking lot space from late November until Christmas Eve and sell trees at retail prices in the range of $50 to $100. Good locations include grocery store parking lots, busy intersections, gas station lots, and basically any other piece of empty ground that is exposed to lots of passing motorists. Wholesaling trees in mass quantities to seasonal Christmas tree sellers and charity organizations is another highly profitably option. The true entrepreneurial mindset will probably combine more than one of these methods to maximize profit potential.

AT A GLANCE

INVESTMENT: Over $25K

SKILL LEVEL: 1–2

RESOURCES
—May Trees, wholesale seedlings, ☎ (888) 383-3708, ♂ www.maytree
    enterprises.com
—National Christmas Tree Association, ♂ www.christmastree.org
—📖 *Christmas Trees: Growing and Selling Trees, Wreaths, and
    Greens*, Lewis Hill (Storey Publishing, 1999)

Houseplants

Great profits can be earned growing houseplants inside under lights or outside in a greenhouse. How much money can you earn growing and selling houseplants? It depends on several factors, including plant selection, plant quality, number of plants grown, and your marketing ability. But even a small operation can net $10,000 a year after expenses only working a few hours a week. The keys to success: plan ahead to know the best and most profitable plants to grow, as well as the best growing techniques to ensure a high and healthy yield. There are also ways to make profits from growing flowers—selling bulbs such as crocus and tulips, selling cut flowers such as carnations and snapdragons, and selling flowering plants such as roses and violets. Houseplants and flowers can be sold both wholesale and retail—garden shows, flea markets, directly from home supported by local advertising and word-of-mouth referrals, and wholesale to grocery stores. To boost revenues and profits, also sell plant accessories such as pots and containers, plant stands, hanging baskets, fertilizers, soil, peat moss, and perlite.

AT A GLANCE

 INVESTMENT: Under $2K

 SKILL LEVEL: 1

RESOURCES
—Mike's Backyard Growing System, ✂ www.freeplants.com/starting-a-plant-nursery.htm
—📖 *Growing Profits: How to Start and Operate a Backyard Nursery*, Michael Harlan (Moneta Publications, 2000)
—📖 *The House Plant Expert: The World's Best-Selling Book on House Plants*, D.G. Hessayon (Expert Books, 1992)

Landscape Supplies

Much like the recent explosion in do-it-yourself home renovation, homeowners have also taken to do-it-yourself landscaping as a way to save money, improve their property, and stretch their creative green thumbs. People take pride in their homes and want them to look as good on the outside as they do on the inside. The best way to accomplish this is with awe-inspiring landscaping. The business concept is simple: Buy landscaping materials in bulk, repackage into smaller quantities, and sell for a profit. You will need a considerable amount of outdoor workspace, along with proper zoning and suitable delivery transportation. Providing you can meet this criteria, purchase sand, gravel, topsoil, and bark mulch by the dump truck load wholesale, package it into smaller quantities, and resell it directly to consumers at retail prices, or to retailers such as garden centers on a wholesale basis. Additional income can be earned by stocking and supplying natural landscape products such as driftwood and river rock. In addition to consumer and wholesale sales, you can also market your landscape supply products to construction-related businesses such a paving stone installers, foundation installers, and playground equipment installers.

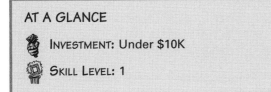

AT A GLANCE

INVESTMENT: Under $10K

SKILL LEVEL: 1

RESOURCES
—Entrepreneur, small business portal, ♂ www.entrepreneur.com
—Coverall Stone, wholesale landscape supplies, ☎ (206) 937-5200,
  ♂ www.caoverallstone.com
—Mulch and Soil Council, ☎ (703) 257-0111, ♂ www.mulchandsoil
  council.org
—National Stone, Sand, & Gravel Association, ♂ www.nssga.org

Firewood

A chainsaw, log splitter, adequate outdoor work and storage space, and a suitable delivery truck are just about all that is needed to start chopping, selling, and delivering firewood. There are a number of sources where you can purchase logs that can be cut, then split into firewood. A few sources include farmers, forestry companies, and tree removal companies. Many municipalities also clear trees from municipally owned lands to make way for development and from the side of highways for safety reasons, and these jobs are generally tendered out to the highest bidders on a yearly basis. Of course, the trees cut down can be turned into valuable firewood. Physical fitness is a definite prerequisite for starting a firewood supply business because even with the aid of a chainsaw and log splitter, this is still very hard, labor-intensive work. The best way to sell firewood is to place Firewood for Sale classified advertisements in your local newspaper as well as to post fliers on bulletin boards throughout the community at locations such as grocery stores, gas stations, community centers, laundries, and libraries. On the upside, once you have customers, repeat business is almost a guaranteed as long as they have wood-burning fireplace.

AT A GLANCE

 INVESTMENT: Under $25K

 SKILL LEVEL: 1

 RESOURCES
—Apache Forest Products, firewood processing equipment and tools,
  ☎ (866) 986-0067, ♂ www.apacheforest.com
—Logsplitters, firewood producers' directory, ♂ www.logsplitters.com/fire
  wood.htm
—Timberwolf Manufacturing, firewood processing equipment and
  tools, ☎ (800) 340-4386, ♂ www.timberwolfcorp.com

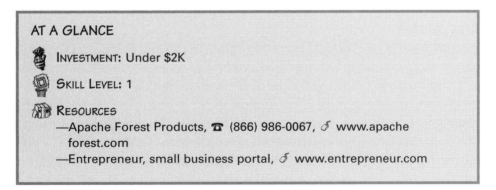

Kindling

Like firewood, excellent profits can also be earned by starting a business specializing in splitting, packaging, and selling kindling. Best of all, this business
requires nothing more than a sharp axe and a strong back to get started. Simply
purchase firewood to split into kindling. Or be a bit more creative, and get lumber to split into kindling for free by visiting construction sites, wood mills, and
manufacturers and offering to haul away their waste woods and cut offs for free.
A walk through a forest will reveal lots of dead ground wood for the taking (with
permission from the landowner, of course). Once you have split the wood into
kindling, it can be packed in bags or shrink-wrapped in plastic for retail sales.
Ideal locations for setting up wholesale accounts include RV camps, campgrounds, gas stations, and grocery stores. Because you can get waste wood for free
to split into kindling, the profit potential is excellent as the only hard costs to produce the product are packaging and transportation.

> **AT A GLANCE**
>
> 🪔 INVESTMENT: Under $2K
>
> 🪔 SKILL LEVEL: 1
>
> 🏚 RESOURCES
> —Apache Forest Products, ☎ (866) 986-0067, ♂ www.apache
>   forest.com
> —Entrepreneur, small business portal, ♂ www.entrepreneur.com

Garden Curbing

Start your own garden curbing manufacturing business, and cash in on the highly
lucrative garden-curbing craze. Labor time, raw materials, and business overheads are very low, which makes this a very profitable opportunity for entrepreneurs prepared to get out and hustle up business. The best way to make concrete
garden curbing is to use a specially designed extrusion machine that produces a
continuous concrete curb right on location, no need to manufacture the curbing in
one location then ship to another. Simply load the equipment onto a truck or
trailer and make the product at your customer's home. The same curbing can be
used to edge flowerbeds, driveways, and walkways and is available in a number
of profiles and color choices. Sell by exhibiting and collecting sales inquiries at
home and garden shows, by advertising in local newspapers and your Yellow

Pages directory, and by building alliances with landscape and building contractors that can refer their clients to your business or hire your business as a subcontracter to supply and install garden curbing.

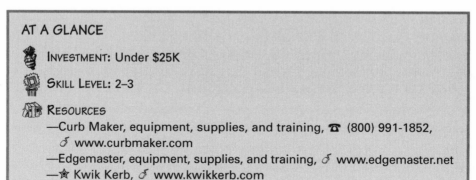

AT A GLANCE

INVESTMENT: Under $25K

SKILL LEVEL: 2–3

RESOURCES
—Curb Maker, equipment, supplies, and training, ☎ (800) 991-1852,
 ♂ www.curbmaker.com
—Edgemaster, equipment, supplies, and training, ♂ www.edgemaster.net
—✦ Kwik Kerb, ♂ www.kwikkerb.com

Fishing Tackle

Fishing enthusiasts take notice; incredible profits can be earned making and selling fishing tackle to other fishing fanatics just like you. There are numerous companies manufacturing fishing tackle components used to make lures, jigs, ties, nets, and custom fishing rods. This make the job of manufacturing fishing tackle very easy because all that is required is to assemble the components using basic hand tools to produce high-quality fishing tackle that is ready to sell for big profits. Fishing tackle can be sold direct to consumers via displays at fishing, hunting, and outdoor recreation shows, as well as online through eBay and fishing tackle marketplaces. Flea markets, community events, and even a homebased fishing tackle shop also provide excellent opportunities to sell high-quality fishing tackle. In larger quantities, tackle can be sold at wholesale prices to bait and tackle shops and outdoor products retailers.

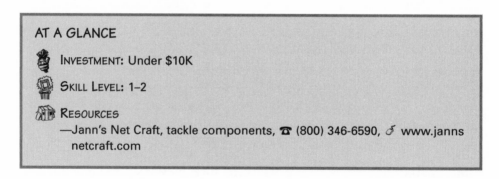

AT A GLANCE

INVESTMENT: Under $10K

SKILL LEVEL: 1–2

RESOURCES
—Jann's Net Craft, tackle components, ☎ (800) 346-6590, ♂ www.janns
 netcraft.com

—Stamina Quality Components, tackle components, ☎ (763) 253-0450, ♂ www.staminainc.com

—Tackle Making, information portal, ♂ www.tacklemaking.com

—📖 *The Complete Book of Tackle Making*, C. Boyd Pfeiffer (The Lyons Press, 1999)

Fishing Bait

Fishing bait is big business in North America, and you can earn serious money raising and selling bait right from your home. To do so, however, you will need to be comfortable handling creepy, crawly things like worms, leaches, and minnows because these are your main profit centers. Bait minnows, like shiners, can be caught in rivers and creeks using traps or a seine net. Or, if you have enough land, you can install a pond for minnow and leach breeding. A license issued by the department of fisheries is generally required to catch or raise fishing bait, so be sure to check regulations in your area before getting started. Dew worms, aka night crawlers, are another bait. They can be raised in soil or moss boxes in a dark area, or you can employ worm-picking crews to pick worms at golf courses and parks after the sun goes down, especially after a rain. To purchase the equipment necessary to store and sell fishing bait from home will require an investment of at least a few thousand dollars, and more if you elect to install a minnow and leach breeding pond. With that said, providing your home is in close proximity to popular fishing lakes or rivers, the investment is quickly returned and rewarded with substantial profits. In addition to selling bait from home, also contact other bait shops in your area and offer to sell bait to them at wholesale pricing.

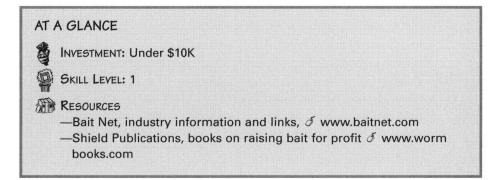

AT A GLANCE

INVESTMENT: Under $10K

SKILL LEVEL: 1

RESOURCES
—Bait Net, industry information and links, ♂ www.baitnet.com
—Shield Publications, books on raising bait for profit ♂ www.wormbooks.com

Marine Canvas

Dodgers, awnings, sail bags, boom tents, boat covers, and canvas knapsacks are just of a few of the high-demand marine canvas products that you can make and sell to the 30 million boaters in the United States and Canada. If you are new to the industry, training and research are definite prerequisites before setting up shop because there's lots to learn about the marine canvas-making trade. Depending on the products you make, workshop space will also be a big consideration, especially if you are going to make sails, as are equipment, material selection, and sources. In the resources section below, you will find links to training, associations, and suppliers. Small and more common marine canvas products like boom tents, bags, and awnings can all be made and sold in standard sizing. However, larger items like dodgers should be made-to-order only, unless you are going to specialize in making canvas products for specific boat manufacturers such as Sea Ray or Hunter, for example. Marine canvas products can be advertised and promoted via advertising online and in boating magazines, as well as exhibited at boat shows. Word travels fast amongst boaters. Therefore, make a great product at fair prices and you can expect lots of referral and repeat business.

AT A GLANCE

INVESTMENT: Under $25K

SKILL LEVEL: 2–3

RESOURCES
—Custom Marine Canvas Training Workshop, ☎ (800) 798-7627, ♂ www. canvastrainingworkshop.com
—Outdoor Textiles, marine canvas equipment and supplies, ☎ (772) 283-4730, ♂ www.outdoortextiles.com
—North East Canvas Products Association, ♂ www.necpa.org
—📖 *The Big Book of Boat Canvas: A Complete Guide to Fabric Work on Boats*, Karen Lipe (International Marine, 1991)

Custom-Fitted Golf Clubs

Golf ranks as one of the most popular and fastest growing sports and recreational pastimes in North America, and you can make a bundle making and selling custom golf clubs. For several reasons, making custom golf clubs is easier than most think. First, there are many golf club building training classes available nationwide.

Second, the required equipment is widely available and relatively inexpensive. Third, you can purchase components such as heads, shafts, and grips wholesale and assemble the clubs at home to meet each customer's specific needs. The sport is so popular that finding customers should not be difficult, especially if you are an avid golfer. This is the type of business that can largely be built and supported by referral and repeat business. Run advertisements locally as well as in specialty golf publications and on web sites. Also forge working relationships with golf courses and pro shops that do not currently offer custom golf club building and sales—you build, they sell, and each profits.

AT A GLANCE

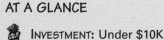 **INVESTMENT:** Under $10K

SKILL LEVEL: 2–3

 RESOURCES
—★ Golf Etc., ☎ (800) 806-8633, ♂ www.golfetc.com/retail_program.cfm
—Kona Golf Sales, golf club components wholesaler, ☎ (905) 366-0212, ♂ www.konagolfsales.com
—Maltby Designs Clubmaking Academy, golf club design and construction courses, ☎ (800) 848-8358
—MGL Golf, golf club components wholesaler, ♂ www.mglgolf.com

---

Canoes

Why paddle only occasionally when you can turn your passion for paddling into a profitable business by building and selling canoes? Without question, there is a learning curve to overcome in terms of having the ability to build high-quality, handcrafted canoes. But with that said, anything worth doing is worth investing the time and money to doing it right. Learn the craft so that you can specialize in building cedar strip, fiberglass, or composites canoes out of materials such as Kevlar. Set up a workshop right at home equipped with tools and equipment needed to make the types of canoes that you want to specialize in. Your workshop can also become a sales showroom, and selling accessories such as paddles, dry bags and gear, rooftop carriers, and life vests can help to boost revenues and profits. In addition to selling from home, you can also sell canoes direct to consumers by exhibiting at sports and recreation shows, online through marketplaces like eBay, and by organizing try-before-you-buy canoe paddling sales events at local lakes and rivers, which provide the paddling-loving public an opportunity to test drive one of your canoes before having to commit to buying. Few will say no after a fun and relaxing afternoon on the water.

AT A GLANCE

 INVESTMENT: Under $10K

 SKILL LEVEL: 2

 RESOURCES
—Kit Guy, canoe plans, www.kitguy.com
—Professional Paddlesports Association, www.propaddle.com
— *Building a Strip Canoe*, Gil Gilpatrick (Delmore Mapping, 2002)

Kayaks

Kayaking provides excellent physical exercise, and it is also fun, which explains why the sport has exploded in popularity over the last decade. Building and selling ocean, river, or white-water kayaks is an excellent choice for people with a keen interest in the sport. Like canoe building, you can specialize in building strip, frame and fabric, fiberglass, or composite kayaks, and again, you can also earn extra profits by selling related accessories such as paddles, dry bags and gear, rooftop carriers, and life vests. Manufacturing kayaks is also a business that will take time to master and time to build a reputation for a high-quality product. But as a rule, kayakers are a tight group, and news travels fast about great products amongst paddlers. Kayaks can be sold from a homebased or factory showroom, online via paddling sites, by exhibiting at sports and recreation shows, and even through a network of retailer dealers.

AT A GLANCE

 INVESTMENT: Under $10K

 SKILL LEVEL: 2

 RESOURCES
—Kit Guy, kayak plans, www.kitguy.com
—Professional Paddlesports Association, www.propaddle.com
— *Kayak Craft: Fine Woodstrip Kayak Construction*, Ted Moores and Jennifer Moores (Wooden Boat Publications, 1999)

Canoe Paddles

All of the millions of recreational canoeists have one thing in common; they need paddles to paddle their canoes. Needless to say, there is huge potential to make big bucks manufacturing and selling wooden canoe paddles. Woodworking skills, equipment, construction plans, and a shop are all that you need to get started. The low end of the canoe paddle industry is competitive because of cheap, mass produced canoe paddles from abroad. You should concentrate on the higher end market, making and selling custom paddles to appeal to the true paddling connoisseur. Avid paddlers can tell you firsthand that there is no shortage of canoeists prepared to part with $100 to $200 for a well-designed and comfortable paddle. Sell directly to consumers via sports and recreation trade shows, eBay, and canoeing-related web sites. If your price point affords, you can also sell to retailers wholesale or on a consignment basis.

AT A GLANCE

INVESTMENT: Under $10K

SKILL LEVEL: 2

RESOURCES
—Mammoth Tools, ☎ (516) 942-0905, ♂ www.mammothtools.com
—Professional Paddlesports Association, ♂ www.propaddle.com
—📖 *Canoe Paddles: A Complete Guide to Making Your Own*, Graham Warren and David Gidmark (Firefly Books, 2001)

Backyard Putting Greens

Real backyard putting greens require mowing, watering, fertilizing, and seeding. Synthetic putting greens are durable and do not require any of that time-consuming maintenance. They are weather resistant, hold up in direct sunlight, and can be used all year (weather permitting). Designing and installing backyard synthetic-turf putting greens is a wonderful full- or part-time opportunity that will appeal to golf fanatics. There are basically two types of backyard putting greens. The first is a sand-filled polypropylene (plastic) synthetic green that can be installed on a compacted aggregate or concrete base. Polypropylene synthetic turfs use fine silica sand to keep the turf fibers in an upright position. The second option is synthetic nylon turf, which can also be installed on a compacted aggregate or concrete base, but nylon turf has memory burned into it, enabling the fibers stand up without the aid of silica sand. Both have advantages and disadvantages, but each can be installed for big profits, especially when you consider material costs are in the range of $3 to $4 per square foot and retail for as much as $15 per square foot. Once established, referrals will be the main source of new business. Therefore, it makes sense to invite neighbors by to see and play each installation.

AT A GLANCE

 INVESTMENT: Under $25K

 SKILL LEVEL: 2–3

 RESOURCES
—Pro Green, synthetic turf supply, ☎ (888) 440-7888, ♂ www.pro green.com
—★ Southwest Putting Greens, ☎ (877) 260-7888, ♂ www.southwest greens.com
—Synthetic Turf Intl., synthetic turf supply, ☎ (800) 405-7455, ♂ www. synthetic-turf.com

Personalized Golf Balls

All you need to get started in the multimillion-dollar personalized golf ball industry is to purchase golf balls in bulk at wholesale prices and a simple and inexpensive pad printer. The rest is pretty easy: Market the business, take orders, print golf balls, and you're away and running. For those not familiar with personalized golf balls, they are nothing more than common golf balls that have been printed with a person's name, a business name and/or logo, or the name of an organization. Personalized golf balls make fantastic gifts for the golf fanatic and for businesses of all sizes to give to clients as an appreciation gift and at golf tournaments. This type of manufacturing business is easy to start, highly profitable, and a low mess and zero noise opportunity that only requires minimal working space—spare bedroom, garage, or basements are all perfectly suitable. Sell via word or mouth, by mail order, through online sales, and by taking orders through prospecting and delivering the balls once printed.

AT A GLANCE

 INVESTMENT: Under $10K

SKILL LEVEL: 1

RESOURCES
—Apiona, golf ball manufacturer, ✆ www.apiona.com
—KingBo Golf, golf ball manufacturer, ✆ www.kingbo-golf.com
—Printex USA, golf ball pad printing equipment, ✆ www.printex usa.com
—Winon USA, golf ball pad printing equipment, ☎ (716) 400-8966, ✆ www.winonusa.com

Party Tents

The party tent rental industry generates millions in annual sales in North America, and all party tent rental companies have one thing in common: they need tents to rent. A fantastic opportunity awaits entrepreneurs who decide to start a party tent manufacturing and sales business. Party tents range from ten feet square to those that cover the better part of a football field. They are comprised of a steel or aluminum frame with a fabric cover. Both frame and cover have to be outfitted with fasteners to allow for quick, yet sturdy assembly and disassembly. In addition to considerable manufacturing space, you also need metal cutting and welding equipment and commercial grade sewing equipment. Sell party tents by advertising in publications catering to the industry and online and through a factory direct showroom. In addition to making and selling party tents, you can also rent them to companies and organizations that routinely need large tents for outdoor events, groups such as wedding planners, catering companies, event and corporate planners, charity organizations, retailers hosting under-the-tent sales and clearance events, and sports teams and clubs. Depending on tent size, rental rates are in the range of $200 to $400 per day including delivery, set-up, and disassembly.

AT A GLANCE

 INVESTMENT: Over $25K

 SKILL LEVEL: 2

 RESOURCES
—Astrup, tent making equipment and supplies, ✆ www.astrup.com

—Entrepreneur, small business portal, ♂ www.entrepreneur.com
—Ontario Sewing Automation, tent-making equipment and supplies,
☎ (905) 850-3537, ♂ www.ontariosewingautomation.ca

Saunas

Nothing relieves the day's stresses like a nice relaxing sauna. There are a couple ways to make and sell home-use saunas for big profits. First, design and build wet or dry ready-to-assemble sauna kits, which can be sold directly to consumers via online marketplaces such as eBay and internet malls, as well as by exhibiting assembled sauna display models at home and recreation shows to take orders. Second, build wet or dry saunas at your customer's location. This option would allow for more creativity in terms of the size and style of the sauna. Both options have advantages and disadvantages, but each can be equally profitable. Saunas are easy to make because design and construction plans are readily available, and there are also numerous companies manufacturing and selling sauna component parts. Therefore, all that needs to be manufactured from scratch is the cedar-insulated shell, door, and accessories such as cedar benches; the balance of the job is assembly work. A well-equipped, suitably sized workshop space will be needed, along with standard carpentry tools and equipment.

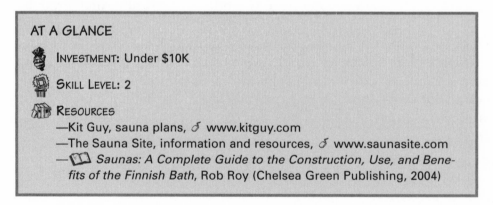

AT A GLANCE

INVESTMENT: Under $10K

SKILL LEVEL: 2

RESOURCES
—Kit Guy, sauna plans, ♂ www.kitguy.com
—The Sauna Site, information and resources, ♂ www.saunasite.com
—📖 *Saunas: A Complete Guide to the Construction, Use, and Benefits of the Finnish Bath*, Rob Roy (Chelsea Green Publishing, 2004)

Hot Tub Replacement Covers

Although modern acrylic shell hot tubs are designed to last for as long as 25 years, the insulated hot tub covers they come with do not. Vinyl hot tub covers get ripped, worn, fade, and generally breakdown in appearance and function from constant use. Insulated hot tub covers are a very important accessories for outdoor hot tubs because they keep heat from escaping when the tub is not being used, thereby reducing energy consumption. Most covers have a locking mechanism to keep kids, pets, leaves, and pests out when not in use. Making hot tub covers is not terribly difficult. You can use rigid foam insulation cut-to-size and covered in vinyl fabric, or a mold and insulating foam injection also covered in vinyl and sewn with piping on the seams. The first method is easier and cheaper, while still providing excellent quality. Because there are many hot tub manufacturers building various sizes and shapes, do not attempt to premake standard sizes. Instead, make each hot tub cover on a made-to-order basis, taking measurements first to ensure proper fit. Market using cheap classified advertisements, by posting fliers throughout the community, and by talking with spa dealers about making replacement hot tub covers for their customers or supplying them on a wholesale basis.

AT A GLANCE

INVESTMENT: Under $10K

SKILL LEVEL: 1

RESOURCES
—Ontario Sewing Automation, awning-making equipment and supplies, ☎ (905) 850-3537, ✂ www.ontariosewingautomation.ca
—Outdoor Textiles, ☎ (772) 283-4730, ✂ www.outdoortextiles.com

Wooden Toys

Wooden toys provide children of all ages with countless hours of fun. In fact, wooden toys often become treasured family heirlooms passed down for each new generation of children to enjoy. The demand and market for wooden toys is enormous. Fortunately, you do not need much in the way of special skills or equipment to start making and selling handmade, high-quality wooden toys so that you can cash in and profit on the demand. Requirements are minimal. You will need workshop space outfitted with basic hand and power tools, and wooden toy construction plans so you can build wooden pull toys, wagons, soldiers, animals, puzzles, trucks, boats, trains, airplanes, tractors, and a variety of animals. Construction plans are widely available from a number of sources. Because wooden toys attract so much attention, they are hot sellers and can be sold just about anywhere. You can sell them online through eBay and internet malls, at craft shows, toy shows, flea markets, and mall kiosks, especially near Christmas time, and even factory direct by setting up a small wooden toy boutique at your home or manufacturing location.

 AT A GLANCE

 INVESTMENT: Under $2K

 SKILL LEVEL: 2

 RESOURCES
—Toy Industry Association, ☎ (212) 675-1141, ♂ www.toy-tia.org
—U-Bild, wooden toy plans, ♂ www.u-bild.com
—Wooden Toy Plans, ♂ www.woodentoyplans.com
— 📖 *30 Toy Vehicles Made of Wood*, Ronald D. Tarjany (Tarjany Publications, 1999)
— 📖 *Making Heirloom Toys*, Jim Makowick (Taunton Press, 1996)

Toy Boxes

Manufacturing and selling themed toy boxes is a wonderful full- or part-time homebased business venture with terrific upside profit potential for entrepreneurs with basic carpentry skills and a bit of a creative flair. You will need to make a small investment into tools, equipment, and raw building materials, but even a couple thousand dollars will be sufficient to get started. You will also need to set up a workspace. Garages or well-vented basement workspaces are two great choices. To ensure success, aim to create unique and original toy box designs using high-quality building materials, brightly painted colors, and themes that kids can eagerly relate to, such as outer space, race cars, fire trucks, dinosaurs, and animals. Sell the toy boxes on a wholesale basis to retailers or direct to consumers through toy trade shows, at flea markets and public markets, and through interior designers. You can also sell online via eBay, internet malls, and e-commerce sites focused on toys and other products for children.

AT A GLANCE

 INVESTMENT: Under $2K

SKILL LEVEL: 1

 RESOURCES
—Toy Directory, database listing toy manufacturers, ♂ www.toydirec tory.com
—Toy Industry Association, ☎ (212) 675-1141, ♂ www.toy-tia.org
—U-Bild, toy box plans, ♂ www.u-bild.com
—Woodworkers Workshop, toy box plans, ♂ www.woodworkerswork shop.com

Dolls

Next to stamp collecting, doll collecting is the most popular collectible hobby in the United States, which means there are millions of potential customers ready to buy the dolls you make. The starting point is to determine the type(s) of doll you will make and sell—rag, wooden, cloth, toy, artistic, and so forth. Regardless of the type of dolls you make, equipment and tool requirements are minimal as is the amount of workspace needed: a spare bedroom, garage, or basement workspace are all suitable for doll making. Doll components are also widely available if you elect not to manufacture the complete doll, but instead want to concentrate on assembling and selling dolls. Designing and sewing interchangeable fashion accessories such as clothing, hats, and handbags for your doll line is also advisable because sales of these items will greatly increase revenues and profits. Dolls can be sold in a number of ways, including via eBay and internet malls, craft fairs, doll collectible and toy shows, and to retailers on consignment.

AT A GLANCE

 INVESTMENT: Under $2K

 SKILL LEVEL: 1–2

 RESOURCES
—The Doll Net, database listing doll manufacturers and supplies, ♂ www. thedollnet.com
—Toy Industry Association, ☎ (212) 675-1141, ♂ www.toy-tia.org
— *Designing the Doll: From Concept to Construction*, Susanna Oroyan (C&T Publishing, 1999)

Dollhouses and Accessories

The dollhouse and miniatures marketplace is exploding as more and more people are turned on to doll, dollhouse, and miniatures collecting. Now is your best opportunity to profit from this highly lucrative marketplace by starting your own dollhouse and miniatures manufacturing and sales business. Plans that will assist you in building scaled dollhouses, furniture, and décor are widely available on the internet. Even weekend novice woodworkers armed with only basic tools and a small workspace can get started and master the craft with a bit of trial and error and practice. Because the marketplace is so hot, selling the finished product is easy, and there are a number of sales avenues you can puruse, including selling online through eBay and doll collecting marketplaces, exhibiting at doll shows, advertising in doll collectible magazines for mail order sales, and displaying at arts and crafts shows, especially close to Christmas.

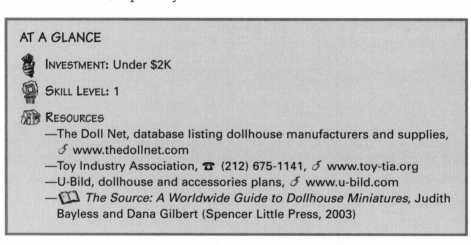

AT A GLANCE

INVESTMENT: Under $2K

SKILL LEVEL: 1

RESOURCES
—The Doll Net, database listing dollhouse manufacturers and supplies, ♂ www.thedollnet.com
—Toy Industry Association, ☎ (212) 675-1141, ♂ www.toy-tia.org
—U-Bild, dollhouse and accessories plans, ♂ www.u-bild.com
—📖 *The Source: A Worldwide Guide to Dollhouse Miniatures*, Judith Bayless and Dana Gilbert (Spencer Little Press, 2003)

Rocking Toys

Everything old is new again, which makes building and selling authentic children's rocking toys a timely moneymaking opportunity. You can design and build your rocking toys to resemble trains, boats, fire engines, cars, tractors, airplanes, rocket ships, farm animals, and a horse, of course. Not much is needed to get started making rocking toys in terms of equipment or experience. You will need to purchase a scroll saw, miter saw, table saw, drill press, bench sander, router, clamps, and construction plans, which are widely available from a number of sources, including the ones listed below. You will also need to set up a small workshop; a garage or space in the basement is adequate, providing the noise does not bother the neighbors and you can install a simple ventilation system. Selling rocking toys is just as easy as making them. Sale venue choices include online sales, mail order via specialty publications and catalogs, craft shows and flea markets, as well as the possibility of wholesaling to retailers of specialty children's furniture and toys.

AT A GLANCE

INVESTMENT: Under $2K

SKILL LEVEL: 2

RESOURCES
—Scrollsaw, rocking toy plans, ☌ www.scrollsaw.com
—Toy Directory, database listing toy manufacturers, ☌ www.toydirectory.com
—Toy Industry Association, ☎ (212) 675-1141, ☌ www.toy-tia.org
—U-Bild, rocking toy plans, ☌ www.u-bild.com

Piñatas

Piñatas aren't just for kids' birthday parties any more. There are piñatas available for just about any special occasion and function imaginable—anniversary parties, weddings, bachelor and bachelorette parties, baby showers, and more. The big difference between many of these piñatas and their kid-friendly counterparts is the prizes hidden inside. You definitely won't find the same prize in a birthday piñata that you will in a bachelor party piñata. Therefore, if you are going to design, make, and sell piñatas for profit, keep your inventory divided so the right piñata goes to the right occasion. Sell the completed piñatas online, at flea markets, and in malls with kiosk space. You can sell the piñatas to retailers on a wholesale basis. Also be sure to build alliances with wedding planners, day-care centers, event planners, and restaurants that host birthdays and other special occasions.

AT A GLANCE

INVESTMENT: Under $2K

SKILL LEVEL: 1

RESOURCES
—Piñata Design, ♂ www.pinatadesign.com
—Family Sweets Distribution, candy wholesale, ☎ (800) 334-1607, ♂ www.familysweets.com
—The Piñata Store, ♂ www.thepinatastore.com

Little League Cards

Basketball, football, soccer, hockey, and baseball—there are literally thousands of little league teams playing in these sports and more across the nation. Producing and selling little league team photograph and stats trading cards is an outstanding business opportunity, and one that could prove to be great fun. Little league trading cards are just like the pros, complete with the player's photograph, name, and team name on the front and player and team statistics on the back. The investment needed to start adds up to little more than the cost of a digital camera, computer, desktop publishing software, and marketing supplies. This is because a local print shop can be enlisted to print the cards. One of the better ways to market the cards is not to charge the players or their parents for the cards, but to charge the current team sponsor or new sponsor in exchange for having their business name also emblazoned across the front and back of the trading card.

AT A GLANCE

 INVESTMENT: Under $10K

 SKILL LEVEL: 1

 RESOURCES
—Art & Advertising, custom printing, ☎ (631) 912-9787, ♂ www.artandadvertising.com
—Little League Online, ♂ www.littleleague.org
—Print Quote USA, custom printing, ♂ www.printquoteusa.com

Kites

You can get started making and selling kites for peanuts. In fact, a few hundred dollars is all that is needed to cover the cost of construction materials and basic marketing materials, such as fliers, signs, and business cards. A great promotional idea is to host the occasional try-before-you-buy kite-flying event. Set up at a local park, beach, or parking lot (with permission), and let potential customers fly a kite of their choice before committing to buy. Advertise the event by informing the local media in the form of a press release, and when creating the press release, think in terms of family fun. Given the unique nature of the event, there should be no problem in securing free and valuable media exposure. Likewise, on the day of the event, it will not take long until a crowd assembles to see what is going on. These kinds of events really build excitement and clearly demonstrate the end-user benefit to consumers—in this case, fun. In addition to try-before-you-buy sales events, you can also sell your kites online, at sports and recreation shows, during community events, and at flea markets and public markets.

AT A GLANCE

INVESTMENT: Under $2K

SKILL LEVEL: 1–2

RESOURCES
—American Kite Fliers Association, ♂ www.aka.kite.org
—Toy Industry Association, ☎ (212) 675-1141, ♂ www.toy-tia.org
—📖 *The Kite Making Handbook*, Rosella Guerra and Giuseppe Fer-lengna (David & Charles Publishers, 2004)

Playhouses

Every child dreams of having a backyard playhouse to fuel his or her creative imaginations and entertain friends, and you can help fulfill these dreams by starting a playhouse manufacturing and sales business. Before you get started, you should know playhouses are big business, generating millions in sales annually. It is common for well-heeled parents to spend upwards of $25,000 for high-end playhouses complete with electricity, running water, hardwood floors, gabled roofs, and even air conditioning. Mid- to high-end is definitely the best segment of the market to cater to because there are many manufacturers flooding the market with inexpensive plastic playhouses. In addition to a well-equipped shop, you will also need construction plans. You will also have to decide if you will build and sell playhouses in kit form ready for customers to assemble or build playhouses on site. The best sales methods are exhibiting at home and garden shows, displaying at home, and building alliances with homebuilders, designers, and architects to secure referral business.

AT A GLANCE

 INVESTMENT: Under $10K

 SKILL LEVEL: 2

 RESOURCES
—Handyman Plans, playhouse plans, ✆ www.handymanplans.com
—U-Bild, playhouse plans, ✆ www.u-bild.com
—📖 *Playhouses You Can Build: Indoor & Backyard Designs*, David R. Stiles and Jeanie Stiles (Firefly Books, 1999)

Handcrafted Switch Plate Covers

Believe it or not, custom crafted electrical outlet and light switch plate covers are big sellers and fetch retail prices ranging from $5 to more than $100 each! Cashing in on the demand is easy, providing you have basic tools, a workshop, and a creative flair. Handcrafted switch plate covers can be manufactured from numerous materials including metals such as copper, brass, and tin, or from ceramics, glass, mirror, or hand-painted plastic. However, switch plate covers crafted from hardwoods such as cherry, oak, maple, and walnut are the most popular because they can be used to match existing wood. I would suggest that you manufacture a line of standard switch plate covers in the most popular configurations, as well as offering custom covers for unique applications. Handcrafted switch plate covers can be sold directly to consumers via online marketplaces, such as home improvement internet malls, internet craft malls, eBay, and your own web site. You can also sell directly to consumers in the brick-and-mortar world by exhibiting your products at home shows and craft fairs. Selling direct to business can be tackled in a few ways. You can set up accounts with independent and/or chain home improvement and décor retailers and sell in bulk at wholesale pricing. Or, target and sell directly to custom homebuilders and renovation contractors.

AT A GLANCE

 INVESTMENT: Under $2K

 SKILL LEVEL: 1–2

Backyard Play Structures

Like playhouses, backyard play structures have almost become a necessity for families across North America, and for good reason. They keep kids playing in the safety of the backyard instead of roaming the streets in search of fun. The days of the simple swing set are long gone. Today's play structures resemble mini-amusement parks complete with spiral slides, cargo net bridges, fireman's poles, rings, bungee swings, and fort-like turret lookouts. They are also much safer than the old metal swing sets and feature rounded edges, concealed fasteners, arsenic-free woods, chemical-free paints, and rubber landing mats under the main play stations. You might decide to design your own. Again, like playhouses, you will also have to decide if you will build and sell in kit form ready for customers to assemble or build and install at your customer's location. Exhibiting at home and garden shows, online sales, and displaying at home are your best bets for landing customers, and also don't overlook the possibility of selling into nonresidential markets: schools, day-care centers, campgrounds, RV parks, churches, and municipal playgrounds.

AT A GLANCE

 INVESTMENT: Under $10K

 SKILL LEVEL: 2

 RESOURCES
—A Better Plan, play structure plans, ♂ www.abetterplan.com
—Creative Playthings, ☎ (800) 444-0901, ♂ www.creativeplay
things.com
—Wood Zone, backyard play structure plans, ♂ www.woodzone.com
— 📖 *The Backyard Playground: Recreational Landscapes & Play Structures* (Creative Publishing, 2003)

Personalized Storybooks

Every child loves a good story, and the market for personalized storybooks for kids is gigantic. What makes creating personalized storybooks so unique is that each customer's child (or children) becomes the main character in the story. Software applications are available with story reprint rights that make this business a snap. Basically, you change the names of the characters to suit, print, and sell. Alternately, if you are a wordsmith, you can create your own story lines, changing the names of the characters to those of your customer's children. To operate the business, you will need a computer, a good quality printer, and a digital camera if you are going to include images of the children in your stories. It can be a mobile business, too, by setting up at malls, flea markets, craft shows, and community events to offer clients personalized storybooks while they wait. Or, you can operate from home and market the business via networking and advertising, mailing out completed orders.

AT A GLANCE

INVESTMENT: Under $10K

SKILL LEVEL: 1

RESOURCES
—Create-A-Book, business opportunity, ☎ (800) 732-3009, ✆ www. hefty.com
—My Family Tales, business opportunity, ☎ (801) 794-0678, ✆ www. myfamilytales.com

Cake Making and Decorating

Making, decorating, and selling one-of-a-kind cakes for every imaginable occasion is a great opportunity for the hobby baker to pursue, and potentially a very profitable one. On a small scale, you can work right from your kitchen, baking specialty cakes for weddings, birthdays, anniversaries, and corporate events. To get started on a shoestring promotional budget, contact wedding planners, photographers, bridal shops, event coordinators, restaurants, and catering companies to let them know about the specialty cakes you bake and sell. But don't forget to bribe them with an occasional cake now and then just to make sure they send business your way. You can also rent kiosk space at farmers' markets, public markets, and community events to sell cakes. On a large scale, you can rent commercial kitchen space so you have enough room to mass produce cakes that can be sold wholesale to restaurants and groceries.

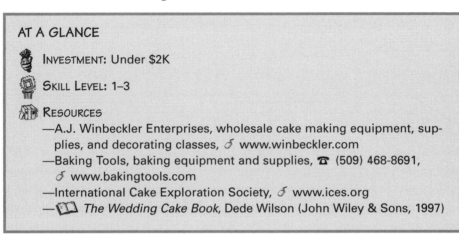

AT A GLANCE

INVESTMENT: Under $2K

SKILL LEVEL: 1–3

RESOURCES
—A.J. Winbeckler Enterprises, wholesale cake making equipment, supplies, and decorating classes, ✆ www.winbeckler.com
—Baking Tools, baking equipment and supplies, ☎ (509) 468-8691, ✆ www.bakingtools.com
—International Cake Exploration Society, ✆ www.ices.org
— 📖 *The Wedding Cake Book*, Dede Wilson (John Wiley & Sons, 1997)

Party Ice

Making and selling party ice is a unique business opportunity with huge growth and profit potential, but at the same time, it requires a substantial financial investment to purchase commercial ice cube machinery, a refrigerated delivery truck, and multiple ice chests for dealer locations. In total, the investment could easily reach six figures, especially if all of the needed equipment is purchased new. The business concept is very straightforward. Make and bag the ice cubes at your business location and deliver the ice to your retail account locations—gas stations, convenience stores, campgrounds, liquor stores, and grocery stores. Ice is typically placed on consignment in your ice chests at these locations, although some locations will supply their own freezer space. Every week you return to restock the ice chest and bill the retailer for the amount of ice sold, less his or her commission. Additionally, ice cubes can also be sold to restaurants, hotels, catering companies, nightclubs, and organizations hosting summertime events.

AT A GLANCE

INVESTMENT: Over $25K

SKILL LEVEL: 1

RESOURCES
—Canadian Association of Ice Industries, ☎ (416) 924-4702
—Ice Machine World, ice cube making equipment and supplies, ☎ (800) 821-9153, ✆ www.icemachineworld.com
—ITC Corp, ice cube making equipment, ✆ www.itcpack.com
—Northeastern Ice Association, ✆ www.northeasterniceassociation.com

Cotton Candy

Thomas Patton received a patent for the first cotton candy machine in 1900, and although cotton candy machines have become more technologically advanced, the process for making cotton candy has not changed for over 100 years. Cotton candy is made using melted sugar and a cotton candy spinning machine. Liquid sugar is poured into the machine, and as the machine spins, the liquid is forced through tiny holes creating the spider web or floss thread effect. The candyfloss cools and is served on a cone or stick. Cotton candy machines are very inexpensive, with tabletop models starting at $400 and up to fully functioning portable cotton candy vending carts costing in the range of $2,000. Because the only ingredient is sugar, about 90 percent of every sale is profit. Cotton candy can be made and sold at community events, fairs, flea markets, beach locations, sporting events, parades, and just about any other place where children gather.

AT A GLANCE

 INVESTMENT: Under $2K

 SKILL LEVEL: 1

 RESOURCES
—Fun Food Depot, cotton candy machines and supplies, ☎ (800) 284-4237, ✆ www.funfood-depot.com
—Gold Medal Products, cotton candy machines and supplies, ☎ (513) 769-7676, ✆ www.gmpopcorn.com
—Old Tyme Food, cotton candy machines and supplies, ☎ (800) 356-6533, ✆ www.oldtymefood.com

Candy

Young or old, everybody loves candy, which is why making and selling candy is a fantastic business opportunity. The first step is to decide what types of candies to make and sell—fudge, chocolate, taffy, hard candies, soft candies, or a combination. Making candy is easy. You need candy-making recipes, molds, ingredients, packaging supplies, and a sales plan. Wholesale sales to convenience stores, grocery stores, gift retailers, and candy boutiques is one option. A second is to open a candy retail shop or sell factory direct. There are also other ways to sell candies directly to consumers by renting mall kiosks, selling from a vending cart at flea markets, community events, and farmers' markets, or selling candy online. Yet another option is to concentrate on the corporate and charity market. Many corporations routinely buy candies of all sorts in packaging emblazoned with their business name and logo to give to customers and employees as appreciation gifts. Likewise, many charitable organizations and schools purchase candy in bulk to resell and raise funds for their various causes.

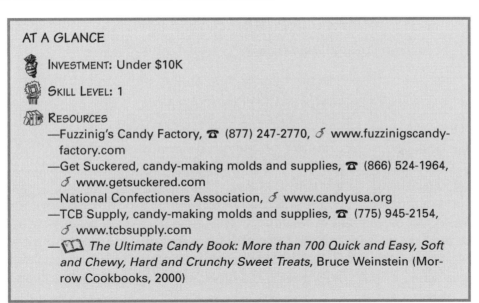

AT A GLANCE

INVESTMENT: Under $10K

SKILL LEVEL: 1

RESOURCES
—Fuzzinig's Candy Factory, ☎ (877) 247-2770, ♂ www.fuzzinigscandy-factory.com
—Get Suckered, candy-making molds and supplies, ☎ (866) 524-1964, ♂ www.getsuckered.com
—National Confectioners Association, ♂ www.candyusa.org
—TCB Supply, candy-making molds and supplies, ☎ (775) 945-2154, ♂ www.tcbsupply.com
—📖 *The Ultimate Candy Book: More than 700 Quick and Easy, Soft and Chewy, Hard and Crunchy Sweet Treats*, Bruce Weinstein (Morrow Cookbooks, 2000)

Hot Dogs

Incredible profits can be earned on weekends, or any day of the week for that matter, making and selling hot dogs at community events, sporting events, concerts, auction sales, the beach and flea markets, and in parking lots of busy retailers such as building supply centers. So what do you need to start making money selling hot dogs? The list is actually very short. You need a hot dog cart, a vendor's permit, a health board certificate, and food stock such as hot dogs, condiments, buns, and soft drinks. In total, expect to invest about $5,000 if you purchase a used hot dog cart and about $10,000 if you decide to buy a new one. Return on investment is quick, as it is not uncommon for hot dog vendors to have sales of $1,000 per day or more in busy locations and keep half that for themselves after expenses. Providing you secure the right location, you can potentially earn $50,000 per year or more working only a few hours a day every weekend.

AT A GLANCE

 INVESTMENT: Under $10K

 SKILL LEVEL: 1

 RESOURCES
  —All American Hot Dog, hot dog vending equipment and supplies,
    ☎ (800) 808-1396, ♂ www.allamericanhotdog.com
  —American Hot Dog Carts, hot dog vending equipment and supplies,
    ☎ (727) 321-3847, ♂ www.americanhotdogcarts.com
  —★ Willy Dog, ☎ (800) 915-4683, ♂ www.willydogs.com

Popcorn

Like hot dogs, excellent part-time profits can be earned making and selling popcorn at community events, sporting events, concerts, auction sales, the beach, and flea markets. The list of supplies and equipment needed to start is also short—a popcorn vending cart, vendor's permit, a health board certificate, popcorn, and packaging. An investment of less than $10,000 will get you on your way to earning fabulous weekend profits. There is also the possibility of establishing a wholesale popcorn business supplying retailers with prepopped and packaged popcorn. To set up wholesale accounts that can be serviced on a weekly basis, call on video stores, convenience stores, groceries, and gas stations. The wholesale side of the business will require addition investment to get started, but you will also have the potential to double your sales and profits if you sell both retail and wholesale.

AT A GLANCE

 INVESTMENT: Under $10K

 SKILL LEVEL: 1

RESOURCES
—Classic Carts, manufacturers specialty food vending carts, www.classic-carts.com
—Pop Corn Guys, pop corn supplies and equipment, ☎ (800) 617-2676, www.popcornguys.com
—★ Pop Culture, ☎ (877) 767-2858, www.popcult.com/franchise info.htm

Snow Cones

Nothing beats the summertime heat like a nice refreshing snow cone treat, which makes snow cones one of the better products to produce and sell for big profits. Snow cone equipment and vending carts are cheap. In fact, a top-end model with all of the bells and whistles will only set you back about $2,000. Using flavored syrup, you can offer customers more than 50 tasty flavors, and selling other treats such as soft drinks and chips will help to boost revenues. For the most part this is a summertime business in northern climates but can be operated year round in the sunny South. Location, location, and location is the name of the game for any retail business, and selling snow cones is no different. The best locations are high-traffic and highly visible areas such as supermarkets, malls, sporting events, the beach, concerts, fairs, parades, rodeos, and parks. There is also the possibility of vending snow cones at corporate events, grand openings, retail sales events, and large family gatherings.

AT A GLANCE

 INVESTMENT: Under $10K

 SKILL LEVEL: 1

 RESOURCES
—1-800-Shaved Ice Company, snow cone equipment and supplies, ☎ (800) 742-8334, www.1-800-shaved-ice.com
—Columbia Jobbing, snow cone equipment and supplies, ☎ (800) 818-0897, www.columbiajobbing.com
—Gala Source, snow cone equipment and supplies, ☎ (888) 521-4252, www.galasource.com

Gourmet French Fries

French fries are without question the most popular and widely consumed fast food in North America, and absolutely huge profits can be earned making and selling gourmet French fries with specialty toppings like cheese, salsa, sour cream, chili, gravy, and family secret sauce recipes. The best French fires are cut from fresh potatoes daily, not frozen from a bag. Equipment needed to make gourmet French fries are minimal in comparison to most restaurants. You will need potato chippers, deep fryers, an exhaust hood and extinguishing systems, soda machines, and other basic equipment, all of which can be purchased secondhand in good condition to keep start-up costs down. The best locations for a gourmet French fry stand are mall food courts or retail storefronts in a high-traffic area such as the beach. Another option is to convert a trailer or van into a portable gourmet French fry stand and operate (with permission) at the beach, auction sales, flea markets, fairs, sports events, concerts, and parades.

AT A GLANCE

INVESTMENT: Under $25K

SKILL LEVEL: 1

RESOURCES
—Boardwalk Fries, www.boardwalkfries.com
—New York Fries, www.newyorkfries.com
—Restaurant Equipment World, (800) 821-9537, www.restaurant equipment.net

Submarine Sandwiches

Blimpy, Subway, Quiznos, and Mr. Sub are all proof you do not have to start big to end big. These are just a few of the once small sub shops that have grown into multinational corporations generating billions annually selling submarine sandwiches. Making and selling submarine sandwiches is a classic example of why you should not try to reinvent the wheel to succeed. Just stick with the time-tested and proven system—make a good quality sandwich, choose the right location, sell at fair prices, and provide excellent customer service. Providing you follow the system, you will succeed and make money selling sandwiches, whether you operate a franchise operation or start your own shop. The main considerations are location, equipment, décor theme, and marketing. Many successful restaurant owners often advise would-be restaurateurs that they should work in the type of restaurant they want to open prior to opening one. This advice is wise.

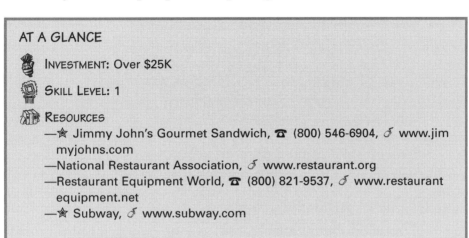

AT A GLANCE

INVESTMENT: Over $25K

SKILL LEVEL: 1

RESOURCES
—☆ Jimmy John's Gourmet Sandwich, ☎ (800) 546-6904, ♂ www.jimmyjohns.com
—National Restaurant Association, ♂ www.restaurant.org
—Restaurant Equipment World, ☎ (800) 821-9537, ♂ www.restaurantequipment.net
—☆ Subway, ♂ www.subway.com

Herbs

Herbs are always in demand, which creates a fantastic opportunity to grow and sell herbs for big profits. Start-up costs are minimal, and even a small herb garden can generate a substantial income. Herbs can be divided into three primary categories: (1) culinary herbs, such as basil, sage, chives, dill, parsley, rosemary, and thyme; (2) fragrant herbs, such as tansy, clove, rue, thyme, and chamomile; and (3) medicinal herbs, such as borage, catnip, ginseng, pennyroyal, and valerian. The first step is to get educated about herbs by reading books, joining herb-growing clubs, and obtaining information about herb gardening online. Next, devise a plan outlining which herbs you will grow and how these will be marketed. Herbs can be sold in a wide variety of ways, including direct to the customer as plants or as a finished product, wholesale to retail stores and bulk herb buyers, and direct to restaurants.

AT A GLANCE

INVESTMENT: Under $2K

SKILL LEVEL: 1

RESOURCES
—Herbs Depot, industry information and resources, ✆ www.
herbs-depot.com
—Herb Growing and Marketing Network, industry information and
resources, ✆ www.herbworld.com
— 📖 *Start Your Own Herb and Herbal Products Business* (Entrepreneur Press, 2003)

Pizza

Making and selling pizza is an opportunity that pizza-loving entrepreneurs can really sink their teeth into. By the slice or by the pie, fantastic profits can be earned making and selling pizza. There are many issues to consider when opening a pizza shop, but the main ones are operating location—mall food court, strip plaza, or a free-standing building—and style of pizzeria—dine in, take out, or a combination. Likewise, you will also need to decide if you will buy a pizza shop, purchase a franchise operation, or start a independent pizza shop. All have advantages and disadvantages. It should be noted, however, that often the most profitable pizza restaurants offer only delivery and pick-up options with no dining in, especially ones in close proximity to office buildings and schools. Another option is to make and sell pizza on a mobile basis, working from a converted van or trailer and setting up at auction sales, beaches, sporting events, outdoor fairs, and community events, basically anywhere a hungry crowd gathers.

AT A GLANCE

INVESTMENT: Under/over $25K

SKILL LEVEL: 1

RESOURCES
—Buck's Pizza, ✆ www.buckspizza.com/franchising.htm
—Instawares Restaurant Supply Superstore, ☎ (800) 892-3622, ✆ www.
instawares.com
—National Restaurant Association, ✆ www.restaurant.org
— 📖 *Getting Your Slice of the Pie: A Definitive Source for Prospering
in Pizza*, Tracy Powell (Empowered Innovations, 2001)

Ice Sculptures

If slicing, chipping, carving, and otherwise transforming blocks of ice into beautiful sculptures appeals to you, chances are an ice sculpting business will be right up your alley. Ice sculptures have become so popular that according to the National Ice Carving Association, it is now a $75 million a year industry and growing fast. Full-size ice bars, seafood ice stations, ice serving trays and bowls, ice drinking glasses, and the ever popular table centerpiece ice swan are just a few of the objects that can be carved from ice for big profits. The demand for ice sculptures is huge—weddings, corporate events, private functions, and trade shows are just a few of the events that commonly purchase ice sculptures to dazzle guests. No question, there is a learning curve in terms of being able to sculpt ice into beautiful shapes replicating everything from people to animals to objects. But at the same time, there are also many ice sculpting classes offered across the country catering to novice and advanced ice carvers. Computer-aided carving equipment and software are available that automatically sculpt ice into any design imaginable. Add color, lights, and flowing liquids, and you have ice sculptures that command upwards of $1,000 each.

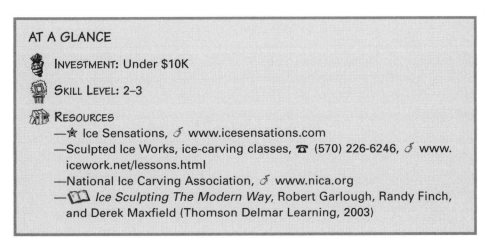

AT A GLANCE

INVESTMENT: Under $10K

SKILL LEVEL: 2–3

RESOURCES
—★ Ice Sensations, ♂ www.icesensations.com
—Sculpted Ice Works, ice-carving classes, ☎ (570) 226-6246, ♂ www.icework.net/lessons.html
—National Ice Carving Association, ♂ www.nica.org
—📖 *Ice Sculpting The Modern Way*, Robert Garlough, Randy Finch, and Derek Maxfield (Thomson Delmar Learning, 2003)

Organic Food Products

Kiss chemicals and preservatives goodbye by growing and selling only the highest quality fresh organic foods available. The potential to make a small fortune growing and selling organic vegetables, fruits, and baked goods is incredible, especially when you consider that more and more consumers are realizing the health benefits of eating organic food products and making the switch. Producing organic foods requires land for farming, appropriate equipment, and organic food producer certification, but even a small garden plot can be productive and profitable to start, and it is easily expanded using the profits you earn. There are a multitude of books, organic food producers' associations, and web sites solely dedicated to organic food production. Therefore, research will enable anyone with an interest in organic food production to get educated on the topic quickly. Sell your organic food products at farmers' markets, public markets, online, and wholesale to specialty food retailers. On a smaller scale, you can also offer customers free direct delivery on a regularly scheduled basis.

AT A GLANCE

 INVESTMENT: Under $25K

 SKILL LEVEL: 1–2

 RESOURCES
—Organic Trade Association, www.ota.org
—Seven Springs Farms, industry information, training, and resources, ☎ (540) 651-3228, ♂ www.7springsfarm.com
—📖 *The New Organic Growers: A Master's Manual of Tools and Techniques for the Home and Market Gardener*, Eliot Coleman, Sheri Amsel, and Molly Cook Field, (Chelsea Green Publishing, 1995)
—📖 *The Organic Gardeners Handbook of Natural Insect and Disease Control*, Barbara W. Ellis (Rodale Books, 1996)

Cookies

In spite of the fact that Wally Amos had no business training and zero start-up capital, he ultimately made millions baking and selling Famous Amos® gourmet cookies and so can you. Cookies are big business, and there are a few ways to cash in and profit. One option is to open a cookie-only bakery in a retail storefront location in a shopping mall or strip plaza. A second option is to start a wholesale-only cookie bakery in a suitable commercial building and sell to restaurants, grocery stores, convenience stores, and coffee shops. Another option, the least expensive in terms of start-up costs, is to make and sell gift cookie baskets from home. Delicious and decorative gift cookie baskets can be sold online, to corporations, and from vending carts located in malls, flea markets, and farmers' markets. Gift cookie baskets can also be sold to specialty food retailers on a wholesale basis. There are lots of options for baking and selling cookies for profit.

AT A GLANCE

 INVESTMENT: Under/over $25K

 SKILL LEVEL: 1

 RESOURCES

—All Homemade Cookies, billed as the world's largest collection of cookie recipes, ♂ www.allhomemadecookies.com

—✯ Nestle Toll House Café, ☎ (214) 495-9533, ♂ www.nestlecafe.com

—📖 *From Kitchen to Market: Selling Your Gourmet Food Specialty, 4th Edition*, Stephen F. Hall (Dearborn Trade, 2005)

—📖 *Start a Cookies Business*, downloadable e-book, ♂ www.information tree.com/cookie_business

Packaged Foods

The focus of this opportunity is not manufacturing, but packaging and reselling food products. Buy foods such as nuts, candies, and spices in large quantities at low wholesale prices, repackage into smaller quantities, and sell for a profit. Sales direct to consumers can be accomplished by selling at public markets, farmers markets, retail storefront, or kiosk, via home delivery, online, or advertising in specialty publications for items like gourmet food, and by delivering orders by mail or courier. Alternately, sell direct to grocery stores and convenience stores wholesale by way of "job-racking," which is a consignment sales term, or to restaurants. Depending on the products you decide to repackage and sell, health board approval made be needed for your business location, so be sure to check local ordinances. Likewise, you will need to invest in designing and having packaging products and possibly packaging equipment to create an efficient and cost-effective operating system.

AT A GLANCE

 INVESTMENT: Under $10K

 SKILL LEVEL: 1

 RESOURCES

—Entrepreneur, small business portal, ♂ www.entrepreneur.com

—GNS Foods, candy, nuts, and snacks manufacturing and bulk wholesale, ♂ www.gnsfoods.com

—National Confectioners Association, ♂ www.candyusa.com

—Nuts Online, bulk wholesale nuts, ♂ www.nutsonline.com

Gourmet Meals

Does everybody rave about your cooking? If so, why not put your extraordinary cooking skills to good use making and selling gourmet meals. Prepare gourmet meals for people hosting house parties, special-occasion events such as birthdays or anniversaries, and corporate luncheons. Personal chefs are quickly becoming a popular alternative to professional caterers for people that do not have the budget for a full-scale catered event or for people hosting small gatherings. There are many advantages associated with making and selling gourmet meals—minimal start-up investment, low overheads, flexible work hours, and huge profit potential. Because this is the type of business that can easily be supported by word-of-mouth advertising and repeat business once established, promote the business by joining community social clubs and business associations to network with potential customers. The prices you charge for your meals will vary depending on factors such as the type of foods and associated costs, but on average expect to earn in the range of $35 to $50 per hour.

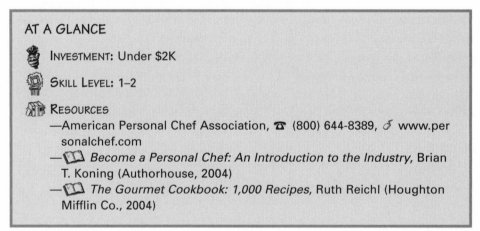

AT A GLANCE

INVESTMENT: Under $2K

SKILL LEVEL: 1–2

RESOURCES
—American Personal Chef Association, ☎ (800) 644-8389, ♂ www.personalchef.com
—📖 *Become a Personal Chef: An Introduction to the Industry*, Brian T. Koning (Authorhouse, 2004)
—📖 *The Gourmet Cookbook: 1,000 Recipes*, Ruth Reichl (Houghton Mifflin Co., 2004)

Coffee Tables

Coffee tables can be constructed from a wide variety of materials, including exotic hardwoods, softwood, plastic, iron, pre-cast cement, marble, stone, fiberglass, fabric covered frames, or a combination. Artistic freedom can also be practiced when designing coffee tables because beauty is in the eye of the beholder. Therefore, stretch your creative wings a bit to come up with a few truly amazing designs incorporating both visual and functional design elements. Aquarium coffee tables, planter coffee tables, coffee tables in the shape of a boat, with built-in storage compartments, made with faux fur, or coffee tables that transform into some other kind of furniture like a chair, bed, or dining table. The sky really is the limit. Coffee tables can be sold online, by advertising in home furnishings magazines, by displaying at home décor and furniture shows, and by making contact with residential and commercial interior designers to secure referral business. Consignment placement with home furnishing retailers and even art galleries is also a possibility. Additionally, don't overlook the commercial market. Unique and finely crafted coffee tables are also needed to furnish offices and waiting rooms.

AT A GLANCE

INVESTMENT: Under $10K

SKILL LEVEL: 2

RESOURCES
—American Home Furnishings Alliance, ☎ (336) 884-5000, ♂ www. afma4u.org
—Kit Guy, coffee table plans, ♂ www.kitguy.com
—U-Bild, coffee table plans, ♂ www.u-bild.com

Entertainment Centers

The proliferation of new high-tech audio and visual entertainment equipment such as flat screen televisions and home theater systems has breathed new life into what was, until a few years ago, a declining electronics industry. With renewed heated consumer demand comes the opportunity for entrepreneurs with basic woodworking skills to profit by making and selling entertainment centers. Like any furniture manufacturing business, you need a workshop, carpentry equipment and tools, and the skills to make high-quality, functional, and visually-appealing entertainment centers. Detailed construction plans are widely available from a number of sources. Or, if you also have a creative flair, you can design your own line of entertainment centers combining unique construction materials such as wood, metal, glass, and ceramics with user-friendly features such as built in CD and DVD storage space. Sell online, at home décor and furniture shows, from a workshop-based showroom, and by wholesaling or consigning pieces with electronics' retailers.

AT A GLANCE

 INVESTMENT: Under $10K

 SKILL LEVEL: 2

RESOURCES
—American Home Furnishings Alliance, ☎ (336) 884-5000, ♂ www.
afma4u.org
—Furniture Plans, ♂ www.furnitureplans.com
—U-Bild, entertainment center plans, ♂ www.u-bild.com

Children's Theme Furniture

All sorts of theme furniture for kids are red-hot sellers! Working from home or a small rental workshop, you can trade on your design and building skills to make and sell furniture for kids in the shape of rocket ships, racecars, tractors, dinosaurs, airplanes, and just about anything else you or, more correctly, kids can imagine. Furniture products can include anything and everything, from beds to toy boxes to bunk beds to dressers and even bedroom forts. All the furniture should be brightly painted to match the furniture's theme, and have kid-safe features such as rounded corners, nontoxic materials and finishes, built-in secret storage compartments, lighting, and options for built-in audio, video, and computer equipment. Themed furniture is so popular with parents and kids alike that it makes it a very easy sale—from home, exhibiting at home décor shows, and on eBay.

AT A GLANCE

 INVESTMENT: Under $10K

 SKILL LEVEL: 2

 RESOURCES
—American Home Furnishings Alliance, ☎ (336) 884-5000, ♂ www.
afma4u.org
—U-Bild, theme furniture plans, ♂ www.u-bild.com
—Wood Zone, theme furniture plans, ♂ www.woodzone.com

Driftwood and Log Furniture

Free or very inexpensive raw materials and huge consumer demand equals big profits for entrepreneurs who choose to manufacture and sell driftwood and log furniture. Recently, there has been a rebirth in the popularity of log furniture for interior and exterior use in the home, cottage, chalet, and even office. Design and manufacture furniture using driftwood, dressed logs, rough logs, and recycled woods, or combine any or all. Just think about the neat products you can manufacture from these materials—coffee tables, patio furniture, bedroom sets, trays, and the list goes on because your only limit is your imagination. There are many options for selling the completed furniture, including wholesale to furniture retailers, factory direct from your own showroom, online at eBay, and exhibiting your furniture at home shows.

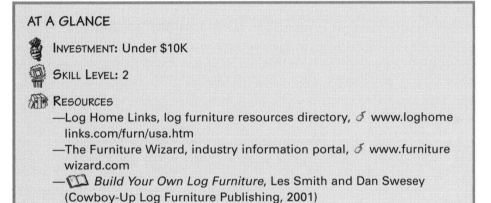

AT A GLANCE

INVESTMENT: Under $10K

SKILL LEVEL: 2

RESOURCES
—Log Home Links, log furniture resources directory, ♂ www.loghome links.com/furn/usa.htm
—The Furniture Wizard, industry information portal, ♂ www.furniture wizard.com
—📖 *Build Your Own Log Furniture*, Les Smith and Dan Swesey (Cowboy-Up Log Furniture Publishing, 2001)

Nursery Furniture

Cribs, cradles, and changing tables are just a few of the in-demand nursery products that you can make and sell for big profits. The requirements for making nursery furniture are the same as for any furniture manufacturing enterprise; you need a workshop, appropriate equipment and tools, skills to make the furniture, and detailed construction plans, which are widely available from a number of sources. Marketing and selling nursery furniture, however, is vastly different than marketing and selling furniture for adults because it is a niche product with a much smaller primary target audience. Consequently, you have to think in terms of the best way to access this market. A few ideas include purchasing mailing lists comprised of newlyweds and expectant parents, as well as mailing lists comprised of grandparents, because they are often the ones doing the buying for their grandchildren. Also, build alliances with midwives and birthing coaches so you can gain access to their clients. Nursery furniture can also be sold through online marketplaces, by exhibiting at home furnishing and baby-related consumer shows, and to independent and chain retailers on a wholesale basis.

AT A GLANCE

  INVESTMENT: Under $10K

 SKILL LEVEL: 2

RESOURCES
—American Home Furnishings Alliance, ☎ (336) 884-5000, ♂ www. afma4u.org
—Furniture Plans, ♂ www.furnitureplans.com
—U-Bild, nursery furniture plans, ♂ www.u-bild.com
—Wood Zone, nursery furniture plans, ♂ www.woodzone.com

Reproduction Antique Furniture

Spend time watching the television program *Antiques Roadshow,* and you will quickly understand why starting a reproduction antique furniture manufacturing business is a wise choice. Real antique furniture sells for prices reaching well into the six-figure range, which means lots of would-be collectors and antique furniture enthusiasts simply cannot afford to purchase the real thing. Instead, they purchase high-quality reproductions as an affordable way to enjoy the furniture without breaking the bank. This is not a business for everyone. You need carpentry and fine furniture making skills and equipment in order to make high-quality antique furniture reproductions. But with that said, those with the necessary skills have the potential to earn substantial profits. The starting point is specialization; pick a period, influence, and country of origin to replicate—early American, French provincial, or English Victorian. Patterns are widely available, or you might elect to use real antique furniture as a guide for replicating. Reproduction antique furniture can be sold online, from a factory showroom, consigned with fine furniture retailers, or even sold wholesale to furniture retailers.

AT A GLANCE

 INVESTMENT: Under $10K

 SKILL LEVEL: 2

 RESOURCES
—Furniture Library, reproduction antique furniture information and construction plans, ♂ www.furniturelibrary.com
—House of Antique Hardware, reproduction hardware, ♂ www.house ofantiquehardware.com
—The Furniture Wizard, industry information portal, ♂ www.furniture wizard.com
—📖 *Making Antique Furniture Reproductions: Instructions and Measured Drawings for 40 Classic Projects*, Franklin H. Gottshall (Dover Publications, 1994)

Futons

Futons are a hip, functional, yet affordable piece of furniture that can serve a multitude of uses and fit into just about any home décor, which has made them a popular purchase for many budget-minded consumers. Futons are also easy to make, requiring only basic tools and equipment, and workshop space such as a garage. Futon furniture plans are widely available online and at retailers selling woodworking equipment and supplies. Standard plans can easily be modified by adding your own personal signature design elements and functional features. To make futon cushions, you will need to invest in sewing equipment, supplies, foam, and fabric. Alternately, cushions can be purchased wholesale, or you can contract this part of the job out to a local seamstress, while still offering fabric selection options. Sell online, at home décor and furniture shows, from a workshop-based showroom, and by wholesaling to or consigning pieces with furniture retailers.

AT A GLANCE

 INVESTMENT: Under $10K

 SKILL LEVEL: 2

> RESOURCES
> —American Home Furnishings Alliance, ☎ (336) 884-5000, ♂ www.
>   afma4u.org
> —Futon Furniture Plans, ♂ www.futonfurnitureplans.com
> —U-Bild, futon plans, ♂ www.u-bild.com

Blanket Boxes

Finely crafted blanket boxes are always a popular home décor choice, making them one of the better products to make and sell for big bucks. The best blanket boxes are covered with hardwood veneers with elegant inlay work and lined with aromatic cedar. Of course, if your carpentry skills are not quite to the level of the fine craftsperson, you can start off making simple blanket boxes constructed solely of pine or cedar wood and better your building skills over time with practice. To get started, you will need to purchase design plans, woodworking equipment, and raw materials, as well as set up a workspace. The best selling venues will include craft shows, home and décor shows, directly from home supported by local advertising and word-of-mouth referrals, and online marketplaces such as eBay, especially those with wedding gift registries. Depending on your profit margin, you might also consider consigning the blanket boxes with local furniture and gift retailers or even selling them to retailers on a wholesale basis.

> AT A GLANCE
>
> INVESTMENT: Under $2K
>
> SKILL LEVEL: 1–2
>
> RESOURCES
> —The Crafters Mall, craft products marketplace, ♂ www.procrafter.com
> —American Home Furnishings Alliance, ☎ (336) 884-5000, ♂ www.
>   afma4u.org
> —Furniture Plans, ♂ www.furnitureplans.com
> —Wood Zone, blanket box plans, ♂ www.woodzone.com

Wall Beds

Designing, building, selling, and installing functional, space-saver wall beds (aka Murphy beds) is a very unique opportunity that will appeal to entrepreneurs with carpentry skills and equipment. The target market for space-saver wall beds is actually very large and continues to grow every year as newly built urban apartments and condominiums shrink in size. Primarily, you will want to aim your marketing efforts at current apartment dwellers, people in the process of buying or renting apartments, condominium developers, interior designers, and architects via advertising and exhibiting products at consumer, trade furniture, and home improvement shows. Wall beds can be designed and constructed in two basic ways. One is as a kit comprised of a steel fold-down bed frame surrounded by a cabinet with doors and drawers that is shipped ready to install on the wall by the homeowner or contactor. The second is a steel fold-down bed frame fastened directly to the wall with the surrounding cabinet built in place (although it may have been prebuilt in a workshop for assembly completed on site).

AT A GLANCE

INVESTMENT: Under $25K

SKILL LEVEL: 2

RESOURCES
—American Home Furnishings Alliance, ☎ (336) 884-5000, ♂ www.afma4u.org
—Kit Guy, wall bed plans, ♂ www.kitguy.com
—✪ More Space Place, ☎ (888) 731-3051, ♂ www.morespaceplace.com

Roll-Top Desks

Handcrafted roll-top desks made of oak, maple, cherry, and walnut hardwood and adorned with inlay work and brass fittings fetch big bucks. You can cash in on the demand by starting a roll-top desk manufacturing and sales business. Build from any of the standard construction plans widely available online, or purchase a few styles of roll-top desks and replicate these designs, adding your own distinct features inside and out. Roll-top desks appeal to a broad range of people—professionals, executives, and homeowners seeking that just-right desk for the home office. A small workshop and basic woodworking tools and equipment are all that's needed to get started. Completed desks can be sold online through handcrafted furniture web sites and marketplaces, via classified ads in newspapers and home furnishings magazines, by displaying at home décor and furniture shows, and by making contact with residential and commercial interior designers to secure referral business.

Wardrobes

Most people are well aware of the fact that you can never have enough closet and storage space, especially when living in tiny urban condos and apartments. Wardrobes have always been hot sellers, which make them excellent products to manufacture and sell for a profit. Design your own line of custom wardrobes, or purchase construction plans to work from, adding your own distinctive features to separate your products from competitors. Both hardwoods and softwoods can be used in the construction process, but be sure to add embellishments such as glass, mirrors, ceramic titles, and unique hardware to increase visual appearance and sales value. In addition to a suitable workspace, equipment and tools such as a table saw, planer, joiner, drill press, band saw, and radial arm saw will be needed, along with basic hand tools like drills, clamps, and pattern jigs. Retail sales options include a workshop-based showroom, furniture show exhibiting, and online sales. Or, if your price point allows, wardrobes can be wholesaled or consigned to furniture and bedding retailers.

RESOURCES
—American Home Furnishings Alliance, ☎ (336) 884-5000, ⚲ www.
    afma4u.org
—The Furniture Wizard, industry information portal, ⚲ www.furniture
    wizard.com
—Furniture Plans, ⚲ www.furnitureplans.com
—U-Bild, wardrobe plans, ⚲ www.u-bild.com

Furniture Slipcovers

People purchase furniture slipcovers for many reasons—to protect furniture from spills and pets, to hide blemishes, or just to renew their furniture with a fresh look while on a budget. Almost any type of furniture is game for slipcovers, including sofas, reading chairs, dinning room chairs, and patio furniture. Designing and making slipcovers for furniture is not difficult, especially if you have sewing skills. There are two approaches you can take. First, design, make, and sell a standard line of slipcovers that fit (within reason) popular sizes of furniture. The second approach is to make and sell tailored slipcovers on a made-to-order basis. Both options have pros and cons. The first is highly competitive, whereas the second allows for more creativity. In addition to sewing skills, you will need sewing equipment, supplies, patterns, and fabric to get started. Slipcovers can be sold online, at home furnishing and décor shows, and wholesale to furniture and linen retailers. If your plan is to concentrate on tailor-made slipcovers, be sure to build working relationships with interior designers, because they will quickly become your best source for new business.

AT A GLANCE

 INVESTMENT: Under $10K

 SKILL LEVEL: 2

 RESOURCES
—Bright Notions, sewing equipment and supplies, ⚲ www.bright
    notions.com
—Slipcover Network, industry information portal, ⚲ www.slipcover
    network.com

> —Slipcover University, training classes, instruction books and videos, and slipcover patterns and supplies, ☎ (817) 923-7160, ♂ www.slip coveruniversity.com
> —📖 *Simply Slipcovers* (Sunset Publishing, 1997)

Junkyard Furniture and Art Creations

Flower vases made from brightly painted old car springs, a sofa built from the backend of a '57 Chevy complete with working turn signals, entertainment centers designed from discarded refrigerators, and a wall clock fashioned from a hubcap, are examples of a few of the products that can be created from junk and sold for big bucks. Artistic flair, basic tools, and a suitable workspace are all that's needed to get started turning junk into cash. Raw materials are easy to find because there are thousands of junkyards and scrap heaps around the country waiting to be scoured for just the right piece of scrap to make into a highly salable piece of furniture, home décor product, or work of art. There are numerous options for selling junkyard creations, including by selling online or from a home-based studio, exhibiting at art, crafts, and home interior shows, and by consigning items with urban furniture retailers, art galleries, and gift retailers.

AT A GLANCE

INVESTMENT: Under $10K

SKILL LEVEL: 1–2

RESOURCES
—Classic Junkyard, junkyard directory, ♂ www.classicjunkyard.com/ junkyards
—Furniture Plans, ♂ www.furnitureplans.com
—National Craft Association, ♂ www.craftassoc.com
—The World Artist Directory, ♂ www.worldartistdirectory.com

Kitchen Racks

Spice racks, spoon racks, wine racks, and pot and pan racks are just a few of the kitchen rack accessories that can be manufactured and sold for a profit. Regardless of experience, these are all easy to make out of wood, metal, or both with nothing more than basic tools. Even better, there is no need to reinvent the wheel because they are proven sellers. Work from standard design plans, or design and build your own racks incorporating unique custom features and materials such as glass and ceramics. Sell your kitchen rack creations on eBay or at home décor and gift shows, flea markets, craft fairs, and in-home parties. Also, don't overlook the possibility of mass-producing various types of racks, which would enable you to establish wholesale accounts with gift and home décor retailers across the county.

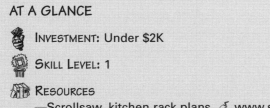

AT A GLANCE

INVESTMENT: Under $2K

SKILL LEVEL: 1

RESOURCES
—Scrollsaw, kitchen rack plans, ♂ www.scrollsaw.com
—Woodcraft Projects, kitchen rack plans, ♂ www.woodcraftplans.com
—Wood Projects Made Easy, kitchen rack plans, ♂ www.easywoodpro jects.com

Boardroom Tables

When it comes time to purchase boardroom furniture, many companies wisely choose to spend a bundle of loot on custom, unique, and one-of-a-kind boardroom tables at prices that can reach into the stratosphere, for good reason. Big deals are made in the boardroom, and first impressions are lasting impressions. Companies need to wow investors, business partners, vendors, and potential employees, and one way to do this is by having an impressively furnished boardroom that projects success. Providing you have a creative flair and experience working in wood, stone, metal, or glass, you can cash in on the demand by designing, building, and selling high-end boardroom tables. Design and construction materials are key to success, and a great deal of research and planning in these areas are necessary. Think also about technology and the need for built-in computer ports, electricity, and lighting. In addition to suitable workspace, tools, equipment, and raw materials are needed to get started. Build alliances with commercial designers and architects to spread the word about your business. Also, display sample boardroom tables at office furniture trade shows and advertise in office furniture magazines and catalogs.

AT A GLANCE

 INVESTMENT: Under $10K

 SKILL LEVEL: 2

 RESOURCES
—The Business and Institutional Furniture Manufacturers' Association, ♂ www.bifma.org
—The Furniture Wizard, industry information portal, ♂ www.furniture wizard.com

Log Homes

Building and selling log homes is a manufacturing business suited to truly ambitious entrepreneurs with a construction background. There are many log home building classes and courses offered in all regions of North America, including two-day weekend classes offered throughout the year by the Log Home Builder's Association of North America. In these classes, you will learn the basic construction principles needed to build log homes and structures, including tool and equipment handling and actual hands-on log home building. It is not necessary to start at the top so to speak. You can start your business by building smaller log structures, such as log garden sheds, gazebos, camping cabins, and garages. Increase the complexity of each new log building project as you hone your skills. Selling log homes and structures is easy, simply because they are in very high demand here and in other regions of the world. On a smaller scale, and if space provides, construct a few sample log structures on your own property to use as display models to secure orders locally. As the business grows, expand into sales and/or installations of complete log home and structure kits.

AT A GLANCE

 INVESTMENT: Over $25K

 SKILL LEVEL: 2–3

 RESOURCES
—★ Lincoln Logs International, ☎ (800) 848-3310, ♂ www.lincolnlogs international.com

—Log Home Builder's Association of North America, ☎ (360) 794-4469, ♂ www.loghomebuilders.org
—📖 *Log Construction Manual: The Ultimate Guide to Building Hand-crafted Log Homes*, Robert W. Chambers (Deep Stream Press, 2002)

Seamless Rain Gutters

Seamless rain gutters have become the gutter of choice for the majority of homeowners, builders, and architects because they are inexpensive, quick to install, and available in a wide range of designer colors and profiles. This creates a fantastic opportunity to cash in on demand by starting a seamless rain gutter manufacturing business. As complicated as this may sound, it is not. There are portable roll form machines available that will form rain gutters in the desired profile and length right at the customer's location. A coil of aluminum in the chosen color is loaded onto a spindle and fed into the gutter-forming machine, and presto, a finished seamless rain gutter comes out the opposite end ready to install. In addition to the extrusion machine, you will also need equipment such as a power miter saw, hand tools, ladders, and suitable transportation. There are two prerequisites for starting this business. One, you should have some construction experience, although most manufacturers of gutter extrusion machines do offer gutter making and installation courses. Two, you cannot be afraid of heights. Market the product to homeowners by advertising in newspapers, coupon books, and fliers and by exhibiting at home improvement shows. Also, be sure to build alliances with new homebuilders, renovation contractors, and architects who can utilize your gutter products and installation services.

AT A GLANCE

 INVESTMENT: Under $25K

 SKILL LEVEL: 2–3

 RESOURCES

—Gutter Works, industry information portal featuring new and used rain gutter machine listings, ♂ www.gutterworks.com
—★ The Gutter Guys, ☎ (800) 848-8837, ♂ www.thegutterguys.com
—The National Rain Gutter Association, ☎ (210) 342-7532, ♂ www. aarcsis.org

Windows

Big bucks can be earned manufacturing and selling wood, aluminum, or vinyl windows. Building windows is actually a very simple manufacturing process, especially aluminum and vinyl windows because most of the required components, such as sealed insulating glass units, rubber gaskets, and aluminum or vinyl extrusion frames can be purchased premade. These materials are cut to the desired size using a power miter saw, gaskets and seals installed, and the frame assembled around the sealed glass unit. Building wood sash windows is a bit more involved because the sash is custom built to size for each window. Regardless of the type of windows you build, all can easily be made in a well-equipped homebased workshop using nothing more than standard carpentry and metal working tools. The market for new construction and replacement double-glazed windows is gigantic, especially as energy costs continue to skyrocket. The primary target audience is renovation contractors, new homebuilders, and do-it-yourself homeowners. The best ways to reach builders and contractors are simply by setting up appointments with them to pitch the benefits of your windows and exhibiting your products at building contractor trade shows. The best way to tap into the do-it-yourself homeowner market is by advertising windows in the Yellow Pages and newspapers at factory-direct prices, as well as by displaying at home improvement shows to collect sales leads and take orders.

AT A GLANCE

INVESTMENT: Under $10K

SKILL LEVEL: 2

RESOURCES
—Canadian Window and Door Manufacturers Association, ☎ www. cwdma.ca
—Glass Links, directory listing window parts and glass suppliers, ☎ www.glasslinks.com
—Window & Door Manufacturers Association, ☎ www.nwwda.org

Custom Doors

If you want to make lots of money building and selling doors, the most lucrative segment of the market is custom wood doors. This includes specialty French doors with stained or etched glass lites, oversize or nonstandard size doors, wood doors with an internal firebreak that can be used in commercial or office applications, antique reproduction doors with authentic reproduction hardware, and arts-and-crafts wood doors with elaborate carved features or embellishments such as copper, glass beading, or mosaic tile inserts. Obviously, the more elaborate the door, the higher the degree of carpentry and artistic skills you need. Custom wood doors can be sold in many ways, although most are made to order. Therefore, you only need to design and build a few doors to use as selling samples at home improvement shows and a workshop showroom. Building alliances with architects, custom homebuilders, and designers are crucial.

AT A GLANCE

 INVESTMENT: Under $10K

 SKILL LEVEL: 2

 RESOURCES
  —Canadian Window and Door Manufacturers Association, ♂ www.cwdma.ca
  —Door Hardware Manufacturers Directory, ♂ www.door-hardware-manufacturers.com
  —House of Antique Hardware, reproduction vintage door hardware, ♂ www.houseofantiquehardware.com
  —Window & Door Manufacturers Association, ♂ www.nwwda.org

Wood Screen Doors

Old-fashioned wood screen doors are in high demand, and if you have a bit of carpentry experience, you can capitalize on that demand by building and selling wooden screen doors right from a homebased workshop. Not much is needed to get started—a workshop, carpentry tools and equipment, design plans, wood, hardware, and screening. Material costs to make screen doors are very low in comparison to the amount of labor time. Therefore, you will need to organize your workspace for maximum productivity and use patterns and jigs to save time and speed up the manufacturing process. Completed doors can be sold in any number of ways, including to retailers on a wholesale basis, direct to builders and renovators, or direct to consumers through online marketplaces, by advertising in specialty publications, and by displaying your product at home and garden shows. To increase revenues and profits, consider making and selling related home improvement products such as wooden patio furniture, window boxes and shutters, and gazebos.

AT A GLANCE

 INVESTMENT: Under $10K

 SKILL LEVEL: 2

 RESOURCES
—Argus Steel Products, screen supplies, ☎ (877) 333-5300, ♂ www.argussteel.com
—Scrollsaw, wood screen door plans, ♂ www.scrollsaw.com
—Window & Door Manufacturers Association, ♂ www.nwwda.org
—Workshop Network, wood screen door plans, ♂ www.workshop.net

Window Screens

Mosquito-spread West Nile virus and ever-present threat of killer bees ensure that window screens will always be in high demand, making this manufacturing business a wise choice for a new start-up. Constructing window screens requires only basic tools and materials to get started—a miter saw, screen rollers, screen rails, various screen replacement parts, and a selection of fiberglass and aluminum screen rolls in various widths. You can manufacture the screens on a mobile basis working from an enclosed trailer or van to provide protection from inclement weather. Or, you can operate from a homebased workshop and measure window screens for repair and replacement at your customer's location, manufacture them at your workshop, and return later to install the new screens. Market the business by contacting companies and individuals that require screen repairs and replacements on a regular basis. These include residential and commercial property management firms, condominium strata corporations, apartment complexes, government institutions, and renovation contractors. The profit potential is excellent because window screens are very inexpensive to make, there is limited competition, and consumer demand for screen repairs and replacements is proven.

AT A GLANCE

 INVESTMENT: Under $10K

 SKILL LEVEL: 2

Security Bars

With property crime and home invasions on the rise, more home and business owners are turning to installing window and door steel security bars to protect their homes, businesses, and families. Security bars are proven to be a very effective deterrent to theft, which is why security bar manufacturers are working around the clock to keep up with demand. The business is very straightforward to start. You need a workshop, welding equipment and supplies, steel, and welding skills, or an employee with welding skills. Selling direct to businesses requires nothing more than advertising locally in the Yellow Pages and putting on a comfortable pair of walking shoes and getting out to talk to store and office owners to pitch the security benefits of your products. Selling to homeowners is best achieved by displaying products at home improvement shows and conducting a local advertising campaign of flier delivery, newspaper ads, and networking nonstop. Building working relationships with alarm and security companies is also wise because they can refer your business to their clients or sell your products to their clients.

AT A GLANCE

 INVESTMENT: Under $10K

 SKILL LEVEL: 2

 RESOURCES
—Entrepreneur, small business portal, ✐ www.entrepreneur.com
—Summit Steel, wholesale steel, ☎ (760) 726-8823, ✐ www.summit steel.net
—Welding Mart, welding supplies and equipment, ✐ www.welding mart.com

Cupolas

Cupolas are a graceful reminder of a proud American heritage and add a classy elegance to residential homes and commercial buildings. Although cupolas can be large domed or square towers reaching 30, 40, and even 50 feet in height, the focus of this opportunity is manufacturing small decorative wooden roof cupolas for homes, sheds, barns, and garages. Most cupolas are constructed of wood with copper, metal, asphalt, or cedar shingle roofs, decorative wood siding sidewalls and bases, and perhaps windows or louvers on the side to let in light or allow hot air to escape from attic spaces. Thus, not only are cupolas decorative, they can also be functional. Constructing cupolas is not difficult. Plans are widely available to aid in design, and only standard carpentry equipment and tools are needed. Cupolas can be sold in a ready-to-assemble kit format reflecting all of the popular roof pitches—six-, eight-, and twelve-twelfths—or on a custom made-to-order basis. Adorning your own roofline with sample cupolas can be one of your best sales and marketing tools. Displaying at home improvement and garden shows to sell and take orders is also effective.

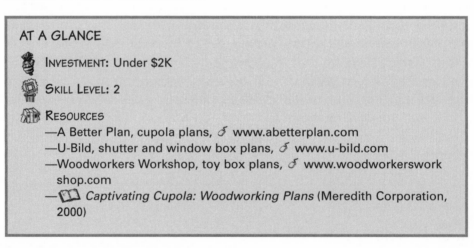

AT A GLANCE

INVESTMENT: Under $2K

SKILL LEVEL: 2

RESOURCES
—A Better Plan, cupola plans, ♂ www.abetterplan.com
—U-Bild, shutter and window box plans, ♂ www.u-bild.com
—Woodworkers Workshop, toy box plans, ♂ www.woodworkerswork shop.com
—📖 *Captivating Cupola: Woodworking Plans* (Meredith Corporation, 2000)

Window Boxes and Shutters

Inexpensive window boxes overflowing with flowers and decorative window shutters add charm and curb appeal to any home, which is why they have become such a popular purchase for homeowners. Trade on your basic carpentry skills and workshop tool inventory to build and sell window boxes and shutters and make lots of profits in the process. Window boxes and window shutters are not particularly difficult to make. In fact, once you have designed and constructed a few, you have pretty much mastered the learning curve. On a small scale, window boxes and shutters can be sold directly to homeowners by advertising locally in your newspapers posting fliers on bulletin boards, exhibiting your products at home and garden shows, and advertising for mail order sales in specialty home improvement and gardening publications and catalogs. On a larger scale, providing you have the required production space and equipment, you can mass produce the product and sell wholesale to building and garden centers.

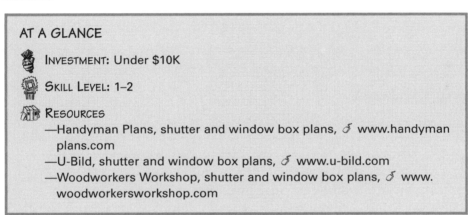

AT A GLANCE

INVESTMENT: Under $10K

SKILL LEVEL: 1–2

RESOURCES
—Handyman Plans, shutter and window box plans, ✆ www.handyman plans.com
—U-Bild, shutter and window box plans, ✆ www.u-bild.com
—Woodworkers Workshop, shutter and window box plans, ✆ www. woodworkersworkshop.com

Sundecks

One of the fastest growing sectors of the home improvement industry is designing and building custom sundecks, which can easily reach $40,000. Custom sundecks can include features such as built-in flower and shrub planters, sunken hot tub complete with a four-season gazebo, glass or cast iron handrails, stone barbeques and kitchenettes, natural gas heaters, built-in sound systems, atmosphere lighting, and custom-manufactured wood patio furniture to match the deck's design. So what is needed to get started building and installing custom sundecks for big profits? Probably less than you think. You need design and construction experience and a creative flair so that you have the ability to build truly one-of-a-kind decks, which in turn greatly increases word-of-mouth advertising and referral business. Likewise, you need carpentry equipment such as a table saw, compound miter saw, drills, hand tools, ladders, and suitable transportation. If funds are limited, most of the equipment can be rented on an as-needed-basis to get started. Also keep in mind, in most municipalities of the United States and Canada, sundecks must meet building codes and require a building permit to install.

AT A GLANCE

 INVESTMENT: Under $25K

 SKILL LEVEL: 2

 RESOURCES
—Deck Industry Association, ☍ www.deckindustry.org
—✫ Garden Structures, ☎ (888) 293-8938, ☍ www.gardenstructures.com
—Handyman Plans, deck plans, ☍ www.handymanplans.com
—📖 *Deck Design: Plus Railings, Planters and Benches*, Steve Cory (Creative Homeowner Press, 2000)

Victorian Millwork

Every year across North American thousands of heritage and Victorian homes are restored to their former glory. There are also thousands more homes built each year to resemble heritage and Victorian homes. Needless to say, the time could not be better for starting a business manufacturing and selling reproduction interior and exterior Victorian millwork moldings and decorative items. To get started, you will need some carpentry skills, a well-equipped woodworking shop, and various Victorian millwork product plans, which are widely available from a number of sources, such as the ones listed below. Millwork items that you can reproduce include porch trim, ceiling moldings, window grills, cornices, fish scale shingles, fretwork, mantels, capitals, and balustrades. Product sales can be both directly to consumers and directly to business. Options for selling direct to home-owners include selling online through specialty building products web sites and marketplaces, exhibiting products at home renovation shows, and advertising in publications catering to heritage home restoration. Potential wholesale customers include building centers, specialty building products retailers, and renovation contractors.

AT A GLANCE

 INVESTMENT: Under $10K

 SKILL LEVEL: 2

 RESOURCES
—Architectural Antiques, buy-and-sell marketplace, ☍ www.architecturals.net

—Used Equipment Network, ☎ (800) 526-6052, ♂ www.buyused.com
—📖 *Victorian Domestic Architectural Plans and Details: 734 Scale Drawings of Doorways, Windows, Stairways, Moldings, Cornices, and Other Elements*, William T. Comstock (Dover Publications, 1987)

Architectural Antique Reproductions and Refurbishment

You can make a fortune buying reclaimed building products such as bricks, lumber, kitchen cabinets, plumbing fixtures, windows, doors, hardware, ceiling tins, fireplace mantels, light fixtures, patio stones, and hardwood flooring cheap, refurbishing, and reselling for a profit. The value of used building products has soared in recent years as the price of new materials has skyrocketed. Especially valuable are architectural antiques such as clear stock casings, stained glass windows, columns and capitals, claw-foot bathtubs, and cut glass doorknobs. Your main buying sources will include contractors specializing in renovation, flooring installers, window replacement companies, demolition companies, plumbers, and homeowners doing their own renovations. Build alliances with these companies so that you can get first dibs on the best and most valuable reclaimed building products as they become available. Equally valuable are other reclaimed building products such as barn board, barn timbers, and split cedar rail fencing. Go for a drive in the country and strike deals with farmers—they demolish old barns and you refurbish and sell the products, splitting the proceeds on a 50–50 basis. The vast majority of refurbishment work needed to bring the old building materials and fixtures back to life will be minor, things like cleaning, removing paint, and making minor repairs. Therefore, only basic skills and equipment will be needed to get started. Sell to homeowners, collectors, interior designers, and architects through online marketplaces, by advertising in specialty building publications, at flea markets, and by building a network of alliances that can refer your business to others.

AT A GLANCE

 INVESTMENT: Under $10K

 SKILL LEVEL: 2

 RESOURCES
—Architectural Antiques, buy-and-sell marketplace, ♂ www.architec turals.net

—National Demolition Association, ☎ (215) 348-4949, ✇ www.demolition association.com

—The Used Building Materials Association, ✇ www.ubma.org

Window Coverings

Fabric draperies, wood or PVC shutters, roll blinds, horizontal or vertical blinds are all choices to consider if you are thinking about making and selling window coverings. Manufacturing each type has advantages and disadvantages. Wood and PVC shutters are the most difficult to make. Draperies require sewing skills. And although making vertical blinds is easy because you can buy and assemble components, at the same time they are the most competitive and least profitable. Ultimately, you will have to decide which type is best for you to design, make, and sell. Custom made-to-order is by far the best approach to marketing for all types because there is lots of competition in the industry, especially in off-the-shelf window coverings at the bottom end of the market. Working on a made-to-order basis will enable you to keep start-up costs to a minimum as well as earn the most profit on each sale. Market your products by creating samples that can be displayed at home improvement shows and shown to prospective clients at a homebased showroom. Working with interior designers and custom homebuilders is also wise.

AT A GLANCE

INVESTMENT: Under $10K

SKILL LEVEL: 2

RESOURCES
—★ Budget Blinds, ☎ (800) 420-5374, ✇ www.budget-blinds.com
—Window Coverings Association of America, ☎ (314) 770-0229, ✇ www.wcaa.org
—📖 *The Encyclopedia of Window Fashions*, Charles T. Randall and Patricia M. Howard (Randall International, 2002)

Closet Organizers

Designing, building, and installing closet organizing systems is a fantastic business opportunity for entrepreneurs with basic carpentry skills and equipment to start. Closet organization products and installation services are in very high demand. Built-in dressers, shelving, garment racks, shoe racks, laundry hampers, and trinket drawers are only a few of the most requested features sought by homeowners. If you have carpentry skills and equipment, you will have no problem starting a closet organizer business from scratch. If not, you might consider purchasing a closet organizer franchise, mainly because all provide the necessary training, equipment, and supplies to get started. Regardless of the route you choose, selling closet organization products and installation services can be done in a number of ways. You can set up a showroom at your manufacturing location and advertise locally to promote your products. You can build displays featuring all the products you make and exhibit at home improvement shows to take orders and requests for estimates. You can also sell direct to interior designers, new homebuilders, and renovation firms, and provide installation services.

AT A GLANCE

INVESTMENT: Under/over $25K

SKILL LEVEL: 2–3

RESOURCES
—☆ Closet Factory, ☎ (310) 715-1000, ♂ www.closetfactory.com
—National Closet Group, ☎ (866) 624-5463, ♂ www.closets.com
— *Closets Magazine*, ☎ (847) 634-4347, ♂ www.closetsmagazine.com

Cabinetmaking

Turn your passion for cabinetmaking into a profitable venture by designing, producing, and selling quality kitchen cabinets, bookcases, and gun cases. Particularly profitable is building and selling high-end custom kitchen cabinets constructed from cherry, oak, maple hardwoods, and select clear softwoods. Cabinetmaking is not for the novice woodworker. It takes a great deal of practice to master the craft, but those that do are rewarded with annual incomes that can reach well into six figures. Build and sell a standard line of cabinet products, although it's best to concentrate on the made-to-order custom cabinet market. Design and build highly elaborate samples and showcase them at home improvement shows to generate interest and orders. Likewise, develop a cabinet showroom at your manufacturing location and invite architects, designers, and custom homebuilders to view your workmanship and products, because these could provide the alliances that can easily become your primary sources of new business and referrals.

AT A GLANCE

INVESTMENT: Over $25K

SKILL LEVEL: 3

RESOURCES
—Cabinetmakers Association, ♂ www.cabinetmakers.org
—Used Equipment Network, ☎ (800) 526-6052, ♂ www.buyused.com
—📖 *Cabinetmaking Procedures for the Small Shop*, Kevin Fristad, John Ward, and Gina Roman (Independent Publishers Group, 2001)

Roof Trusses

Prebuilt engineered roof trusses are used in most new home construction today. Building and selling roof trusses is one of the more costly and highly specialized manufacturing opportunities listed in this chapter, but at the same time, making and selling roof trusses has the potential to be very financially lucrative. The main issues to consider when starting a truss manufacturing business are business location, equipment, workforce, transportation, blueprint comprehension, and building and truss load codes. Each state and province has codes of acceptable truss design and construction materials. Consequently, you will need to familiarize yourself with these codes as part of the due diligence process. The primary target audience is new homebuilders, architects, and renovation contractors. In most instances, roof trusses are manufactured once an order has been placed.

AT A GLANCE

INVESTMENT: Over $25K

SKILL LEVEL: 2

RESOURCES
—Entrepreneur, small business portal, ♂ www.entrepreneur.com
—The Wood Truss Council of America, ♂ www.woodtruss.com
—📖 *Design of Building Trusses*, James Ambrose (Wiley, 1994)

Countertops

Become known as the King (or Queen) of countertops by starting a business manufacturing, selling, and installing custom kitchen and bathroom vanity countertops so you can cash in on the multimillion dollar kitchen and bathroom renovating boom. Build the business by working closely with interior designers, architects, cabinetmakers, and kitchen and bath renovation contractors. All can utilize your products or refer their clients to your business. Also sell direct to homeowners by exhibiting samples of your custom countertops at home and décor shows and by establishing a countertop showroom at your manufacturing location. Manufacturing countertops is not for everyone. You will need carpentry and cabinetmaking experience to truly flourish in the business, as well as the required tools and workshop space. But with that said, custom countertops sell for as much as $100 per square foot. Needless to say, the profit potential is excellent for people with the necessary skills. There is a wide variety of materials used in custom countertop construction. Laminates, marble, granite, concrete, wood, ceramic tiles, metal, or a combination of these materials are all popular. So you will probably need to specialize in one or two of these in order to master the trade and become known as a specialist.

AT A GLANCE

INVESTMENT: Under $10K

SKILL LEVEL: 2

RESOURCES
—Entrepreneur, small business portal, ♂ www.entrepreneur.com
—Used Equipment Network, ☎ (800) 526-6052, ♂ www.buyused.com

Custom Washroom Vanities

Custom washroom vanities are hot sellers. Providing you have carpentry experience and the needed equipment and workshop space, you can earn big bucks building and selling them to homeowners, building contractors, designers, and architects. The choice is yours. Design and build traditional style washroom vanities using exotic hardwoods and exquisite hardware, or go one step farther and build vanities using antique dressers or sideboards, which are in huge demand right now and being snapped up for thousands of dollars by people restoring heritage homes. Regardless of the design and construction materials, the key to success is to produce a high-quality product and to go after the high-end market. You can sell direct to homeowners through advertisements, a showroom, or home improvement and décor shows. You can also go after the commercial market by presenting your products to luxury homebuilders, interior designers, and architects.

AT A GLANCE

INVESTMENT: Under $10K

SKILL LEVEL: 2

RESOURCES
—Kit Guy, washroom vanity plans, ♂ www.kitguy.com
—U-Bild, washroom vanity plans, ♂ www.u-bild.com

Glass Etching

There are several techniques that can be used to etch decorative glass—acid wash, engraving, laser etching, and sandblasting. At present, sandblasting remains the most popular choice. This is accomplished by covering the glass with a stencil pattern and blowing sand against the surface; the area not protected by the pattern becomes etched. Glass etching is a great moneymaking opportunity because glass etching is easy to learn, equipment and supplies are inexpensive, you can work from a garage workshop, and demand is high. Products that can be etched with elegant designs, patterns, and images for resale include window and cabinet glass, glass awards, tables, signs on doors and windows, automotive, mirrors, glassware, and sun catchers. Glass can also be etched with codes and identification marks for security purposes. You can buy ready-made etching stencil designs and letter stencils or make your own. In addition to selling etched glass products online and at home décor shows, you can also do custom one-of-a-kind glass etching work for interior designers, kitchen cabinet installers, and automotive dealers.

AT A GLANCE

INVESTMENT: Under $2K

SKILL LEVEL: 1–3

 RESOURCES
—The Crafters Mall, craft products marketplace, ♂ www.procrafter.com
—Martronics Corporation, glass etching tools and supplies, ☎ (800) 775-0797, ♂ www.glass-etching-kits.com
—SCM Systems, glass etching tools and supplies, ☎ (800) 755-0261, ♂ www.scmsystemsinc.com
— 📖 *Easy Glass Etching*, Marlis Cornett (Sterling, 2004)

Kitchen Islands

Thanks to the recent explosion in kitchen renovation and replacement, custom kitchen islands have become a highly sought after product. Designing and manufacturing kitchen islands is much easier than manufacturing a full line of kitchen cabinetry. Not as much workshop space or as many specialized tools are required. Kitchen islands can be manufactured from a kit, making them very easy to sell and ship around the globe direct to consumers or retailers. Considerably less skill is required to design and build custom islands as opposed to a complete custom kitchen. And, the market is arguably larger because custom kitchen islands can be purchased and used by homeowners that do not want to replace their entire kitchen. Think creatively when designing islands, and incorporate handy features such as easy-clean surfaces, drawers, pot and pan storage, slide-out chopping boards, built-in trash bins, and wheeled models that can be easily folded and/or stored when not in use. Also think about incorporating unique and visually appealing materials in the construction process—exotic hardwoods, metal, glass, ceramics, and laminates. Sell direct to consumers by displaying at home improvement shows, online in internet malls, and from a homebased or factory-direct showroom. The product is also perfect for mass sales to independent and chain retailers of home improvement products and furnishings.

AT A GLANCE

 INVESTMENT: Under $2K

 SKILL LEVEL: 1–2

RESOURCES
—Handyman Plans, ♂ www.handymanplans.com
—U-Bild, kitchen island plans, ♂ www.u-build.com
—Woodworkers Workshop, kitchen island plans, ♂ www.woodworker
  sworkshop.com

Appliance Refurbishment

Refurbishing and selling secondhand and antique appliances is a great money-making opportunity for mechanically-inclined entrepreneurs. Stoves, fridges, dishwashers, washers, dryers, and freezers are all appliances that can be purchased very cheaply, or even taken away for free, repaired and cleaned up so they are in good working order, and sold for big profits. Refurbishing antique stoves from the '40s and '50s with modern gas fittings is especially profitable, as these are now fetching prices in the $2,000 to $3,000 range. You will need home appliance repair training, but certification courses can be completed in less than a year, and you can contact the associations listed below to find classes available in your area. Sources for acquiring appliances in need of refurbishment include posting classified ads in your local paper offering to "take away appliances, working or not," and by attending auction sales. Common appliances with no antique value can be sold in the same fashion once refurbished—by posting classified ads as well as fliers on bulletin boards. For ease of salability, be sure to provide a 90-day unconditional warranty on all appliances sold. Refurbished antique appliances can be advertised online and in specialty publications catering to home restoration.

AT A GLANCE

 INVESTMENT: Under $10K

 SKILL LEVEL: 2–3

 RESOURCES
—Canadian Electronic & Appliance Service Association, ☎ (905) 629-
  7907, ♂ www.ceasa.org
—★ Mr. Appliance, ♂ www.mrappliance.com
—National Appliance Repair Association, ☎ (765) 453-1820, ♂ www.
  nasa1.org

Refurbishing Washroom Fixtures

Big bucks can be earned by refurbishing washroom fixtures, especially antique claw foot bathtubs and pedestal sinks, which routinely command as much as $2,000 each! Amazing, when you consider that they can be purchased in less than perfect condition for as little as $50 each, and sometimes absolutely free. Given the incredible profit potential you probably have there are three burning questions right now: What do you need to start? Where do you get bathroom fixtures to refurbish? And, how do you sell the refurbished fixtures? First, you will need to purchase reglazing equipment and learn how to use it. Companies like Midwest Chemicals sell reglazing equipment and supplies, and they also provide reglazing training. Second, antique claw foot tubs and pedestal sinks can be bought cheaply from a number of sources, including plumbers, used building material dealers, demolition contractors, and homeowners renovating bathrooms. Third, once refurbished, you can sell the fixtures through specialty publications, by exhibiting at home décor shows, placing ads in your local newspaper, and building alliances with interior designers, architects, and companies specializing in the restoration of heritage homes.

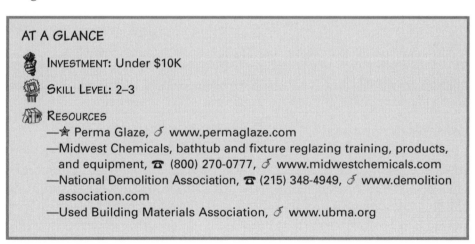

AT A GLANCE

INVESTMENT: Under $10K

SKILL LEVEL: 2–3

RESOURCES
—✫ Perma Glaze, ♂ www.permaglaze.com
—Midwest Chemicals, bathtub and fixture reglazing training, products, and equipment, ☎ (800) 270-0777, ♂ www.midwestchemicals.com
—National Demolition Association, ☎ (215) 348-4949, ♂ www.demolition association.com
—Used Building Materials Association, ♂ www.ubma.org

Carpentry Shop

A terrific opportunity exists for carpenters of every skill level to earn a substantial full- or part-time income by setting up a fully equipped carpentry shop at home, if space and zoning permits, or from a rented workshop space. Offer customers various woodworking and carpentry services, including lumber milling, planning, joining, sawing, and gluing, as well as custom work such as shaping, cabinetmaking, and sash construction. Commercial grade carpentry equipment will be required. Most items can be purchased in good condition secondhand and for about half the cost of new through auction sales, newspaper classified ads, and shop closeouts. The best aspect about this manufacturing business is the fact that you do not need to invest in raw material to produce a product as materials are either supplied by customers up front or paid for by customers before you make the product. In addition to homeowners in need of custom milling and woodworking, other potential customers will include building contractors and antique dealers. The sale of exotic woods, patterns and plans, carpentry related tools, and carpentry supplies to hobbyist woodworkers and craftspeople can also help boost sales and profits.

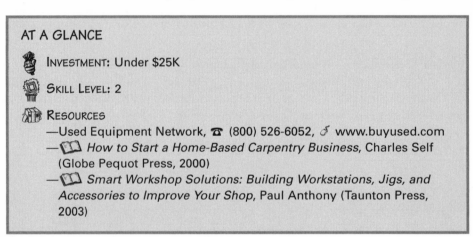

AT A GLANCE

INVESTMENT: Under $25K

SKILL LEVEL: 2

RESOURCES
—Used Equipment Network, ☎ (800) 526-6052, 🖰 www.buyused.com
—📖 *How to Start a Home-Based Carpentry Business*, Charles Self (Globe Pequot Press, 2000)
—📖 *Smart Workshop Solutions: Building Workstations, Jigs, and Accessories to Improve Your Shop*, Paul Anthony (Taunton Press, 2003)

Custom Workbenches

Every home workshop needs a workbench to keep tools, bits and pieces, and projects organized, as well as to maximize floor space. A terrific and potentially very profitable opportunity awaits entrepreneurs who choose to design and build custom workbenches constructed mainly of wood. Make your designs unique, and incorporate handy features such as built-in clamps, cutting extensions, tool drawers, dust collection systems, power outlets, work lighting, and casters for easy portability around the workshop. The primary target audience is hobby woodworkers and weekend handypeople. Custom, made-to-order workbenches for businesses are also a market. Locally, custom workbenches can be promoted via classified advertising, by posting fliers on bulletin boards, and by exhibiting at home improvement and woodworking shows. If you think big, there is no reason why custom workbenches cannot be sold to building centers wholesale and sold online in a ready-to-assemble kit format.

AT A GLANCE

 INVESTMENT: Under $10K

 SKILL LEVEL: 2

 RESOURCES
—Entrepreneur, small business portal, ✂ www.entrepreneur.com
—Free Woodworking Plans, workbench plans, ✂ www.freeww.com/
workbenches.html
—How to Build a Workbench, workbench plans, ✂ www.how-to-build-
a-workbench.com

Metal Flashing

A wide variety of metal flashings are used every day in the building and renovation industry, and making and selling flashings is very easy, especially for people who have basic metalworking skills and experience. The best types of metal flashings to make and sell are window, door, roof, chimney, wall, siding, and 6-, 8-, and 10-inch standard fascia and bargeboard cap flashings. Metal flashings are made with rolled or flat aluminum or tin stock in the desired color, cut to length using hand or power sheers, and bent to the desired profile using a metal brake. Flashings can be made in standard sizes and profiles and sold to renovation contractors, roofing companies, window and door installers, siding installers, and chimney masons. These same companies often also need custom made-to-order flashings, which can become an additional revenue source. You can also sell to building supply retailers on a wholesale basis.

AT A GLANCE

 INVESTMENT: Under $10K

 SKILL LEVEL: 2

 RESOURCES
—American Douglas Metals, ✂ www.americandouglasmetals.com
—Metal Suppliers Online Directory, ✂ www.metalsuppliersonline.com
—Wholesale Tools, ✂ www.wttool.com

Stairs

Providing you have the required skills and equipment, huge profits can be earned designing, building, and selling stairs. The most popular stair construction materials include hardwoods such as oak or maple, softwoods such as pine and poplar, or more durable materials such as stone, concrete, and steel. A combination of these materials can also be used. The first order of business is to determine a specialty, such as residential stair design and construction, commercial stairs, safety stairs such as fire escapes, or specialty stairs such as spiral stairs or pull-down attic stair kits shipped ready to assemble. The primary target audience for custom stair design and construction includes homebuilders, contractors, renovation companies, designers, and architects. In addition to making and selling stair treads, risers, and stingers, related products such as spindles, handrails, and pickets can also be manufactured and sold to building centers wholesale. The profit potential for a stair design and manufacturing business is excellent; it is common for custom staircases for luxury homes to sell for $20,000 or more.

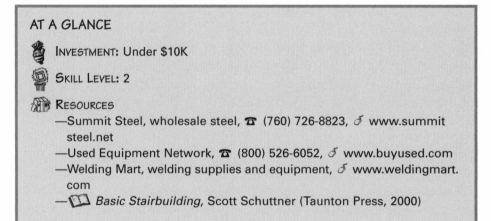

AT A GLANCE

INVESTMENT: Under $10K

SKILL LEVEL: 2

RESOURCES
—Summit Steel, wholesale steel, ☎ (760) 726-8823, ♂ www.summit steel.net
—Used Equipment Network, ☎ (800) 526-6052, ♂ www.buyused.com
—Welding Mart, welding supplies and equipment, ♂ www.weldingmart. com
—📖 *Basic Stairbuilding*, Scott Schuttner (Taunton Press, 2000)

Roll Form Metal Roofing

Manufacturing and selling metal roofing panels is a very unique business opportunity with excellent growth and profit potential. Best of all, no previous metal roofing experience is needed to start the business because manufacturers and distributors of metal roofing panel machines provide operator training when machines are purchased. Metal roof panel machines are equipped with mounting brackets enabling large coils of metal (aluminum, zinc, steel, and copper) to be automatically fed into one end of the machine and come out the opposite end in the desired profile and length. They also automatically cut fastener slots. Machines are available in both stationary and portable models allowing for flexibility in terms of manufacturing location—at your shop or the customer's job site. There are two primary target audiences for metal roofing panels—roofing contractors and building supply retailers.

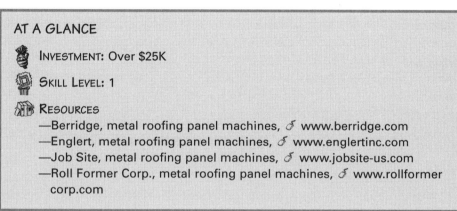

AT A GLANCE

INVESTMENT: Over $25K

SKILL LEVEL: 1

RESOURCES
—Berridge, metal roofing panel machines, ♂ www.berridge.com
—Englert, metal roofing panel machines, ♂ www.englertinc.com
—Job Site, metal roofing panel machines, ♂ www.jobsite-us.com
—Roll Former Corp., metal roofing panel machines, ♂ www.rollformer corp.com

Storm Boards

The changing global climate has noticeably increased the ferocity and frequency of hurricanes, tornadoes, tropical storms, blizzards, and gales, resulting in millions of dollars in property damage every time these weather phenomena occur. You cannot prevent these storms, but you can help home and business owners be prepared when the weather turns foul by making and selling storm boards. Building storm boards is easy because all that's required is to measure your customers' windows, cut plywood panels to fit, label each panel for the corresponding window, and install quick-assembly hardware on the exterior window trim. And presto, the next time the weather turns ugly, your customers can have their windows professionally boarded-up in a matter of moments, potentially saving them thousands in damage. No more long waits at the lumber yard for them with hundreds, possibly thousands, of anxious people trying to buy plywood and fasteners to board up their windows before the storm hits. Market the business by advertising locally, distributing promotional fliers, talking to business owners in person to pitch the benefits of your product, and exhibiting at home shows.

AT A GLANCE

INVESTMENT: Under $2K

SKILL LEVEL: 1

RESOURCES
—Entrepreneur, small business portal, ♂ www.entrepreneur.com
—Mammoth Tools, ☎ (516) 942-0905, ♂ www.mammothtools.com

Handbags

If you have a flair for design and want to break into the fashion handbag industry, then what's stopping you? Go for it. Pick a specialty. Design, produce, and sell everything from high fashion, glamorous totes to adorable tropical beach bags, to vintage reproduction handbags by top designers like Fendi, Gucci, and Prada. The fashion handbag and tote market is red hot, but at the same time very competitive. Give careful thought to how you are going to make a big promotional splash—namely a launch that attracts the attention of the media and garners lots of free and valuable publicity. Along those lines, think creatively—celebrity endorsements, unique construction materials, dazzling original designs, or new uses like the now infamous designer bags for dogs made famous in the movie *Legally Blonde*. Selling options are numerous—home purse parties hosted by sales reps, online sales via internet fashion malls and eBay, wholesale to fashion retailers, and direct to consumers via fashion shows and a homebased showroom.

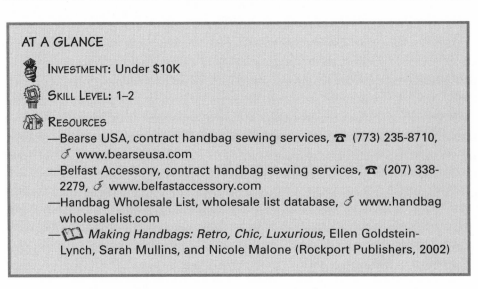

AT A GLANCE

INVESTMENT: Under $10K

SKILL LEVEL: 1–2

RESOURCES
—Bearse USA, contract handbag sewing services, ☎ (773) 235-8710, ♂ www.bearseusa.com
—Belfast Accessory, contract handbag sewing services, ☎ (207) 338-2279, ♂ www.belfastaccessory.com
—Handbag Wholesale List, wholesale list database, ♂ www.handbagwholesalelist.com
—📖 *Making Handbags: Retro, Chic, Luxurious*, Ellen Goldstein-Lynch, Sarah Mullins, and Nicole Malone (Rockport Publishers, 2002)

Designer Fashions

The vast majority of internationally known fashion designers were once just like you are now, dreaming of starting their own fashion houses and sharing their designs with fashion enthusiasts around the world. If they can make it big, so can you! What does it take to break into the world of high-fashion clothing? Great designs, a determination to succeed, and a persistence to ensure you do succeed. To get started, there are basically three routes you can choose. One, design and manufacture fashion clothing to sell to department stores or chain fashion retailers. Two, design and manufacture fashion clothing to sell to small independent fashion boutiques. Or three, design and manufacture fashion clothing for private clients. Each route has advantages and disadvantages, but all three share a common thread: great fashions start with great designs. Initially, concentrate on creating sketches of the clothing you want to make. Pick a few of your best designs and make sample garments that can be shown to fashion buyers. If you do not sew at the level needed for fashion clothing, contract with a local seamstress to sew the garments. Once you have secured orders, you can interview and contract with a suitable clothing manufacturer able to sew garments in larger quantities.

AT A GLANCE

 Investment: Under $10K

 Skill Level: 2–3

 Resources
—Bright Notions, sewing equipment and supplies, ✂ www.brightno
    tions.com
—Fashion Schools Online, fashion schools and programs directory,
    ✂ www.fashionschools.com
—National Association of Fashion and Accessory Designers, ✂ www.
    nafad.com
—📖 *High Fashion Sewing Secrets from the World's Best Designers:
    A Step-By-Step Guide to Sewing Stylish Seams, Buttonholes, Pockets,
    Collars, Hems, and More*, Claire B. Shaeffer (Rodale Books, 2004)

Belts

Belts are more than a tool to keep your britches up, they are also a statement for many fashion-conscious consumers. Fashion belts can be made of many materials or combinations of materials—leather, wood, plastic beads, glass beads, ceramics, fabric, and metal. Equipment requirements will depend on the types of belts you make, but regardless of construction materials, equipment needs are minimal. Belts are easily designed and made with a bit of practice. If you opt not to manufacture your own belt buckles or clasps, take comfort in the knowledge that there are many wholesale sources for these, including the ones listed below. Belts are just as easy to sell as they are to make, and great sales venues include fashion shows, craft shows, and online fashion internet malls, eBay, wholesale sales to independent and chain fashion and accessories retailers, and consignment placements with fashion retailers.

AT A GLANCE

INVESTMENT: Under $2K

SKILL LEVEL: 1

RESOURCES
—Belt Buckle Shop Wholesale, ☎ (800) 962-5003, ✆ www.beltbuckle
shop.com
—Fun Buckles Manufacturing, ☎ (514) 421-6238, ✆ www.funbuckles.com

Silk-Screened T-Shirts

Silk-screening and selling T-shirts and other garments right from the comforts of home can earn you big bucks. How much profit? Lots, especially when you consider that you can buy T-shirts in bulk for as little as $2 each wholesale, spend another 50 cents in the silk-screening process, and retail each shirt for up to $20. That's a whopping $17.50 gross profit on every sale! Retail sales of silk-screened clothing and products is only one avenue. You can also silk-screen clothing and sell it to retailers wholesale or directly to corporations, clubs, and sports teams. Other products and garments that can be silk-screened include mouse pads, sweaters, sports bags, hats, and aprons. In total, you will have to invest about $15,000 into equipment and supplies to get started, unless you buy used silk-screening equipment, which can cut your start-up costs by about $5,000. Retail direct to consumers at flea markets, sports and recreation shows, concerts, community events, eBay and other online marketplaces, kiosks at malls, and at the beach.

AT A GLANCE

 INVESTMENT: Under $25K

 SKILL LEVEL: 1–2

 RESOURCES

—Atlas Screen Supply, silk screening equipment and supplies, ☎ (800) 621-4173, ♂ www.atlasscreensupply.com
—Silkscreen Biz, equipment and supplies, ☎ (877) 260-7422, ♂ www.silkscreen.biz
—United States Screen Printing Institute, information and resources, ♂ www.usscreen.com
—📖 *How to Print T-Shirts for Fun and Profit*, Scott O. Fresener (St. John Books, 2000)

Children's Clothing

Adult-sized profits can be earned by making and selling pint-sized designer clothing for kids. So what do you need to get started in the multi-billion dollar children's clothing industry? You need sewing equipment and supplies, fabric, sewing patterns, a suitable workspace, creative designs, and a solid marketing plan. Children's clothing is a very competitive industry, so it is wise to develop a specialty in terms of the types of clothing you design and make, as well as how the clothing is sold. A few selling ideas include organizing and hosting a monthly fashion show and enlisting neighborhood kids as models. Or, hire contract sales representatives to organize and host children's designer fashion sales parties in their own homes and split the profits with them on all sales. Additional sales avenues include establishing a homebased boutique or retail storefront and selling online or through mail-order catalogs. Finally, wholesale or consignment sales through children's clothing and products retailers are not out of the question either, providing your pricing and production capabilities allow you to pursue these opportunities.

AT A GLANCE

 INVESTMENT: Under $10K

SKILL LEVEL: 2

 RESOURCES
—Bright Notions, sewing equipment and supplies, ✄ www.brightno
tions.com
—Children's Apparel Manufacturers' Association, ✄ www.cama-apparel.org
—Sewing Patterns, ✄ www.sewingpatterns.com

Maternity Clothing

When you stop to consider more than four million babies are born each year in the United States and Canada, you quickly realize a great opportunity exists to make and sell maternity fashions to moms-to-be. The major prerequisite to get this venture up and rolling is the ability to design and produce maternity fashions and the funds to purchase the required equipment and materials. One of the better ways to sell maternity fashions is to hire contract sales representatives to organize and host maternity fashion sales parties in their own homes. Ideal candidates, of course, are moms-to-be. Remuneration to the party hosts can be by way of commission, revenue split, free product, or any combination. Establishing a homebased boutique is also a great way to sell. Advertise locally and build alliances with midwives and day-care centers, which can refer their clients to your business. Also, don't overlook the possibility of selling to a global audience by creating your own e-commerce web site as well as selling on eBay and other online marketplaces.

AT A GLANCE

 INVESTMENT: Under $10K

 SKILL LEVEL: 2

 RESOURCES
—Bright Notions, sewing equipment and supplies, ✄ www.bright
notions.com
—Patterns That Fit You, ☎ (800) 883-2348, ✄ www.patternsthatfityou.com
—Sewing Patterns, ✄ www.sewingpatterns.com

Embroidery

Multihead embroidery machines are available that will embroider six items or more at a time, greatly increasing productivity and profitability. Modern embroidery equipment is also computer assisted. Designs can be created using a computer and software and then automatically transferred to the embroidery machine to complete the stitching of the design onto the chosen garment. Making and selling embroidered items is an easy business to operate from home with the aid of a small showroom to display samples. Popular products for embroidery include hats, T-shirts, sweaters, fleece garments, leather jackets, sports bags, and towels and linens, all of which can be purchased wholesale in bulk. Market custom embroidery work by creating a product catalog or brochure and distribute it to potential customers, such as sports associations, schools, corporations, government agencies, organizations, and charities, basically any business or organization that routinely purchases embroidered garments for employees and customers. Or, create standard designs and embroider garments that can be sold directly to consumers from your homebased showroom by renting kiosk space at malls, and through online garment marketplaces and internet malls.

AT A GLANCE

INVESTMENT: Under $25K

SKILL LEVEL: 2–3

RESOURCES
—☆ Embroid Me, ☎ (800) 727-6720, ♂ www.embroidme.com
—Embroidery Trade Association, ☎ (888) 628-2545, ♂ www.embroidery
    trade.org
—📖 *Embroidery Monogram Business Magazine Online*, ♂ www.emb
    mag.com

Wedding Gowns

When you stop to consider that more than two million people tie the knot every year in the United States, it quickly becomes apparent there is great potential to earn substantial profits by designing, producing, and selling wedding gowns. Wedding gowns embellished with beadwork and lace are not easy to design or sew. It takes great skill, but at the same time, with practice the art can be mastered.

In addition to sewing skills and equipment you will also need an outgoing personality, the type of person who is not afraid to call and set appointments with wedding professionals such as wedding planners, because these are the people that have the ability to send lots of business your way. A homebased bridal gown boutique stocked with your designs will also be needed, especially if you plan to work on a smaller scale and only sell locally. Additional ways to sell wedding gowns include online wedding-related marketplaces, bridal shows, and consignment and wholesale sales to established bridal boutique retailers.

 AT A GLANCE

 INVESTMENT: Under $10K

 SKILL LEVEL: 2–3

RESOURCES
—All Wedding Companies, wedding products and services marketplace, ♂ www.allweddingcompanies.com
—Fashion Schools Online, fashion schools and programs directory, ♂ www.fashionschools.com
—National Association of Wedding Professionals, ♂ www.nawp.com
—Wedding Gown Search, wedding gown designers directory, ♂ www.weddinggownsearch.com
—📖 *Bridal Couture: Fine Sewing Techniques for Wedding Gowns and Evening Wear*, Susan Khalje (Chilton Books, 1997)

Bridal Veils

To make her wedding day special, every bride needs the perfect wedding gown, shoes, makeup, hair, and bouquet. But wait, something is missing: the perfect bridal veil, of course. A bridal veil is like a cake topper; it completes the picture. You can cash in on the multibillion-dollar wedding garment industry by starting your own custom bridal veil design and production business. Working from home, you can produce and sell all of the most popular veil styles in the most popular fabric selections, including lace, satin cord, embroidered, motif, and rhinestone and sequin embellished veils. But offer to make clients veils in any design and fabric selection they wish. There are primarily two ways to sell bridal veils, wholesale and retail. Selling wholesale to bridal boutiques will require a bit of legwork to get out and present samples of your designs to shop owners to secure orders or to attend business-to-business wedding products trade shows. Selling retail, or direct to consumers, means you need to take the time necessary to get well-connected in the wedding industry with wedding planners, gown designers, wedding photographers, and more, as all can become a source of referral business. Additional direct-to-consumer selling options include online sales via wedding products marketplaces, selling at wedding shows, and selling from a homebased showroom supported by print, electronic, and word-of-mouth advertising.

> ### AT A GLANCE
>
> INVESTMENT: Under $2K
>
> SKILL LEVEL: 1
>
> RESOURCES
> —All Wedding Companies, wedding products and services marketplace, ♂ www.allweddingcompanies.com
> —National Association of Wedding Professionals, ♂ www.nawp.com
> — *"I Do"—So Can You! A Step-by-Step Guide to Making Bridal Headpieces, Hats, and Veils with Professional Results*, Claudia Lynch (Harpagon Productions, 1996)

Costumes

Making and selling costumes is an opportunity to combine fun with earning profits. Although most costumes are sold leading up to Halloween, costumes can be sold year round; it just takes a bit of innovative marketing. You can specialize in one particular type of costume or period or choose to offer a wide range of costume designs as well as accept made-to-order custom costume orders for television productions, stage productions, corporate mascots, event costumes, theme park costumes, and restaurant serving staff costumes. In addition to sewing equipment and skills, you need costume patterns or the ability to create your own designs. The most popular costumes continue to be ones replicating police uniforms, soldier uniforms, super hero costumes, witches, clowns, ghosts, historical, space creatures, western icons, and dance costumes. Sell from home, online via eBay, and direct to costume rental businesses. You can also rent costumes to earn additional income.

AT A GLANCE

 INVESTMENT: Under $2K

 SKILL LEVEL: 2

 RESOURCES
—Denver Fabrics, costume patterns and fabrics, ♂ www.denver fabrics.com
—Entrepreneur, small business portal, ♂ www.entrepreneur.com
—Sewing Patterns, costume patterns, ♂ www.sewingpatterns.com

Tie-Dyed Clothing

As the name suggests, creating tie-dyed clothing is the process of tying clothing using elastics or folds and rinsing the garment in one or more clothing dye solutions to create permanent colorful patterns on the clothing. There are three basic tieing techniques used to create the designs: spirals, accordion folds, and sunburst. All are easily learned with practice, which means everyone is qualified to make and sell tie-dyed clothing. The most popular garments to tie-dye and sell are T-shirts, sun hats, cotton pants, and shorts, although just about any type of garment, especially those made of cotton fabrics, can be tie-dyed. Outside of clothing blanks, dyes, and laundry tubs for dye washing and rinsing, there are few other requirements to get started. Tie-dyed clothing can be sold in various ways including online, at flea markets, at concerts and community events, and from a retail storefront located in a mall or beach arcade.

AT A GLANCE

 INVESTMENT: Under $2K

 SKILL LEVEL: 1

 RESOURCES
—G.S. Dye, clothing dye supplies and garment blanks, ☎ (800) 596-0550, ♂ www.gsdye.com
—Jacquard Products, clothing dye supplies, ☎ (800) 442-0455, ♂ www.jacquardproducts.com
—Standard Dyes, clothing dye supplies, ☎ (800) 859-1240, ♂ www.standarddyes.com

Lingerie

Sexy and profitable are the best two words to describe starting a business designing, producing, and selling lingerie. Using fabrics such as Lycra®, silk, and cotton, you can produce a full line of lingerie from your own designs or from standard patterns. Right now, vintage lingerie fashions from the '30s, '40s, and '50s, are red-hot sellers, as is plus-size lingerie. Opportunities to sell lingerie are nearly limitless. Wholesale sales to fashion and lingerie retailers is one approach, so is selling lingerie online, mail order via magazine ads, at fashion shows, and from a home-based lingerie boutique. Another sales method is to hire contract sales consultants to organize and host lingerie sales parties in their homes and pay them a commission on their total sales. Choosing this route provides an excellent avenue to expand the business nationally, and even internationally, very quickly and at minimal cost.

AT A GLANCE

INVESTMENT: Under $10K

SKILL LEVEL: 2

RESOURCES
—Sew Sassy Fabrics, lingerie fabrics and patterns, ♂ www.sew
  sassy.com
—Sewing Lingerie, lingerie sewing patterns, supplies and how-to
  instructional books and videos, ♂ www.sewinglingerie.com
—The Blue Gardenia, vintage lingerie sewing patterns, ♂ www.the
  bluegardenia.com

Fine Art

If you have the artistic ability to create fine works of art, then why not share this gift with the world and make a great living at the same time? Regardless of the medium—oil and watercolor paintings, ink drawings, sculptures in stone, wood, or iron—creating and selling fine art can be a very profitable and personally rewarding lifestyle. The hard work is producing the art; the easy work is selling it. People love art. In the virtual art world, you can develop your own web site for sales, sell through eBay, or sell through any number of virtual art galleries online. In the bricks and mortar world, you can sell your art through established art galleries, through art auction sales, from a homebased art studio, and by exhibiting your work at art shows, home décor shows, and renting mall kiosk space, especially in the weeks leading up to Christmas. Also contact interior designers to give them first viewing and the first opportunity to purchase your art for their clients on a semi-exclusive basis. It's probably best to combine all of these selling methods, along with accepting commissioned assignments, to ensure maximum exposure and maximum profitability.

AT A GLANCE

INVESTMENT: Under $2K

SKILL LEVEL: 3

RESOURCES
—Art Schools, online directory of art schools, ♂ www.artschools.com
—The World Artist Directory, ♂ www.worldartistdirectory.com
—Opus Framing and Art Supplies, ♂ www.opusframing.com

Folk Art

By definition, folk art is a product of an artistic nature created by people who have little or no formal art education. Folk artists may work within established traditions or have their own distinct art forms. Typically, they demonstrate great creativity in overcoming technical limitations. What this means is just about any handcrafted, one-of-a-kind product imaginable can be classified as folk art, including furniture, paintings, carvings, jewelry, textiles, sculpture, pottery, toys, dolls, and clothing. The beauty lies within the eye of the beholder. This is what makes producing and selling folk art such a wonderful opportunity for creative people. There are just as many ways to sell folk art as there are folk art products—selling online via folk art marketplaces and eBay, selling from a homebased folk art studio, displaying folk art at craft shows and home décor shows, and renting mall kiosk space, especially near Christmas.

AT A GLANCE

INVESTMENT: Under $2K

SKILL LEVEL: 1

 RESOURCES
—Folk Art, folk art marketplace, www.folk-art.com
—Folk Art Central, folk art marketplace, www.folkartcentral.com
—Folk Art Society of America, ☎ (800) 527-3655, www.folkart.org
—John C. Campbell Folk School, folk art classes, ☎ (800) 365-5724,
    www.folkschool.com

Woodturning Products

Finely crafted ornamental woodturning products, such as bowls, plates, and lamp bases, can fetch as much as $500 each, which is incredible when you figure there is little cost associated with making them, other than time. Granted, the woodturning craft is not something that can be mastered overnight, but this is a great opportunity to start as a hobby and turn into a profitable venture as your skills grow. In addition to the time investment, you will also need to make a financial investment to purchase the tools of the woodturners' trade, including a lathe, shaping tools, wood blanks, and sanding blocks. The bestselling venues include arts and craft shows, home décor shows, directly-from-home sales supported by local advertising and word-of-mouth referrals, and online marketplaces such as eBay. You might also consider consigning with local home décor and gift retailers, or even selling to retailers wholesale.

AT A GLANCE

 INVESTMENT: Under $10K

 SKILL LEVEL: 2–3

 RESOURCES
—Amazon Exotic Hardwoods, woodturning blanks, ☎ (866) 339-9596,
    www.amazonexotichardwoods.com
—Craft Supplies USA, woodturning tools and supplies, ☎ (800) 551-
   8876, www.woodturnerscatalog.com
—John C. Campbell Folk School, woodturning classes, ☎ (800) 365-
   5724, www.folkschool.com
—American Association of Woodturners, www.woodturners.org
—U-Bild, woodturning plans, www.u-bild.com

Woodworking Project Plans

Share your creative woodworking projects with the world by putting pen to paper and making detailed construction plans. Include helpful resources in your plans such as detailed material lists, tool and equipment requirements, approximate costs to build, and supplier contact information for the materials needed to build the project. Sell your woodworking project plans to the millions of hobby woodworkers around the globe. How, you might be wondering? There are a few approaches you can take in terms of distribution. First, sell your plans to an established publisher that specializes in producing and selling woodworking plans. Second, become your own publisher and produce and sell the plans. Third, digitize the plans and sell electronically via the internet. Of course, you might decide to persue all routes. In addition to online sales, you can also exhibit at woodworking shows and arts and crafts shows to sell the plans, and advertise in specialty woodworking magazines for mail-order sales. Depending on the complexity of the project, woodworking plans typically sell in the range of $10 to $50 per set, which makes this a potentially very profitable business opportunity, especially if you have an interesting and appealing woodworking project to share with the world.

AT A GLANCE

INVESTMENT: Under $2K

SKILL LEVEL: 2

RESOURCES
—Entrepreneur, small business portal, ☌ www.entrepreneur.com
—Garlinghouse Publishing, ☎ (800) 235-5700, ☌ www.garling house.com
—Summerset House Publishing, ☎ (800) 444-2540, ☌ www.summer sethouse.com

Candles

Become known as the candle guru by making and selling aromatherapy, scented jar, floating, wedding, novelty, 100-percent beeswax, citronella, and decorative bowl and crock candles. Of course, you can specialize in one kind, but why, when candles are so easy to make and sell? Sell your candle creations on eBay and create your own candle web site. Display and sell at home and gift shows, and advertise in magazines for mail-order sales. You can even sell at flea markets, in-home parties, and from mall kiosks at holiday times. To increase sales and profits, buy candle accessories such as holders and stands, snuffers, coil incense, and lamp oils wholesale, and resell these products along with your wide selection of candles at retail prices. Also, don't overlook the possibility of mass-producing candles so that you can establish wholesale accounts with gift and home décor retailers right across the county. The candle making learning curve is short, which makes this an excellent opportunity for everyone.

AT A GLANCE

 INVESTMENT: Under $2K

 SKILL LEVEL: 1

 RESOURCES
—☆ Candleman, ☎ (800) 328-3453, ♂ www.candleman.com
—National Candle Association, ♂ www.candles.org
— *Candlemaking for Fun & Profit*, Michelle Espino (Prima Lifestyles, 2000)

Picture Frames

Put your creative energies to work earning money by starting a simple picture frame manufacturing business. Use unique and interesting materials in the construction of the picture frames—copper, exotic woods, ceramics, glass, plastic, injection foam, or a combination of materials. Set up your workshop in the basement, garage, or even a garden shed; you do not need a lot of space or expensive equipment and tools to get started making picture frames. In total, adding up building materials, equipment, glass, and hand tools, you should easily be able to get started on an initial investment of less than $1,000. On a small scale sell direct to consumers by exhibiting your frames at craft, gift, photography, and home décor shows, and from a homebased studio or rented mall kiosk space. If you decide to produce on a large scale, sell wholesale to picture framing shops, gift retailers, home décor retailers, photo shops, and independent photographers.

AT A GLANCE

 INVESTMENT: Under $2K

SKILL LEVEL: 1

 RESOURCES
—American Picture Framing Academy, ☎ (888) 840-9605, ♂ www.pictureframingschool.com
—⭐ Big Picture Framing, ☎ (800) 315-0024, ♂ www.bigpictureframing.com
—Scrollsaw, picture frame plans, ♂ www.scrollsaw.com
—📖 *Picture Framing: Library of Professional Picture Framing*, Vivian C. Kistler (Columbia Publishing, 2001)

Mosaic Creations

Mosaic products are in high demand; they are unique, colorful, great gifts, and fantastic home, garden, or office decorations. More important to you, mosaic products can become the basis of a very profitable business venture. Mosaic products are made out of broken ceramic titles and/or glass put together to form an abstract design or scene and placed over a substrate such as wood or plastic mesh and held together with grout in the cracks. Mosaic products can include tabletops, floor and wall tiles, planters, picture and mirror frames, wind chimes, wall plaques, garden fountains, inlay floor and wall tiles, inlay patio and walkway tiles, and other unique interior or exterior decorative items. The learning curve to make mosaic products is quick and mostly obtained through practice. But with that said, artistic abilities and a creative flair are definite assets. Selling mosaic products is also very easy; sell them where people go to shop for gifts and home decorations—craft shows, home shows, flea markets, online marketplaces, and mall kiosks. Consigning or wholesaling your products to gift retailers, garden centers, and building stores are also viable options.

AT A GLANCE

 INVESTMENT: Under $2K

 SKILL LEVEL: 1

 RESOURCES
—Mosaic Art Supply, ♂ www.mosaicartsupply.com
—Mosaic Basics, tools and supplies, ♂ www.mosaicbasics.com

—Mosaic Tile Supplies, ♂ www.mosaictilesupplies.com
—📖 *Mosaics: Inspiration and Original Projects for Interiors and Exteriors*, Kaffe Fassett, Candace Bahouth, and Debbie Patterson (Taunton Press, 2001)

Pottery

Huge bucks can be earned making and selling decorative art and functional pottery and ceramics products. However, creating fabulous pottery products is not a craft that is mastered overnight; it takes lots of practice to hone your skills. There are, of course, pottery classes available in every community, as well as a plethora of pottery training books and videos available to get you up and running in your own pottery business. What types of pottery and ceramic products can you make and sell? Lots, including planting pots, window boxes, picture frames, stoneware, jugs, plaques, vases, candlesticks, decorative tiles, sculptures, and the list goes on and on because just about any product can be made from pottery. You will need to invest in the tools of the potter's trade, such as a pottery wheel, slab roller, clay extruder, kiln, mixers, glazing tools, and ware racks, all of which are widely available through pottery supply companies. Pottery can be sold in many ways, including consigned with home furnishing, garden, and gift retailers, or sold wholesale to these same retailers at discounted prices. Alternately, pottery products can be sold to consumers by establishing a homebased pottery showroom, selling at craft fairs and home and garden shows, and utilizing online marketplaces such as eBay and internet craft products malls.

AT A GLANCE

INVESTMENT: Under $10K

SKILL LEVEL: 1–3

RESOURCES
—American Art Pottery Association, ♂ www.amartpot.org
—Art Schools Online, pottery schools directory, ♂ www.artschools.com
—Axner Pottery Supply, pottery equipment and supplies, ☎ (800) 843-7057, ♂ www.axner.com
—Bailey Pottery, pottery equipment and supplies, ☎ (800) 431-6067, ♂ www.baileypottery.com
—Pottery Auction, ♂ www.potteryauction.com

Stained Glass Products

Making and selling stained glass products such as lamps, window and door inserts, cabinet inserts, and sun catchers is an excellent way to supplement your income, or even replace your income entirely. Don't worry if you have no experience. Affordable stained glass classes are available in every community across the country, and the leaning curve is quick. Likewise, equipment and start-up raw materials are inexpensive; for a total investment of less than $2,000, you can set up making great stained glass products and earning excellent profits. Completed products can be sold in a number of ways, including internet malls, eBay, wholesale to retailers, direct to interior designers and builders, and directly to consumers from a homebased showroom, at crafts shows, and at home shows. Also keep in mind that you can target businesses, such as restaurants, retailers, and professionals seeking to jazz up their shops and offices with artistic stained glass items for sales as well.

AT A GLANCE

 INVESTMENT: Under $2K

 SKILL LEVEL: 2–3

 RESOURCES
—Delphi Glass, stain glass supply and equipment, ☎ (800) 248-2048, ♂ www.delphiglass.com
—Stained Glass Association of America, ☎ (800) 888-7422, ♂ www.stainedglass.org
—📖 *390 Traditional Stained Glass Designs*, Hywel G. Harris (Dover Publications, 1996)

Wood Sash Mirrors

Making wooden sash mirrors is very easy, and they are even easier to sell because they make such wonderful gifts and great designer home décor items. To make wooden sash mirrors, you will first need to source a good supply of old wooden window sashes. The best place to start your search is window replacement companies, glass shops, renovation contractors, and used building materials retailers. Expect to pay in the range of a few dollars each to as much as $50 for large and highly decorative wooden window sashes. Once you have acquired the sashes, the next steps are to remove the glass, putty, and paint, then refinish in a stain or natural finish, and install mirrors in the individual mullioned lites. Window sashes converted to mirrors are currently selling in the range of $75 to as much as $400 for large sashes with curved tops and other decorative features. They can be sold directly to interior designers, at flea markets, craft shows, online, and from home.

AT A GLANCE

 INVESTMENT: Under $2K

 SKILL LEVEL: 1

 RESOURCES
—Architectural Antiques, buy-and-sell marketplace, ☌ www.architec turals.net
—The Crafters Mall, craft products marketplace, ☌ www.procrafter.com
—National Demolition Association, ☎ (215) 348-4949, ☌ www.demolition association.com
—Used Building Materials Association, ☌ www.ubma.org

Art Jewelry

When we hear the word jewelry, images of shiny gold and brilliant diamonds come to mind, but fine jewelry comprises only a very small percentage of the total jewelry market. The larger portion is comprised of mass-produced costume jewelry and better quality art jewelry that often incorporates some precious stones and materials, such as silver and turquoise. Art jewelry can be created from many raw materials individually or in combination—metals, plastics, stones, ceramics, fabrics, bone and shell, and exotic hardwoods and softwoods. Because of this, art jewelry makers require a wide range of skills, which can include moldmaking, casting, soldering, polishing, gem and stone-cutting, setting, and much more. But don't fret, there are art jewelry classes taught in every backwater berg and big city right across the land, as well as lots of training books and videos available on the subject. Art jewelry can be sold to or consigned with fashion, jewelry, and gift retailers, art galleries, or wholesale at discounted prices. Art jewelry products can also be sold to consumers utilizing a homebased showroom, at craft fairs and fashion shows, by renting kiosk space in malls, by hiring sales reps to host art jewelry sales parties in their homes, and by selling online through eBay and internet malls.

AT A GLANCE

 INVESTMENT: Under $2K

 SKILL LEVEL: 1–3

RESOURCES
—Auntie's Beads, jewelry making equipment and supplies, ✆ www.auntiesbeads.com
—Jewelry Supply, jewelry making equipment and supplies, ✆ www.jewelrysupplies.com
—John C. Campbell Folk School, jewelry making classes, ☎ (800) 365-5724, ✆ www.folkschool.com
—📖 *The Encyclopedia of Jewelry Making Techniques*, Jinks McGrath (Running Press Books, 1995)

Christmas Decorations

Every year consumers around the globe spend millions on handcrafted Christmas decorations, and cashing in on the demand is easier than most people think. Forget about making and selling mass-produced decorations; the marketplace is already flooded with cheap, low quality, and arguably garish Christmas decorations. Instead, concentrate on making and selling high-quality handmade decorations that over time will become cherished family heirlooms. Wreaths, table centers, tree ornaments, tree toppers, and monogrammed mantel stockings are all popular with consumers. Supplies to make decorations are available at craft supply wholesalers, and many of the raw materials, such as pinecones and cedar greens, can be obtained cheaply or for free. Practice makes perfect. So long before the October to December prime selling season, constantly look for ways to make your current designs better and to create new decoration products. Sell direct to consumers from a homebased Christmas decoration boutique, at Christmas craft shows, online marketplaces, and by renting mall kiosks and vending cart space around Christmas. Additional options include consignment sales through gift retailers as well as selling wholesale to independent and chain gift retailers.

 AT A GLANCE

 INVESTMENT: Under $2K

Skill Level: 1

 Resources
—Christmas Mall, Christmas products marketplace, www.christmas mall.us
—Craft Mall, craft products marketplace, www.craftmall.com
— *Christmas Ornaments to Make* (Better Homes and Gardens, 2002)
— *Wreaths for Every Season*, June Apel and Chalice Bruce (North Light Books, 2002)

Quilted Products

Quilted products are a symphony of thread, fabric, shape, color, and creativity, which is why they are hot sellers. Quilted products such as blankets, handbags, throws, linens, chair pads, table runners, placemats, wall hangings, napkins, and clothing can be produced by hand or by quilting machines. The latter are much more economically viable from a business opportunity standpoint. According to the National Quilting Association, on average, quilters can expect to earn about $150 profit on the sale of every machine-sewn queen-size quilt after expenses. Given that a quilt can be made in a day, the potential to earn $40,000 to $50,000 per year doing something you love is a bonus. Quilting is a skill that can be self-taught through practice and reading books or you can take the fast-track method and enroll in quilting classes. Quilted products can be consigned with retailers, sold at craft, gift, and home décor shows, or sold online. If your production is good, you can also hire sales reps to host quilting products sales parties in their own homes, working on a profit-sharing arrangement.

AT A GLANCE

 Investment: Under $2K

 Skill Level: 1–3

 Resources
—Hands On Sewing Schools, ☎ (888) 739-6395 www.handson sewingschools.com
—Quilters Coupon, quilting equipment and supplies, www.quilters coupon.com

—Start Your Own Machine Quilting Business, ♂ www.machine-quilting-business.com
—National Quilting Association, ☎ (614) 488-8520, ♂ www.nqaquilts.org

Hand-Knitted Products

Turn your knitting hobby into a profitable part-time business by making and selling hand-knitted items, such as sweaters, mittens, hats, vests, blankets, shams, dog sweaters, scarves, and even clothing for dolls and stuffed animals. The opportunities are endless, and all hand-knitted items sell like crazy and for big bucks. All you need to get rolling are knitting skills, patterns, knitting needles, yarn, and a plan for selling your hand-knitted goods. A few of the best venues for selling hand-knitted crafts and garments are craft shows, gift shows, flea markets, eBay and internet malls, and even right from a homebased showroom supported by local advertising and word-of-mouth referrals. Likewise, items can also be placed on consignment with gift and fashion retailers, and if you are really ambitious, not to mention a very fast knitter, hire sales reps to host knitting product sales parties at their homes and split the profits with them on all products sold.

AT A GLANCE

INVESTMENT: Under $2K

SKILL LEVEL: 2

RESOURCES
—John C. Campbell Folk School, knitting classes, ☎ (800) 365-5724, ♂ www.folkschool.com
—Spin Craft Patterns, ♂ www.spincraftpatterns.com
—Knitting Guild Association, ☎ (740) 452-4541, ♂ www.tkga.com

Seashell Crafts

Seashell craft products such as shell wind chimes, shell-covered jewelry boxes, shell costume jewelry, and shell lamps are hot sellers in all regions of the country. Cashing in on the demand is simple because shell craft products are easy to make, and even easier to sell. All you need to get started is an idea about the types of seashell craft products you are going to make, a good supply of seashells, a glue gun, basic hand tools, and appropriate fasteners determined by the products you make. Fortunately, making seashell craft products is not messy, so you can set up shop in just about any room of the house. There are numerous companies selling seashells in bulk at wholesale prices. Sell your completed seashell creations online utilizing eBay, internet malls, and your own web site, as well as through offline sales venues, such as flea markets, arts and crafts shows, and at community events. Another option is to sell your products wholesale to home décor, gift, and fashion retailers, or place products with retailers on a consignment basis.

AT A GLANCE

INVESTMENT: Under $2K

SKILL LEVEL: 1

RESOURCES
—Sanibel Seashell Industries, seashell craft information and supplies, ☎ (239) 472-1603, ♂ www.seashells.com
—Shell Horizons Wholesale, ☎ (727) 536-3333, ♂ www.shell horizons.com
—The Shell Store, seashell craft information and supplies, ☎ (727) 360-0586, ♂ www.theshellstore.com
—U.S. Shell Wholesale, ☎ (956) 554-4500, ♂ www.usshell.com

Twig Furniture and Crafts

Have fun and earn extra money on weekends, or even full-time, by making and selling twig furniture, garden products, and crafts. Outdoor Adirondack furniture, birdhouses, tables, chairs, bentwood arbors, trellis, planters, mirror frames, picture frames, and lots more, can all be easily made from willow and birch twigs and branches. The learning curve is quick, and a walk through the woods collecting branches (with permission) will supply you with all the raw materials you need to get going. Tools and fasteners add up to nothing more than basic hand tools, a power saw, and a drill press, along with carpenter's glue, wire, and screws. Sell finished products online, at flea markets, craft shows, garden shows, and even set up wholesale accounts with retailers, or consign twig products with retailers. There are virtually no material costs associated with making twig furniture and products, which means there are no financial risks, yet huge profit potential.

 AT A GLANCE

 INVESTMENT: Under $2K

 SKILL LEVEL: 1

 RESOURCES
—The Crafters Mall, craft products marketplace, ♂ www.procrafter.com
—Twig Factory, information and twig furniture and product plans,
  ♂ www.twigfactory.com
—Woodworking Plan Finder, twig product plans, ♂ www.woodworking
  planfinder.com
—📖 *Making Twig Furniture and Household Things*, Abby Rouff (Hartley & Marks Publishers, 1999)

Leather Crafts

Making and selling leather crafts is not only a very enjoyable hobby business, but also one with great potential to earn some serious extra cash. Leather goods and crafts such as gloves, wallets, pet collars, clothing, bookmarks, key fobs, jewelry, art, billfolds, business card holders, cellular telephone cases, belts, knife sheaths, and business organizers are just of few of the items you can produce and sell. Leather craft tools, patterns, instructional classes, books, and videos, as well as leather crafting supplies are readily available through many offline and online businesses. Leather crafts are just as easy to sell as they are to make, and one option, especially for entrepreneurs looking to grow their businesses big, is to consign products with retailers or sell products to retailers on a wholesale basis. Alternately, you can sell the products you make directly to consumers utilizing online marketplaces such as eBay, internet malls, and your own web site, or to consumers in the bricks and mortar world utilizing venues such as flea markets, craft fairs, and hunting, fishing, and fashion consumer shows.

AT A GLANCE

 INVESTMENT: Under $2K

Skill Level: 1

 Resources
—Craft Mall, craft products marketplace, ✆ www.craftmall.com
—eLeather Supply, leather craft tools and supplies, ✆ www.eleather supply.com
—John C. Campbell Folk School, leather craft classes, ☎ (800) 365-5724, ✆ www.folkschool.com
—Leather Craft Supplies, ✆ www.leather-craft-supplies.com
—Tandy Leather, leather craft supplies, ✆ www.tandyleather.com

Model Craft

There are primarily two ways to profit making and selling models: designing, constructing, and selling handcrafted models or purchasing, assembling, and selling models from kits. Both can be equally profitable, but handcrafting models from scratch requires considerably more artistic skill and equipment. If you choose to assemble models from kits, take heart in the fact that for the most popular subjects, such as boats, ships, automobiles, trains, airplanes, and military machinery, model kits can be purchased in bulk at wholesale prices. Assembling model kits only requires basic modelers' tools, a workbench, and good lighting. Once completed, they can be mounted on a base or under glass to increase the value and sold online, at craft and hobby shows, and from a homebased showroom. If you elect to design and construct models from scratch, you will first need to choose a construction medium—wood, stone, metal, ceramic, die cast, fabric, or injection plastic. Tool requirements will be in direct relationship to the types of construction materials utilized. Because building from scratch is an artistic endeavor, the models can be exact scale replicas or abstract, capturing the spirit of the subject more than the exact image. Like kit models, handcrafted models can also be mounted on a base, plaque, or under glass to increase value and sold in the same ways—online marketplaces, craft and hobby shows, from a homebased showroom, and through art galleries.

AT A GLANCE

 Investment: Under $2K

 Skill Level: 1–2

RESOURCES
—Gatto Plan Supply, model construction plans, ✆ www.gatto plans.com
—Spacecraft International Manufacturing, ready-to-assemble, plastic model kits, ☎ (626) 398-4800, ✆ www.spacecraftkits.com
—📖 *Ship Modeling Simplified: Tips and Techniques for Model Construction from Kits*, Frank Mastini (International Marine, 1990)

Decorative Table Centerpieces

If you are looking for a simple, yet potentially highly profitable business to start, look no further than making and selling decorative table centerpieces. Decorative table centerpieces are commonly purchased by event planners for social and corporate gatherings, by restaurant owners and catering companies, and by wedding coordinators to create visually appealing tables for guests. In addition to great profit potential, two aspects of this business are very exciting. One, many of the materials needed to create jaw-dropping gorgeous table centerpieces can be acquired for free by scouring beaches, meadows, and forests in search of wild flowers, beach glass, stones, pine cones, and twigs. Two, you can spread your creative wings because there is no step-by-step manual dictating how table centerpieces should look or what materials can be used in crafting them. Use glass, metal, wood, ceramics, stone, fabrics, herbs, flowers, water, and just about anything else that you can imagine to arrive at an attractive end product. Again, table centerpieces can be sold to restaurants, catering companies, wedding and event planners, banquet halls, hotels, and to homeowners looking for an attractive table feature for their next dinner party.

AT A GLANCE

 INVESTMENT: Under $2K

 SKILL LEVEL: 1

 RESOURCES
—Craft Mall, craft products marketplace, ✆ www.craftmall.com
—Entrepreneur, small business portal, ✆ www.entrepreneur.com
—The Crafters Mall, craft products marketplace, ✆ www.procrafter.com
—National Association of Wedding Professionals, ✆ www.nawp.com

Hand-Painted Storage Boxes

Many people look for interesting and unique ways to organize and store their personal items, kitchenware, and business documents, which is why one-of-a-kind, hand-painted storage boxes have become big sellers. Using wood, metal, plastic, fabric, cardboard, or a combination of these, you can design and build storage boxes and paint them to suit every décor or storage application. Depict landscapes, abstract designs, animals, or let your customers choose the types of images they want painted on the storage boxes. Don't worry if you lack artistic skills, you can concentrate on building and marketing the storage boxes and hire an artist to paint them on a per-unit basis or profit-sharing basis. Good places to track down artists are at local schools and through community art programs. There are numerous options for selling the finished product, including online sales, on a wholesale basis to retailers, by exhibiting at home décor and gift shows, direct to interior designers and professional organizers, and by renting sales space at public markets, mall kiosks, and flea markets.

AT A GLANCE

 INVESTMENT: Under $2K

 SKILL LEVEL: 1–2

 RESOURCES
—Craft Mall, craft products marketplace, www.craftmall.com
—Mammoth Tools, ☎ (516) 942-0905, www.mammothtools.com
—Woodworkers Workshop, storage box plans, www.woodworkers workshop.com
—Wood Zone, storage box plans, www.woodzone.com

Bamboo Products

In bulk quantities, bamboo is cheap to buy and can be made into a wide variety of highly saleable products, including indoor and outdoor bamboo furniture, mirror and picture frames, room dividers, birdhouses, garden arbors, planters, and wind chimes. The wood is also very easy to work with, and all of the products listed can be manufactured using basic tools and fasteners, at home or in a rented workshop. The products that can be made from bamboo are nearly unlimited. Be creative in terms of what you make and design because it is the lasting quality and striking visual appearance of bamboo that appeals to many people and makes bamboo products very easy to sell. Consider selling bamboo products on eBay, at home décor, garden, and gift shows, and craft fairs and flea markets. Products can also be consigned with retailers or sold to retailers at wholesale.

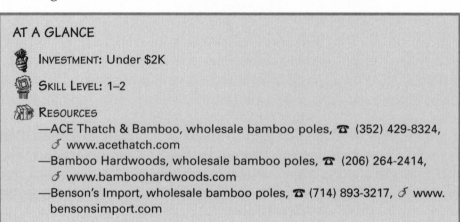

AT A GLANCE

INVESTMENT: Under $2K

SKILL LEVEL: 1–2

RESOURCES
—ACE Thatch & Bamboo, wholesale bamboo poles, ☎ (352) 429-8324,
✆ www.acethatch.com
—Bamboo Hardwoods, wholesale bamboo poles, ☎ (206) 264-2414,
✆ www.bamboohardwoods.com
—Benson's Import, wholesale bamboo poles, ☎ (714) 893-3217, ✆ www.
bensonsimport.com

Party Balloons

An investment of less than $1,000 can get you on your way to earning big profits selling helium and cold-air party balloons. Corporate events, grand openings, children's birthday parties, special occasions, graduations, retailer sales, weddings, and community events, the demand for party balloons is gigantic and continually growing. Selling party balloons is best achieved by creating a basic, yet detailed brochure describing your business and distributing it to party and event planners, wedding planners, children's stores, restaurants, banquet facilities, daycare centers, and catering companies. There are also many balloon manufacturers offering custom printing services, thereby enabling you also to sell to businesses that want to advertise sales and special events with their names and logos emblazoned on the balloons. You will need equipment such as helium tanks for gas-filled balloons and air compressors for inflating cold-air balloons, along with reliable transportation for delivery purposes.

AT A GLANCE

INVESTMENT: Under $2K

SKILL LEVEL: 1

Papermaking Crafts

Papermaking crafts is a little-known business opportunity that can generate exceptional profits. What is really good about this opportunity is that there are two revenue sources: making custom paper from scratch or producing and selling papermaking craft products. Both are relatively easy to learn using training aids such as papermaking classes, books, and videos. Handmade paper is used in papermaking craft products as well as by artisans producing specialty gift, place, note, and birthday cards, gift tags, wedding invitations, birth announcements, wrapping paper, watermarked stationery, watercolor paintings, matting art, pressed flower art, and calligraphy. A few of the handcrafted paper products you can produce are mobiles, lampshades, lanterns, window shades, and jewelry. Handmade paper can be sold directly to artisans; papermaking craft products can be sold to gift retailers wholesale or directly to consumers utilizing online venues such as eBay and internet craft malls or by exhibiting products at craft fairs.

AT A GLANCE

 INVESTMENT: Under $2K

 SKILL LEVEL: 1

 RESOURCES
—Hand Papermaking, industry information and resources, ♂ www.hand
papermaking.org
—International Association of Hand Papermakers and Paper Artists,
♂ www.iapma.info
—Paper Making, industry information and resources, ♂ www.paper
making.net

Photo Albums

Making and selling custom photograph albums is a simple business that anyone can tackle, especially people looking for a profitable outlet for their artistic abilities. Using interesting materials such as exotic hardwoods, carved softwoods, copper, tin, fabric, stained glass, beads, stone, ceramics, or hand-painted canvas, you can make designer photo album covers and appeal to customers that are searching for a special way of housing their cherished photo memories. Armed with samples of your most elaborate photo albums, visit wedding photographers and portrait photographers to present your work and enlist their assistance in marketing your products to their customers on a profit-sharing basis. Also sell photo albums through online marketplaces such as eBay, at craft fairs, and at home décor and gift shows. Consignment sales through gift retailers, bookstores, photography studios, and camera retailers will also go a long way to boost revenues and profits.

AT A GLANCE

INVESTMENT: Under $2K

SKILL LEVEL: 1

RESOURCES
—Craft Mall, craft products marketplace, ♂ www.craftmall.com
—Wedding Photojournalist Association, ♂ www.wpja.org
—The Crafters Mall, craft products marketplace, ♂ www.procrafter.com

Mirror Art

Mirror art is simply assembling small pieces of different color tints of mirrors in various design patterns to create an image that resembles a landscape, an animal, an action such as skier carving a hill, or an abstract design. Mirror art is becoming very trendy for both residential and commercial applications because of its unique and eye-appealing qualities. In most cases, a trip to your local glass shop will supply you with most of the mirror you need very cheaply, because glass shops dispose of mirror cutoff pieces that are too small to sell, but are perfect for creating mirror art. Equipment needed to make mirror art includes a glasscutter, glass pliers, and a small glass grinder similar to ones used in the stained glass craft; in total, about $200 will be sufficient to purchase the required equipment. Once you have created a pattern, the next step is to transfer it to the mirror and cut out each piece of the design and polishes any sharp edges. The final steps are to glue each mirror piece using construction adhesive to a piece of plywood to create a solid backing and frame it. Mirror art can be sold at craft fairs, online, from a home-based studio, and consigned with gift and art retailers.

 INVESTMENT: Under $2K

 SKILL LEVEL: 1

 RESOURCES

—Craft Mall, craft products marketplace, ✆ www.craftmall.com
—National Craft Association, ✆ www.craftassoc.com
—The Crafters Mall, craft products marketplace, ✆ www.procrafter.com

AT A GLANCE

Baskets

Although basket making is a centuries old craft, little has changed in the way hand-made baskets are made today; they are still handwoven by the craftsperson. What has changed is the way baskets are used. At one time baskets were used every day to carry goods and to measure quantities of goods such as eggs. Today, baskets are more artistic than utilitarian, which is reflected in the prices. It is not uncommon for highly artistic handcrafted baskets to fetch $500 or more. Learning to make baskets can be accomplished in two ways: You can teach yourself the craft through trial and error with the aid of instructional books and videos, or you can enroll in basket-making classes. Regardless, you will need to invest in basic tools such as a measuring tape, scissors, water bucket, awl, knife, and clamps, as well as raw materials. Sell baskets directly to consumers utilizing online marketplaces such as eBay, internet malls, and your own web site, or sell to consumers in the bricks and mortar world utilizing venues such as flea markets, craft fairs, and gift shows.

AT A GLANCE

 INVESTMENT: Under $2K

 SKILL LEVEL: 1

RESOURCES
—Basket Makers, industry information and resources, ✆ www.basket makers.org
—Basket Makers Catalog, supplies, ✆ www.basketmakerscatalog.com
—Basket Patterns, ✆ www.basketpatterns.com
—Handweavers Guild of America, ✆ www.weavespindye.org
—John C. Campbell Folk School, basket-making classes, ☎ (800) 365-5724, ✆ www.folkschool.com

Pet Memorials

The loss of a pet can be a very emotional experience for the owner. Many choose to purchase a memorial that can be placed in the yard or garden as a permanent reminder of their cherished friend. Making and selling pet memorials is a fantastic business to start, especially for pet-loving entrepreneurs. Pet memorials are very similar to people memorials—a stone marker inscribed with the pet's name, a message, and often an image of the pet. You can use natural field or river stone, granite, marble, or whichever type of stone your customers choose. You will need to purchase a sandblaster and teach yourself how to use it, but don't worry, the learning curve is short. If you have the creative abilities, you can design and cut the stencils used in the sandblasting process. If not, hire an art student on piecework to draw and cut the stencils. The best way to market pet memorials is to make sample markers, which can be displayed at veterinary offices and pet shops along with price lists and order forms. Customers simply complete the form and include the information and image they want on the memorial. You fulfill the order by delivering the completed memorial back to your dealer or directly to the customer.

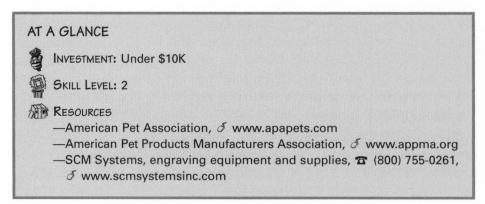

AT A GLANCE

INVESTMENT: Under $10K

SKILL LEVEL: 2

RESOURCES
—American Pet Association, ✆ www.apapets.com
—American Pet Products Manufacturers Association, ✆ www.appma.org
—SCM Systems, engraving equipment and supplies, ☎ (800) 755-0261, ✆ www.scmsystemsinc.com

Pet Leashes and Collars

Turn your passion for pets into a profitable pastime by manufacturing and selling custom pet leashes and collars. Working from a small homebased workspace with basic hand tools, you can design pet collars and leashes using materials such as leather, metal, or fabric and decorate each with studs, beads, and other visually appealing embellishments. How do I know that there are big profits to be earned in this type of manufacturing business? Simple, my wife and I spend a small fortune every year purchasing many new collars and leashes for our dog, Dana. So do all of our friends and family with pets. And so do millions of other pet owners here in the United States and Canada, and around the rest of the globe. Pet products are big business, period. Sell your creations online via internet malls and eBay, and at pet fairs and craft shows. There is also great potential to build a wholesale arm of the business by contacting pet product boutiques to carry your line, or at least consign a few products to test the waters.

AT A GLANCE

INVESTMENT: Under $2K

SKILL LEVEL: 1–2

RESOURCES
—American Dog Owners Association, ✆ www.adoa.org
—American Pet Association, ✆ www.apapets.com
—The Bow Wow Boutique, dog products marketplace, ✆ www.
  dog-products.dogs-central.com

Clothing for Dogs

Americans spend more than 30 billion annually on their pets, and big bucks can be earned by designing, making, and selling designer duds for dogs. Sweaters and rain jackets are sure bets to become top sellers, but dog lovers around the globe are also buying designer doggie hats, goggles, shirts, booties, and scarves for their beloved furry friends. The criteria for getting started are minimal—design skills, sewing skills and equipment, patterns, and a bit of gumption to get out and pitch your fabulous designer fashions for mutts and pedigrees alike to pet shop retailers, especially if your ambitions are to establish wholesale accounts with chain and independent pet shop retailers. If not, there are still many ways to sell direct to dog owners. These include exhibiting and selling at pet fairs, online sales via dog-related web sites, mail order sales supported by newspaper, catalog, online, and magazine advertising, and establishing a doggie clothing boutique at home or in a retail storefront location. As dog owners know, word travels fast amongst dog owners, and when a great product for a pet is found, he or she is quick to spread the word to other dog owners.

AT A GLANCE

 INVESTMENT: Under $10K

 SKILL LEVEL: 1–2

 RESOURCES
—American Dog Owners Association, ☎ www.adoa.org
—The Bow Wow Boutique, dog products marketplace, ☎ www.dog-products.dogs-central.com
—The Pet Professor, dog products marketplace, ☎ www.thepetprofessor.com

---

Furniture for Pets

North Americans love to spoil their pets as evidenced by the plethora of pet spas, gourmet foods, and tailored clothes. And, of course, no truly cherished pet can be without custom-manufactured furniture to lounge around on all day. What types of furniture can you design, build, and sell for pets? Couches, chairs, beds, ottomans, squeaky toy boxes, and baskets all have appeal. You will need the basics to get started—workshop, tools, catchy business name, and a solid marketing plan. Likewise, you will need to decide if you are going to build a standard line of furniture for pets or concentrate on custom made-to-order furniture for pets. You can even show your customers numerous fabric swatches and let them choose to match their décor. There are many ways to sell furniture for pets, including online venues such as eBay, exhibiting at pet shows and fairs, directly to retailers on a wholesale basis, marketing through veterinarians and pet groomers, and right from a home-based pet furniture boutique supported by local advertising and referrals. Making and selling a line of pet fabric covers to protect household furniture and car seats can also earn additional revenues for the business venture.

AT A GLANCE

 INVESTMENT: Under $10K

SMALL LEVEL: 2

 RESOURCES
—American Pet Association, ♂ www.apapets.com
—American Pet Products Manufacturers Association, ♂ www.appma.org
—Furniture Plans, ♂ www.furnitureplans.com
—U-Bild, furniture plans, ♂ www.u-bild.com

Dog Treats

The fastest growing, and arguably most profitable, segment of the pet foods industry is gourmet dog treats. There is a lot of money to be made in this business because the profit margin is very high and people are willing to pay for the best dog treats money can buy. I know because I am one of these people who blow a bundle every month pampering my pooch with the best treats money can buy. As people become more health conscious of their own diets, they begin to scrutinize their pet's diets as well, and many are turning to naturally-made food and biscuits for their dogs, even though all-natural handmade biscuits cost as much as ten times more than commercially produced biscuits. Making dog biscuits at home is easy; all you need to get started are dog biscuit recipes, healthy ingredients, biscuit molds (shaped like bones and cats are dog favorites), a catchy name, and packaging materials. Baking and selling specialty dog treats is a fantastic opportunity for pet-loving entrepreneurs who want to work from home and have a lot of fun. Selling options are plentiful. Sell to independent and chain pet food retailers on a wholesale basis or to consumers via online pet products marketplaces, at pet fairs, and from your home supported by word-of-mouth advertising. The advertising is very easy to get, providing dogs love your treats.

AT A GLANCE

 INVESTMENT: Under $2K

 SKILL LEVEL: 1

RESOURCES
—American Dog Owners Association, ♂ www.adoa.org
—American Pet Products Manufacturers Association, ♂ www.appma.org
—Gourmet Sleuth, 200 dog biscuit recipes, ♂ www.gourmetsleuth.com/recipe_dogbiscuit.htm

Scratch Posts

People who get cats are quick to realize that $30 spent to buy a scratch post can potentially save them hundreds, if not thousands, of dollars in damage that cats can inflict on furniture while sharpening their claws. No special skills are needed to make scratch posts. Tool requirements are basic, raw materials involve nothing more than cheap softwood and carpet ends. Of all of the products listed in this book, scratch posts are one of the easiest products to make and sell. Granted, you would be hard pressed to get rich making scratch posts. But, if your goal is to earn an extra few hundred dollars each month, then this may very well be the opportunity to help you reach that goal. Scratch posts can be sold by renting table space at pet fairs and flea markets and by getting them into pet shops on a consignment or wholesale basis.

AT A GLANCE

 INVESTMENT: Under $2K

 SKILL LEVEL: 1

 RESOURCES
—American Pet Association, www.apapets.com
—American Pet Products Manufacturers Association, ♂ www.appma.org
—Cat Furniture, scratch post construction plans, ♂ www.pusscats.com/
  Cat_Furniture.htm

Doghouses

A workshop, doghouse construction plans, and basic woodworking equipment such as a table and miter saw are all that are needed to start a doghouse manufacturing and sales business. Doghouses can be constructed from standard plans, or you can design your own doghouses to suit each customer's individual needs and aesthetic preferences. You may even want to consider going after the high-end market, building and marketing custom one-of-a-kind doghouses complete with luxuries like heated floors, air conditioning, running water, lighting, and eye-pleasing design elements like gabled rooflines. Doghouses can be sold in kit format ready for customers to assemble, or you can offer a complete package, including delivery and installation. Much will depend on the style of doghouses you design and build, as well as your target audience. Sale methods include online sales, establishing wholesale and/or consignment accounts with pet supply retailers, sales through building centers, displaying and selling from home supported by community advertising, and exhibiting doghouse displays at pet shows and fairs.

AT A GLANCE

INVESTMENT: Under $2K

SKILL LEVEL: 1

RESOURCES
—American Dog Owners Association, ♂ www.adoa.org
—American Pet Products Manufacturers Association, ♂ www.appma.org
—Woodworkers Workshop, doghouse plans, ♂ www.woodworkers workshop.com
—📖 *Building a Doghouse*, Mary Twitchell (Storey Books, 2000)

Cat Condos

Cats have an instinctual desire to jump, scratch, and explore dark places, which is why many cat owners buy a cat condo to provide a lifetime of enjoyment for their cats. A cat condo is nothing more than a plywood or strand board frame covered with carpet, designed to include multiple levels, scratching surfaces, perches, cubby hole hiding places, catwalks, and attached swinging toys. Because play can get rough, especially if there are more than one cat in the house, cat condos must be sturdily built on a wide-base platform to prevent tipping. Some cat condos can reach six feet high. Cat condos are cheap to build yet can retail for as much as $250 for highly elaborate designs with all the bells and whistles. Tool and equipment requirements add up to nothing more than a skill or table saw and basic hand tools. Cat condos can be sold online, at pet shows, at fairs, consigned in local pet shops, and wholesaled in bulk to chain and independent pet products retailers.

AT A GLANCE

INVESTMENT: Under $2K

SKILL LEVEL: 1

> RESOURCES
> —Cat Condos, cat condo building plans, ♂ www.cat-tree-plans.com
> —Cat Tree Plans, cat condo building plans, ♂ www.cattreeplans.com
> —Entrepreneur, small business portal, ♂ www.entrepreneur.com

Aquariums

Make an excellent full- or part-time income constructing and selling small- to medium-sized custom aquariums for both residential and commercial applications right from a homebased workshop. Granted, if you have no previous experience working with glass and acrylic, there will be a bit of a learning curve to get up and running, but with self-training and lots of practice, you should be building and selling custom fish tank aquariums in no time. Accessories such as tank stands, canopies, filters, food, lights, aquatic plants, skimmers, ornaments, and cleaning supplies can also be purchased wholesale and sold retail to add a valuable source of extra revenue. If you concentrate on building custom made-to-order fresh water and salt water tanks, market through specialty publications, by networking with residential and commercial contractors and renovators, and by designing and building sample tanks that can be displayed and sold through pet shop retailers on a made-to-order and profit-sharing basis.

> AT A GLANCE
>
> INVESTMENT: Under $10K
>
> SKILL LEVEL: 2
>
> RESOURCES
> —American Pet Products Manufacturers Association, ♂ www.appma.org
> —Florida Tropical Fish Farms Association, ♂ www.ftffa.com
> —Tropical Fish Net, industry information and links, ♂ www.tropical-fish.net

Engraved Pet Tags

To get started making and selling engraved tags for pets, you will need to purchase blank tags or make your own by purchasing flat metal stock and using tools such as power sheers or a band saw to create interesting tags in the shapes of bones, hearts, and animal-specific breeds. Whether you buy blank tags in bulk or make your own, the equipment needed to engrave metal tags is cheap and widely available, with not much workspace needed. In fact, you can even operate on a portable basis, engraving tags for customers while they wait. Ideal locations include setting up at pet fairs, pet retailers on weekends, renting kiosk space at malls, and displaying at flea markets. Of course, engraved tags for pets can also be sold online and shipped to customers once completed. This simple manufacturing business has the potential to be very profitable as material costs are minimal and tags are quick to engrave, yet can retail as for as much as $20 each for name, contact information, and message engraved on custom-designed tags.

AT A GLANCE

INVESTMENT: Under $2K

SKILL LEVEL: 1

RESOURCES
—Net Signs, blank pet identification tag wholesaler, ☎ (954) 517-9007, ♂ www.netsigns.net
—NingBo Guiyou Pet Products, blank pet identification tag manufacturer, ☎ 0086-574-8793-2496 (Taiwan), ♂ www.guiyou.com
—SCM Systems, engraving equipment and supplies, ☎ (800) 755-0261, ♂ www.scmsystemsinc.com

Soap

With an investment of less than $500, you can be in the specialty soap business, making and selling anything from aromatherapy, hypoallergenic, dermatological, novelty, and herbal soaps, as well as soap gift baskets and sets. There are just as many ways to sell soap as there are different kinds of specialty soaps. For instance, you can sell part time from a homebased soap boutique, hire salespeople to organize and host in-home soap sales parties, sell through eBay and internet malls, and display your soaps at craft shows, farmers' markets, and health shows. You can also sell direct to the public by renting kiosk space in malls and by starting a suds club in which you collect customer information and send out a new bar of specialty soap every month as a free gift while including a product catalog and order forms: one for the person and two for friends. On a larger scale, you can also make and package specialty soaps and sell to retailers such as gift shops, bed and bath retailers, and natural health products retailers on a wholesale basis.

AT A GLANCE

 INVESTMENT: Under $2K

 SKILL LEVEL: 1

 RESOURCES
—Handcrafted Soap Makers Guild, ☎ (866) 900-7627, ♂ www.soap guild.org
—John C. Campbell Folk School, soap making classes, ☎ (800) 365-5724, ♂ www.folkschool.com
—National Craft Association, ♂ www.craftassoc.com
— 📖 *Soapmaking for Fun & Profit,* Maria Nerius (Prima Lifestyle, 1999)

Natural Cleaning Products

In all probability, many of the traditional cleaners you use daily to clean your home contain potentially dangerous toxins that promote illness, fatigue, and disease and can be especially harmful to people with allergies, to children, and to pets. But don't fear, starting a business that manufactures and sells natural cleaning products for residential and commercial use is your opportunity to eliminate this deadly risk and get rid of stubborn dirt and grime in your own home as well as customers' homes and offices. Natural cleaning products use only citrus-based oils, ingredients from corn and other renewable materials and contain no dyes, artificial fragrances, or pesticide residues. In short, natural cleaning products are very people, pet, and planet friendly. Great, but what do you need to get started? You need a catchy "eco friendly name," as well as recipes for natural cleaning products and containers made of recycled materials to hold your products. Natural cleaning products can be sold in a number of ways, including wholesale to grocery stores and eco-products retailers, direct to office and residential cleaning services, and direct to consumers via online "eco-friendly marketplaces" and by selling at home shows. Another sales tactic is to hire sales reps to organize and host natural cleaning products sales parties in their own homes and pay a commission on all sales.

AT A GLANCE

 INVESTMENT: Under $2K

Skill Level: 1

 Resources
—Eco Mall, natural products marketplace, ✂ www.ecomall.com
—Nancy's Natural Cleaning Resources, industry information and resources, ✂ www.nancysnatural.expage.com
— *The Naturally Clean Home: 101 Safe and Easy Herbal Formulas for Non-Toxic Cleaners*, Karyn Siegel-Maier (Storey Books, 1999)

First-Aid Kits

Assembling and selling first-aid kits has tremendous upside profit possibilities, especially when you consider the vast number of people who might need quick access to a well-stocked first aid kit on a regular or emergency basis. People like hikers, campers, sports enthusiasts, families, boaters, motorists, workers, and pet owners need this product. There are lots of wholesalers where you can purchase medical supplies at rock-bottom prices. The next step is to assemble the kits with first-aid medical items specific to your target customers and their needs. Once completed, the kits can be sold directly to businesses or consumers online, or at industry-specific shows such as auto, home and garden, and sports and recreation shows, depending on your target customer. This is a great opportunity for retirees, homemakers, or for anyone else seeking to earn a few extra bucks every month working part time and mainly from the comforts of home.

AT A GLANCE

 Investment: Under $2K

 Skill Level: 1

 Resources
—Entrepreneur, small business portal, ✂ www.entrepreneur.com
—First Aid Supplies Online Wholesale, ☎ (800) 874-8767, ✂ www.firstaidsuppliesonline.com
—MP First Aid Wholesale, ☎ (888) 332-4863, ✂ www.mpfirstaid.com

Body and Bath Products

Entrepreneurs seeking a simple, yet potentially very profitable enterprise should look no further than making and selling body and bath products. Gels, scrubs, salts, and aromatherapy oils for the bath, and creams, balms, and powders for the body after the bath are all red-hot sellers. Make the products from your own recipes, or use recipes found on the internet and in books to get started. Tweak these along the way as your knowledge of the products increases. Selling body and bath products is just as easy as making them. Start with a unique and interesting package that describes the products' most beneficial points. Hire salespeople to organize and host body and bath product sales parties from their homes, sell products online, exhibit at health and beauty shows, and make body and bath gift baskets and sell from kiosks in malls, especially close to Christmas, Mother's Day, and Valentine's Day. Also think big and develop wholesale accounts and sell in bulk to spas, health stores, and cosmetics retailers—locally, nationally, and internationally.

AT A GLANCE

 INVESTMENT: Under $2K

 SKILL LEVEL: 1

 RESOURCES
—Eco Mall, natural body care products marketplace, ☞ www.ecomall.com
—Eco Business Links, natural body care products manufacturers' directory, ☞ www.ecobusinesslinks.com/natural_bodycare_skincare.htm
—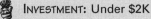 *Natural Beauty at Home: More than 250 Easy to Use Recipes for Body, Bath, and Hair*, Janice Cox (Owl Books, 2002)

Essential Oils

By definition, essential oils are the volatile essences extracted from aromatic plants by steam, distillation, or expression extraction. Essential oils can be applied topically or inhaled, and act on physical, emotional, and psychological processes. Essential oils are up to 100 times more concentrated than the oils found in dried herbs and can be used as fragrant ingredients in a wide variety of health and beauty products, including cosmetics, body lotions, soaps, candles, aromatherapy burners, perfume, and aromatic potpourri products. There are basically two ways to extract essential oils from herbs and flowers: distillation and expression. Distillation is the most common; it uses steam to break down plant tissue, causing it to release essential oil in a vaporized form. The vapors travel from the distillation chamber into cooling tanks, causing the vapors to become a liquid, which is then separated into water and pure essential oil. You can make your own essential oil distiller, although purchasing a commercial distiller, which will set you back about $1,000, is recommended. The expression, or cold pressing extraction, method involves mixing the plants with citrus oils and pressing the mixture. The resulting liquid is then filtered to separate the pure essential oils. But this method yields much less essential oil than distillation. The retail selling price of essential oils is directly related to how much plant material is needed for distillation. Essential oils can be sold in bulk to companies manufacturing and selling health and beauty products or sold to consumers online, at craft fairs, and via mail-order sales.

AT A GLANCE

 INVESTMENT: Under $2K

 SKILL LEVEL: 1

 RESOURCES
—National Association for Holistic Aromatherapy, ♂ www.nhha.org
—The Essential Oil Company, professional distillation equipment,
   ☎ (800) 729-5912, ♂ www.essentialoil.com
—The Journal of Essential Oil Research, ♂ www.perfumerflavorist.com
— *The Complete Book of Essential Oils and Aromatherapy*, Valerie
Ann Worwood (New World Library, 1991)

Gift Baskets

Profit from your creative and marketing skills by making and selling one-of-a-kind gift baskets. Simply select items such as specialty foods, cosmetics, bath products, chocolates or candies, flowers, or just about any other type of product depending on your target audience and arrange in attractive wicker baskets or unique containers, wrap in foil or colored plastic, and the gift basket is complete. Gift products for the baskets are readily available from a number of wholesale sources. Concentrate your marketing efforts on securing repeat clients such as corporations, professionals, small business owners, realtors, and sales professionals. Basically, focus on individuals and companies that would have reason to regularly send out gift baskets to existing and new clients to thank them for their business.

Promote your gift basket business in a number of ways, including direct mail, exhibiting at gift shows, and networking with your target audience at business and social functions in your community; places like the chamber of commerce are excellent. Also, sell the gift baskets online and through local gift retailers and flower shops on a consignment or wholesale basis.

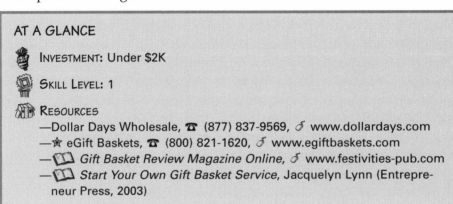

AT A GLANCE

INVESTMENT: Under $2K

SKILL LEVEL: 1

RESOURCES
—Dollar Days Wholesale, ☎ (877) 837-9569, ♂ www.dollardays.com
—★ eGift Baskets, ☎ (800) 821-1620, ♂ www.egiftbaskets.com
—📖 *Gift Basket Review Magazine Online*, ♂ www.festivities-pub.com
—📖 *Start Your Own Gift Basket Service*, Jacquelyn Lynn (Entrepreneur Press, 2003)

Cactus Arrangements

For creative entrepreneurs, making and selling unique cactus arrangements offers an excellent opportunity to earn a few extra dollars every week. Cactus arrangements make great gifts for the home and office, and making them is easy. Collect things such as small rocks, gravel, shells, pinecones, and small pieces of driftwood or bark, which often can be obtained free if you are prepared to go for a hike in the woods or on the beach. Arrange these items with planted dwarf cactuses in a terra cotta or similar pot. That is about all that is required to make cactus arrangements. Sell your arrangements online via specialty gift and gardening sites, as well as your own web site. You can also sell the cactus arrangements at craft, gift, Christmas, and gardening shows. Likewise, target potential volume buyers like corporations, small business owners, professionals, and salespeople who routinely send clients unique appreciation gifts.

AT A GLANCE

INVESTMENT: Under $2K

SKILL LEVEL: 1

RESOURCES
—Arizona Pottery, wholesale pots, ☎ (800) 420-1808, ♂ www.arizona
pottery.com
—Cactus Ranch, wholesale cactus plants, ☎ (903) 567-5042
—Kactus Korral, wholesale cactus plants, ☎ (830) 540-4521, ♂ www.
kactus.com
—📖 *Complete Book of Cacti & Succulents,* Terry Hewit (DK Publish-
ing, 1997)

Clocks

Grandfather, wall, mantle, cuckoo, carriage, pendulum, novelty, toy, or advertising clocks, your options are almost unlimited in terms of the various styles that
can be made and sold for big profits. Custom clock building is easier than most
people think; all you have to do is build the case or clock surface and assemble
and install clock mechanisms such as motors, faces, and hands, which can be purchased relatively inexpensively through many clock parts wholesalers. Some
skills, however, are still needed in order to design and build cases and surfaces
made from wood, metal, glass, or plastic, depending on the types of clocks you are
going to build and sell. Reproduction collectible clocks sell particularly well, as do
grandfather and novelty clocks. Sell through home décor shows, flea markets,
craft and woodworking shows, online via eBay and other e-commerce marketplaces, and directly from home.

AT A GLANCE

INVESTMENT: Under $10K

SKILL LEVEL: 2

RESOURCES
—Mammoth Tools, ☎ (516) 942-0905, ♂ www.mammothtools.com
—Scrollsaw, clock plans, ♂ www.scrollsaw.com
—U-Bild, clock plans, ♂ www.u-bild.com
—📖 *How to Build 35 Great Clocks,* Joseph Daniele (Stackpole Books,
1998)

Religious Products

Regardless of faith, worldwide religion is enjoying a rebirth and may be more popular now than in any time in history. Books, Bible cases, religious bookmarks, crucifixes, plaques, rosary products, religious jewelry, pins, religious games and novelties, art, and figurines are just a few of the religious items that you can make and sell for a profit (with 10 percent going to your church, of course). There are just as many ways to sell religious products, as there are religious products that can be manufactured. In the virtual world of religion, you can set up your own web site for e-commerce sales, sell through eBay, or any number of online "religious" marketplaces. In the bricks and mortar world, you can sell your products direct from a homebased showroom, at craft sales, and at religion-themed trade and gift shows. There is also the potential to establish wholesale sales accounts with retailers of religious products. Follow your faith, and concentrate your manufacturing and marketing efforts on the products and religion you know best.

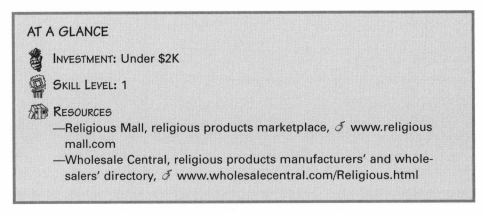

AT A GLANCE

INVESTMENT: Under $2K

SKILL LEVEL: 1

RESOURCES
—Religious Mall, religious products marketplace, ♂ www.religious mall.com
—Wholesale Central, religious products manufacturers' and wholesalers' directory, ♂ www.wholesalecentral.com/Religious.html

Custom Awards and Trophies

Manufacturing and selling custom awards could prove to be fun and profitable. Every year across North America millions of awards are given out for sports, business, and special achievements by businesses, schools, governments, and organizations. The key to success will be in your ability to make very unique awards from a wide variety of materials, including glass, stone, wood, fabric, and metal. Not much workspace is required for manufacturing custom awards, and equipment requirements will vary depending on the materials you use. Engraving equipment, of course, will be needed regardless of the chosen construction material. Design and make sample awards that can be used for marketing and sales purposes. Set appointments with school boards, corporations, clubs, and sports associations to present your products. Also be sure to offer your custom awards for sale online, as well as advertising in your local Yellow Pages under Awards and Trophies categories.

> ## AT A GLANCE
>
> INVESTMENT: Under $10K
>
> SKILL LEVEL: 1–2
>
> RESOURCES
> —Able Engraving Machines and Supplies, trophy engraving equipment, ☎ (800) 383-5185, ✆ www.able-engravers.com
> —Awards and Recognition Association, ☎ (800) 344-2148, ✆ www.ara.org
> —★ Crown Trophy, ✆ www.crowntrophy.com
> —Jon-Ko Trophy Products, trophy engraving equipment and components, ☎ (800) 537-9092, ✆ www.jon-ko.com

Trinket Boxes

Jewelry, coins, keys, and keepsakes, trinket boxes are great for storing these items and lots more. Trinket boxes are also very easy to make, even if you have limited craft and artistic abilities, which makes them a terrific item for just about anyone to build and sell for a profit. Use unique and interesting materials in the construction of the boxes: exotic wood, metals like copper, glass, shells, beads, ceramic tiles, and mirrors. Selling trinket boxes is just as easy as making them, mainly because they are inexpensive to buy and make excellent gifts for birthdays, weddings, Christmas, and anniversaries. Sell them at craft shows, flea markets, and online via eBay and internet malls. Also make a few sample boxes, and visit jewelry shops and gift retailers to make inquiries about placing product in these shops on consignment or to offer them to retailers at wholesale pricing to sell them in bulk.

> ## AT A GLANCE
>
> INVESTMENT: Under $2K

SKILL LEVEL: 1

 RESOURCES
—National Craft Association, ♂ www.craftassoc.com
—U-Bild, trinket box plans, ♂ www.u-bild.com
—Wood Projects, trinket box plans, ♂ www.woodprojects.com
—Wood Zone, trinket box plans, ♂ www.woodzone.com

Reproduction Collectibles

The skyrocketing prices of real vintage collectibles has turned the reproduction collectibles market into a multimillion dollar industry simply because many collectors can no longer afford to buy the real McCoy but will happily part with their hard-earned money to buy a quality reproduction. The starting point is to pick a collectible category and products from that category to reproduce. If you are an avid collector of a certain product, the choice should be easy because you already know the product and market for the product. The most popular collectibles categories include:

- Advertising collectibles such as reproduction tin signs
- Automobilia collectibles such as reproduction classic car emblems
- Petroliana collectibles such as reproduction vintage gas pumps
- Military collectibles such as reproduction metals
- Sports collectibles such as reproduction vintage team jerseys
- Toy collectibles such as reproduction western play sets
- Entertainment collectibles such as reproduction vintage movie posters

In some instances you may have to contact the license holder to get permission and pay a licensing fee if you choose to reproduce a copyrighted or trademarked image or product. Sell your reproduction collectibles online at venues such as eBay and collectible marketplaces, as well as at flea markets, arts and crafts shows, and product or industry specific collectible shows.

AT A GLANCE

 INVESTMENT: Under $10K

 SKILL LEVEL: 2

Metaphysical Products

The category of metaphysical products, also known as new age products, covers a wide range of items, including tarot cards, magnets, zodiac pendants, astrological products, crystals, healing wands, fountains, meditation supplies, yoga mats and books, pagan products, crystal balls, pyramids, hypnosis tapes, and hemp products. Therefore, you might want to specialize making and selling a few items and expand your product line as your business grows. Although there are certainly no prerequisites required to make and sell metaphysical products, retail or wholesale, an interest and belief in new age ideology is suggested. The nature of these products means online marketing will be your best bet. Join new age chat rooms and user groups so that you can network for customers and spread the word about the benefits of your products. Also, sell your goods at flea markets, consumer shows related to metaphysical products, and rental kiosk space in malls on busy weekends.

AT A GLANCE

💰 INVESTMENT: Under $10K

🎰 SKILL LEVEL: 1

🏚 RESOURCES
—Alternative Market Place, products directory, ✆ www.alternativemarket place.com
—Entrepreneur, small business portal, ✆ www.entrepreneur.com
—The New Age Wholesale Directory, ✆ www.newagereseller.com

Gifts-in-a-Can

Making and selling gifts-in-a-can is a unique and potentially very profitable business opportunity. So, what are gifts-in-a-can? Exactly that, gifts-in-a-can, including silk screened T-shirts, stuffed animals, toys, toys for pets, dry flowers, or, for the more risqué, adult novelties, all neatly packaged in a quart- or gallon-size paint-style tin. All of the parts necessary to make the product can be purchased cheaply on a wholesale basis—gifts, paint cans, and labels. You simple assemble the product by packing the gift in the can, sealing the lid, and applying the exterior label. The finished product can be sold wholesale to gift retailers or directly to consumers via online marketplaces and by renting kiosk space at malls and gift shows. There is also a potential to supply corporations, business owners, and professionals with gifts-in-a-can so they can give them away to their customers as appreciation gifts. In this instance, you would simple pack the can with the gift of your client's choice and have exterior labels designed and printed to meet its marketing objective.

AT A GLANCE

INVESTMENT: Under $10K

SKILL LEVEL: 1

RESOURCES
—Dollar Days, wholesale gift products, ☎ (877) 837-9569, ♂ www.dollardays.com
—National Association of Wholesale-Distributors, ☎ (202) 872-0885, ♂ www.naw.org
—SKS Packaging, wholesale paint tins, ☎ (518) 899-7488, ♂ www.sks-bottle.com

Utility Trailers

Home renovations, yard work, and antiquing are just a few of the reasons why owning a utility trailer has become a necessity for many people. With demand comes the opportunity to profit, especially for entrepreneurs with welding skills and workshop space. Building utility trailers is not terribly difficult, mainly because components such as tires, wheels, fenders, lights, and axles are readily available from a number of wholesale sources. Therefore, the job entails welding a steel tube frame, adding a steel plate or wood deck and sides, installing the components, wiring, lights, and a hitch, and the trailer is ready to go. Manufacturing utility trailers on a small scale typically falls under the u-built category for roadworthy registration, but each state and province has its own regulations. Contact your local branch of the department of transportation for registration details in your area. Sell by running trailer-for-sale ads in the classifieds as well as in specialty publications catering to off-road motorcycles and snowmobiles, directly from home with appropriate signage, and by contacting builders, landscape contractors, and other businesses that typically need utility trailers.

AT A GLANCE

 INVESTMENT: Under $25K

 SKILL LEVEL: 2

 RESOURCES
—Champion Trailer Parts Supply, trailer part components and building plans, ☎ (800) 224-6690, ♂ www.championtrailers.com
—National Association of Trailer Manufacturers, ☎ (785) 272-4433, ♂ www.natm.com
—Southwest Wheel, trailer part components and building plans, ☎ (800) 866-3336, ♂ www.utilitytrailerkit.com

---

Packing Crates

Building and selling custom made-to-order packing crates is a fantastic business opportunity with a nearly unlimited supply of potential customers. Every year millions of products are shipped in specially designed and built protective wood packing crates to ensure the cargo does not get damaged in transit. Building packing crates requires nothing more than basic tools such as a table saw, miter saw, drills, and a good supply of c-grade wood. In total, you can be up ad running on less than $10,000 including tools, marketing materials, and sample crates. Landing customers is easy. Design a promotional flier detailing your business and the beneficial features of your packing crates and set appointments with manufacturing firms to pitch your products. In addition to building and selling packing crates, extra money can be earned by building and selling wood shipping pallets, which require the same basic tools to build.

AT A GLANCE

 INVESTMENT: Under $10K

 SKILL LEVEL: 1

RESOURCES
—National Wooden Pallet and Container Association, ☎ (703) 527-7667, ♂ www.nwpca.com
—Pallet Mall, packing crate and pallet information and resources, ♂ www.palletmall.com

Power Equipment Refurbishment

Mechanically inclined entrepreneurs have the opportunity to make big bucks refurbishing and selling outdoor power equipment, all from the comforts of a homebased workshop. Even if you do not have previous power equipment and small engine repair experience, there are numerous schools offering on-site and correspondence courses in small engine repair training. The list of equipment you can refurbish and sell is almost unlimited—lawnmowers, outboard engines, gas trimmers, lawn tractors, snowmobiles, snow blowers, leaf blowers, power tools, and chainsaws. The best thing about refurbishing and selling outdoor power equipment is that more times than not, you can acquire the equipment in need of refurbishment for free, or for very little money. How, you might be wondering? Simply by placing classified ads in your community newspaper and posting fliers on bulletin boards, both stating that you will take power equipment and small engines "working or not" away for free. You can also go garage sale hunting and to auctions in search of power equipment in need of repair. Once repaired and in good working order, simply sell the equipment the same way you got it, by placing inexpensive classified ads in newspapers and by posting fliers on bulletin boards. To maximize sales value, be sure to offer a 30-day unconditional warranty on all of the refurbished power equipment sold.

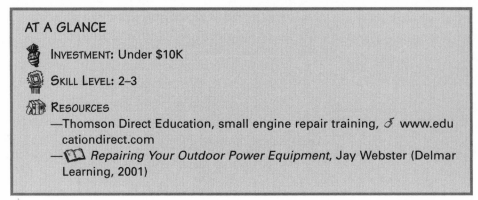

AT A GLANCE

INVESTMENT: Under $10K

SKILL LEVEL: 2–3

RESOURCES
—Thomson Direct Education, small engine repair training, ♂ www.educationdirect.com
—📖 *Repairing Your Outdoor Power Equipment*, Jay Webster (Delmar Learning, 2001)

Signs

Now is your chance to cash-in on the ever-growing demand for advertising signs by starting your own sign-making business. The options are numerous; make and sell wooden, computer-generated and cut-vinyl stick-on, magnetic, hand-painted, sandblasted stone, illuminated box signs, awning, neon, silk-screened banner signs, or mixed-media signs constructed from materials such as plastic, foam, wood, and metal. Even with little experience or basic training you can get started from home and grow your sign-making business as your skills increase. In addition to retail store and office signs, you can also target others that need signs, such as boat owners and trade show exhibitors. Extra income can also be earned by installing signs and by offering monthly, quarterly, or annual sign maintenance services changing light bulbs, cleaning, and painting.

AT A GLANCE

INVESTMENT: Under $25K

SKILL LEVEL: 2–3

RESOURCES
—☆ Sign-A-Rama, ☎ (800) 286-8671, ♂ www.signarama.com
—Sign College, sign-making training courses, ♂ www.signware house.com/sign_college
—Sign Warehouse, sign-making equipment and supplies, ☎ (800) 699-5514, ♂ www.signwarehouse.com
—📖 *Sign Industry Magazine Online*, ♂ www.signindustry.com

Store Fixtures

The retail store fixture industry is very competitive, but at the same time there are thousands of new retail shops opening every month, and store renovations require custom displays and cases built to suit their merchandising requirements and budgets. Designing and manufacturing custom store fixtures and displays as opposed to generic mass-produced fixtures are very much hands-on activities requiring meetings with shop owners, designers, and architects to determine what best fills the needs and budgets of the stores. They are also hands-on in the sense that you need the ability and equipment to work with construction materials such as wood, laminates, glass, stone, and metal. Marketing custom store fixtures is straightforward.

Start by building sample products that can be used as sales aids at your manufacturing location and at trade shows catering to the store fixture merchandising industry. This is a business that also survives and thrives on referrals. Therefore, you need to get actively involved with networking and building relationships with independent and chain retail store owners, managers, and executives and commercial property managers, as well as building alliances with contractors and designers specializing in retail store design, construction, and revitalization.

AT A GLANCE

INVESTMENT: Under $25K

SKILL LEVEL: 2

RESOURCES
—National Association of Store Fixture Manufacturers, ☎ (954) 893-7300, ♂ www.nasfm.org
—National Retail Federation, ☎ (202) 783-7971, ♂ www.nrf.com
—Retail Source, ♂ www.retailsource.com
—📖 *Retail Merchandiser Magazine*, ♂ www.retail-merchandiser.com

Exposition Displays

More than one million companies, organizations, and individuals exhibit everything from products to services to accommodations every year at some 10,000 trade and exhibition shows in the United States alone. All of these exhibitors have one thing in common; they need exposition displays, racks, signs, and props of all sorts to help display and promote their products and services. Capitalizing on the demand for quality trade-show displays is easy because there are many manufacturers building and selling component parts used to construct completed exposition displays, making the job more one of assembly work than actually manufacturing. If you concentrate your manufacturing and marketing efforts on custom one-of-a-kind displays, this is true manufacturing, with the sky the limit in terms of creativity and profit potential. To sell exposition displays and accessories requires a showroom outfitted with samples, a manufacturing/assembly workshop, and basic tools and equipment. A homebased workspace is suitable to get started, providing space and zoning permit. Alternately, you rent commercial space. Design a catalog featuring all of the tradeshow display products you make, as well as a web site also featuring your products, because both are essential sales tools.

> **AT A GLANCE**
>
> INVESTMENT: Under $25K
>
> SKILL LEVEL: 2
>
> RESOURCES
> —Exhibit Designers and Producers Association, ☎ (404) 303-7310,
>   ✆ www.edpa.com
> —Trade Show Displays, industry information, ✆ www.tradeshow
>   displays.biz

Advertising Promotional Products

The advertising promotional products industry generates billions in sales annually and cutting a slice of this very lucrative pie is easier than most people think. Why? One, demand continues to grow for promotional advertising products as more and more businesses look for unique ways to promote and brand their products and services in a cost-efficient, effective way. Two, the equipment and supplies needed to print advertising promotional products are readily available, easy to use, and relatively inexpensive, especially if you scout around for used equipment. Utilizing pad printers, silk-screening equipment, and hot stamping, you can print a wide variety of products for businesses. A few of the products that can be printed for profit range from air fresheners to coffee mugs and flags to magnets.

Promotional advertising products can be sold online, at business-to-business trade shows, and from a homebased showroom. Hire sales reps inside and outside your area to call on businesses to sell products and secure orders.

> **AT A GLANCE**
>
> INVESTMENT: Under $10K
>
> SKILL LEVEL: 1–3
>
> RESOURCES
> —ITW Imtran, printing equipment and supplies, ✆ www.itwimtran.com
> —Pad Printing Machinery of Vermont, printing equipment and supplies,
>   ✆ www.padprintingmachinery.com
> —Press Xchange, used printing equipment marketplace, ✆ www.pressx
>   change.com

—Printex USA, printing equipment and supplies, ♂ www.printexusa.com
—Promotional Products Association International, ☎ (972) 258-3206,
♂ www.ppa.org

Aerial Photographs

Aerial photography equipment is available in various styles, including telescopic aluminum masts outfitted with a camera that can extend to heights reaching over 100 feet, as well as helium-filled blimps outfitted with cameras ranging in size from 5 to 25 feet in diameter that can reach altitudes nearing 1,000 feet while being safely operated from the ground by a tether line or remote control. Good quality blimps complete with photographic gear and trailer cost from $10,000 to $25,000. Whether you choose to use a telescopic mast or a helium blimp, both can be outfitted with film or digital still cameras or video cameras. Clients include any person or business that wants or needs aerial photographs of their homes, buildings, events, or property, which potentially includes government agencies, homeowners, property developers, corporations, marinas, campgrounds, amusement parks, golf courses, outdoor event organizers, mining and forestry sites, and sporting event organizers. To safely operate the blimp, training is recommended, but the blimp manufacturers listed below provide basic training.

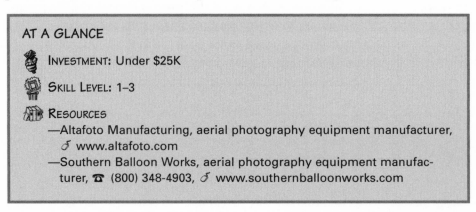

AT A GLANCE

INVESTMENT: Under $25K

SKILL LEVEL: 1–3

RESOURCES
—Altafoto Manufacturing, aerial photography equipment manufacturer, ♂ www.altafoto.com
—Southern Balloon Works, aerial photography equipment manufacturer, ☎ (800) 348-4903, ♂ www.southernballoonworks.com

Logos

Great logos help build and maintain instant brand recognition and consumer awareness, visually linking the logo to the business, product, or service it represents. If you have a creative flair and artistic abilities, you can put these to good use by designing and selling logos. You will need a computer, digital camera, printer, and design software to get started. But outside of these expenditures, startup costs are minimal. The ongoing overhead to operate the business is also minimal because you can work from home, and there are no raw material costs associated with designing and selling logos, just time. There are two easy ways to get started. First, take a broad approach and simply start designing or redesigning logos for businesses in your community. Once finished, set appointments with business owners, and present your work. Close the sale by using the above mentioned persuasions—building brand recognition and consumer awareness. Second, design and create logo samples of fictitious businesses and use these samples to prospect for logo design jobs. Join small business groups to network for business, acquire new business start-up lists, and sell logos online. Basically, market your logo design talents to business owners and professionals, product developers, nonprofit organizations, clubs, and government agencies, that is, to anyone in need of product, service, or personal branding through repetitive use of a logo. The better known you become for your incredible logos that perfectly describe what they represent and the bigger your customers are, the higher your fees will go.

AT A GLANCE

INVESTMENT: Under $25K

SKILL LEVEL: 2–3

RESOURCES
—Guru, online marketplace for freelance talent, ♂ www.guru.com
—📖 _Logo Design Workbook: A Hands-On Guide to Creating Logos_,
   Sean Adams and Noreen Morioka (Rockport Publishers, 2004)

Greeting Cards

In spite of the increasing popularity of electronic greeting cards, the paper greeting card industry generates $7.5 billion in annual sales. Needless to say, a very lucrative opportunity awaits enterprising entrepreneurs who design, produce, and sell greeting cards. One idea is to go after the high-end greeting card market by hiring local artists to paint original watercolor scenes on blank greeting card stock to suit occasions such as seasonal holidays and milestone events, effectively making each card a highly collectible piece of artwork. These could then be sold through retailers on a wholesale or consignment basis, direct to businesses for promotional activities, and directly to consumers via mall kiosks, on eBay, and by establishing alliances with wedding and event planners who can refer your one-of-a-kind artist cards to their clients. You could also concentrate only on business-to-business sales by customizing each greeting card to a specific business, such as house photographs on the outside of the cards for realty companies, car photographs for car dealers, and pet photographs for pet shop retailers. Each card would also be customized on the inside to suit the specific business.

AT A GLANCE

 INVESTMENT: Under $2K

 SKILL LEVEL: 1

 RESOURCES
—Greeting Card Association, ☎ (202) 393-1778, ✆ www.greetingcard.org
—📖 *Designing Handcrafted Cards: Step-by-Step Technique for Crafting 60 Beautiful Cards*, Claire Sun-Ok Choi (Quarry Books, 2004)
—📖 *Making Greeting Cards with Creative Materials*, Mary Jo McGraw (David & Charles Publishers, 2002)

Custom Calendars

There are lots of ways to produce highly saleable paper wall calendars and make big profits in the process. Here are three simple ideas to get you started.

First, capitalize on your artistic skills by purchasing blank wall calendars and hand painting a scene, object, or portrait for each month. Sell the hand-painted art calendars at gift shows and craft fairs, on eBay, and by placing them on consignment with gift and art retailers.

Second, using your photography skills, take people and pet portraits and incorporate the photographs into each month of the calendar. The target audience for this type of calendar is people who want to have a unique product made that can be given to friends and family at Christmas.

Third, initiating your marketing skills, create coupon calendars, and sell advertising space to participating retailers and service providers that want to have a coupon discount featured in the calendar. Each month would feature a new set of coupons, and the calendars could be distributed for free throughout the community every December.

Photo Novelties

Whether you take the picture or your customer does, printing photographs on products such as T-shirts, plates, coffee mugs, mouse pads, and key chains can earn you big cash. Making and selling photograph transfer novelties is a cheap business to start and has great upside profit potential. Required equipment is relatively inexpensive and available through most printing equipment supply companies. The business offers the flexibility to work full time, part time, or only occasionally, and equipment can be set up to work from home, from a retail storefront or mall kiosk, or at flea markets, craft shows, sporting events, concerts, and community events. Costs to produce photograph novelty products vary depending on the item that the image will be printed on, but the profit margin is very high. For instance, T-shirts retailing in the range of $25 to $30 can be produced for about $5 each, including the wholesale shirt and supplies needed to create and print the photograph image on the shirt. Needless to say, you do not need a ton of orders to make some very serious cash.

—Print USA, image transfer and printing equipment, ♂ www.print usa.com

—Printex USA, image transfer and printing equipment, ♂ www.print exusa.com

Articles and Stories

Writing and selling articles and stories is competitive, but it can also be the basis of a very profitable business and fulfilling career for those that stick it out and get published in print or electronic formats. Specialization is the key to success. Pick a topic(s) that you know, write, write some more, and keep submitting your work until you find your voice and an audience. You could specialize in a general area such as business, sports, or entertainment, or focus on more specialized niche markets. When you get published, you will be paid in one of two ways: per word or a fixed amount for each story or article. Sometimes there are further royalties depending on republishing rights. Book writers generally get paid an advance against future royalties. Expect to write a few freebies, especially shorter articles, in order to get your name out there and get publishing credits. The best paying markets tend to be major monthly magazines. The least attractive pay is for content for web publishing.

AT A GLANCE

INVESTMENT: Under $2K

SKILL LEVEL: 1

RESOURCES
—Elance Online, ♂ www.elance.com
—Freelance Online, information and resources, ♂ www.freelance online.com
—📖 2005 Writer's Market, (Writer's Digest Books, 2004)

Business Plans

According to the U.S. Small Business Administration, about 750,000 new businesses are started each year in the United States, and this does not include the many thousands of existing businesses that are purchased during any given year. All of these new start-ups and newly purchased businesses create an outstanding opportunity for entrepreneurs with business planning experience to capitalize by providing research and business plan development services to new and even seasoned entrepreneurs that start or buy a business. Market your service by attending business networking meetings. Also attempt to obtain a list of all new and renewal business registration licenses through your local business service center. Target marketing efforts at existing businesses and professionals that are expanding or need to update or create a new business plan. Be sure to run an inexpensive classified ad in your community paper under the Business for Sale category stating, "Starting or buying a business? Get the right start with a professional business plan" or a similar advertisement. Billing rates vary depending on the size and scope of the business plan being developed, but expect to earn in the $50 to $75 per hour range.

AT A GLANCE

 INVESTMENT: Under $2K

 SKILL LEVEL: 2

 RESOURCES
—Elance Online, outsourcing and services marketplace, ♂ www.elance.com
—Business Plan Writer, information and resources, ♂ www.business-plan-writer-online.com
—Business Plan Pro Software, ♂ www.paloalto.com
— *Rule's Book of Business Plans*, Roger C. Rule (Entrepreneur Press, 2004)

Calligraphy Products

Turn your talent for exquisite handwriting into a profitable business by making and selling calligraphy products. Even people with minimal artistic ability can easily learn calligraphy. There are numerous books and kits available that can help you master the craft, and training classes are offered through the resources listed below. Calligraphy can be used to create one-of-a kind handwritten wedding and event invitations, restaurant menus, gift basket cards, high-end product labels, business cards, award certificates, cards, stationery, and logos. Print shops and stationery retailers are often asked for special designs requiring calligraphy, so building alliances with these types of businesses is wise. Create a portfolio of your calligraphy work, and meet with wedding consultants, restaurants, banquet facilities, associations, and clubs throughout your community, as well as print and stationery shops, to land new business.

AT A GLANCE

INVESTMENT: Under $2K

SKILL LEVEL: 1–3

RESOURCES
—Association for the Calligraphic Arts, ✆ www.calligraphicarts.org
—Society for Calligraphy, ✆ www.societyforcalligraphy.com
—📖 *The Calligrapher's Bible: 100 Complete Alphabets and How to Draw Them*, David Harris (Barron's, 2003)

Photographs

Calling all hobby photographers, start profiting from your hobby by selling your photographs for big bucks. The internet has breathed new life into how the freelance photography industry works and how photographs can now be sold. Using e-mail, it is now very easy to send pictures to publishers, editors, copywriters, marketers, and designers, from around the globe in a matter of moments. Billions of photographic images are needed to fill the more than five billion web pages. In addition to the internet, there are also millions of print publications, media companies, retailers, marketers, organizations, government agencies, and companies who need new photographs every a day to fill newspapers, newsletters, magazines, brochures, catalogs, and presentations. Needless to say, people with fantastic photographic skills have the opportunity to earn a great living producing and selling photographs. You can post your photographs for sale on any one of the many online stock photography services. People browse these sites and purchase photographic images they need, and you are paid a one-time fee or a royalty each time the image is downloaded, depending on your agreement with the image broker. You can also pursue the artist route and frame or mount your best photographs and host gallery shows or sell via mall kiosks, online, and by exhibiting at home décor and art shows.

AT A GLANCE

INVESTMENT: Under $2K

SMALL LEVEL: 2

 RESOURCES
—International Freelance Photographers Organization, ✆ www.ai press.com
—📖 *2005 Photographer's Market* (Writers Digest Books, 2004)

Cartridge Recycling

One of the fastest growing businesses today is ink cartridge recycling. Ink and toner cartridges used in most photocopiers, fax machines, and laser and inkjet printers can be recycled by simply replenishing the ink or toner supply, keeping them out of the landfill and putting big profits in your pockets. This creates a wonderful business opportunity for energetic entrepreneurs to start a toner cartridge recycling business operating from home, on a mobile basis, or from a retail location such as a mall kiosk or storefront. The requirements to operate the business are basic. You will only need simple and inexpensive tools and the ability to refill cartridges with ink, which is easily learned. Customers can save as much as 50 percent off the cost of new cartridges by purchasing recycled ink cartridges, and this fact can become your most convincing marketing tool for landing new business. Offer clients fast free pickup and delivery right to their offices, stores, or homes. Finally, don't be afraid to go after the large accounts with hundreds of machines that need ink and toner cartridges renewed regularly.

AT A GLANCE

 INVESTMENT: Under $2K

 SKILL LEVEL: 1

 RESOURCES
—American Cartridge Recycling Association, ☎ (305) 539-0701
—★ Full Circle Image, ☎ (800) 584-7244, ✆ www.fullcircleimage.com
—📖 *Recharger Magazine Online*, ✆ www.rechargermag.com

How-To Information

How-to information in book, electronic, or tape formats can retail for as much as $100 per product and cost as little as a few dollars to produce, which makes producing and selling how-to information a red hot business opportunity. Many publishers, authors, and media companies sell master copies or reproduction rights to their works cheaply, which means you can purchase and reproduce the work in various print and electronic formats to resell for a profit. You should know that there are two kinds of rights: reprint rights and master rights. Reprint rights means the owner of the copyrighted material authorizes a buyer to reproduce the materials in print or electronic format for resale. Master rights means the copyright owner has also authorized the buyer to sell the reprint rights to anyone they wish. The most popular how-to and self-help information includes topics relating to business, sales, marketing, relationships, child rising, home renovation, health, crafts, and diet and fitness. The best selling methods include online sales, back-of-room seminar sales, trade shows, and mail order.

AT A GLANCE

INVESTMENT: Under $10K

SKILL LEVEL: 1

RESOURCES
—The eBook Directory, www.theebookdirectory.com
—Reprint Rights, ☎ (888) 550-8855, ✆ www.reprint-rights.com
—Total Resale, ✆ www.totalresale.com

Newsletters

People pay big money to have access to the right information. So why not sell your knowledge in electronic newsletter format and get rich in the process? There are two ways to profit from selling your specific knowledge and expertise. First, develop a weekly or monthly newsletter, and distribute it electronically free of charge to subscribers. Revenues would then be generated by selling advertising space in the newsletters to companies that want exposure to your subscriber base. Second, develop a weekly or monthly newsletter, and charge subscribers a fee to receive it. This opportunity is available to just about anyone who has specific knowledge or expertise. For example, if you are an experienced and successful sales coach, develop your newsletter around selling and sales training. If you are an experienced woodworker, develop your newsletter around topics for woodworkers. The sky is the limit in terms of selling specialized information, especially if this information makes your readers wealthier, healthier, and wiser. Salable areas of expertise include information from dating to cooking to religion. You need to invest in a web site, e-mail merge software, time, and a few free sample issues to get started, but the potential financial windfall is well worth the effort.

AT A GLANCE

INVESTMENT: Under $10K

SKILL LEVEL: 2

RESOURCES
—E-Newsletter Pro, newsletter management software, ♂ www.enews letterpro.com
—How to Write a Newsletter, newsletter toolkit software, ♂ www.how towriteanewsletter.com
— Design It Yourself Newsletters: A Step-by-Step Guide, Chuck Green (Rockport Publishers, 2002)

Mailing Lists

For many companies peddling highly specialized products and services, the only viable means of marketing is via print or electronic direct mail. Hence, a great opportunity is available for entrepreneurs to profit by compiling and selling print and electronic direct mail lists. I said sell, but in reality you do not want to sell your mailing lists, but rather you want to rent them over and over to many users. Why get paid once when you can potentially get paid hundreds, if not thousands, of times for the same information? Mailing lists can be rented by creating self-adhesive mailing labels for direct mail print campaigns or server-based electronic lists for electronic direct mail campaigns. There are a few ways that you can collect contact information about people and businesses to build your lists. One way is through opt-in mailing lists, which are compiled from the e-mail addresses of people that have given permission to be included. Another way is via subscription lists, which are composed of individuals and businesses that subscribe to print or electronic publications, magazines, newsletters, trade journals, and so on. A third way is by attendee mailing lists composed of people that have attended a specific event, everything from seminars, or trade shows to time-share pitch sessions. Assembled mailing lists round out the main methods; these lists are compiled from various published information sources such as telephone directories or industry association directories. The key to success in this business is quality. Well-targeted mailing lists rent for substantially more than junk lists, and the vast majority of available mailing lists definitely fall into the junk category. You will need to create a data card for all of your lists. A data card is used as a sales tool to inform and entice marketers to purchase your lists and not a competitor's list. On the data card is information about the cost per one thousand names, the size and minimum order of names, a profile description outlining details such as the source of the list, history of the list, average value of orders, and hotline information like the kinds of products or services that people on the list recently purchased, as well as list usage restriction information. Mailing lists can be sold to business and marketers online using direct sales methods such as e-mail blasts and telemarketing or sold to list brokers that will rent your lists on a revenue sharing basis.

AT A GLANCE

 INVESTMENT: Under $10K

 SKILL LEVEL: 1

RESOURCES
—Email Manager Pro, mail list management software, ✂ www.email-manager-pro.com
—Email Marketing Software, mail list management software, ✂ www.massmailsoftware.com
—List soft, mail list management software, ✂ www.lsoft.com

Career Guides

Career guides have always been hot sellers, are very cheap to produce, yet can retail for as much as $100 each. The best career guides revolve around specialized jobs that are either very high paying or very exciting. Some of the better careers to write about include jobs in the travel industry such as cruise ship, airline, sunny destination, hotel, food, and beverage jobs. Specialized construction jobs and trade careers are popular, as are high-tech, medical service, and television and feature film production careers. So what type of information should be included with each career guide? Lots of information should be included, so excellent research skills will be needed. Create a full description of the career, including job duties, salary range, training courses, industry association and union information if applicable, and lots of contact resources relevant to the career. The guides can either be produced and sold in print by running classified ads for mail-order sales and by exhibiting at career expositions or in a downloadable e-book format to be sold via online marketplaces.

AT A GLANCE

INVESTMENT: Under $2K

SKILL LEVEL: 1

RESOURCES
—Fab Job, 🔗 www.fabjob.com
—Hot Job, 🔗 www.hotjob.com
—Monster, 🔗 www.monster.com

Window Displays

Retailers need elaborate product displays in their windows to grab the attention of passing consumers and draw them in to shop, but not all retailers have the time or the ability to create window displays that get the job done. Starting a business specializing in effective window merchandise displays for retailers is the focus of this opportunity. People with a design and retail background will be well suited to take up the challenge to cash in for big profits. Marketing your talents should not be difficult. Set appointments with retailers, and explain that window space is one of the best and least expensive marketing tools available, a 24-hour silent salesperson that never sleeps. Window space can be used to display new products, demonstrate products, and motivate impulse buying. In short, well-planned and well-executed window displays increase revenues and profits. In addition to an artistic flair, you will need to build an inventory of interesting props, signs, and lighting options. Remember, your goal is not a one-time sale, but a regular schedule for creating new window displays.

AT A GLANCE

INVESTMENT: Under $2K

SKILL LEVEL: 1–2

RESOURCES
—Entrepreneur, small business portal, 🔗 www.entrepreneur.com
—National Retail Federation, 🔗 www.nrf.com
—📖 *Retail Merchandiser Magazine*, 🔗 www.retail-merchandiser.com

Resumes

Wordsmiths with business management or human resources experience take notice; big bucks can be earned creating resumes for the millions of people in search of employment every year. Finding the perfect words to describe why you should get the job is difficult, which is one reason why resume services continue to flourish in spite of the fact that just about everybody has access to a computer and a word processing program. This is not a traditional manufacturing business, but at the same time you will be producing and selling an in-demand product. One of the best aspects about creating and selling resumes is you can start part time and keep costs to a minimum by working from home, which makes this the perfect opportunity for people looking to earn an extra few hundred dollars every month. In addition to creating resumes, also write cover, sales, and follow-up letters for customers as a way to increase revenues. Advertise locally, online, and through career exposition trade shows. Once established, this is the type of business supported mainly through word-of-mouth advertising and repeat business.

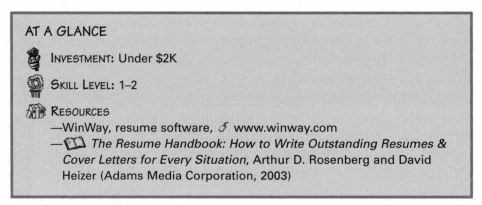

AT A GLANCE

INVESTMENT: Under $2K

SKILL LEVEL: 1–2

RESOURCES
—WinWay, resume software, ♂ www.winway.com
—📖 *The Resume Handbook: How to Write Outstanding Resumes & Cover Letters for Every Situation*, Arthur D. Rosenberg and David Heizer (Adams Media Corporation, 2003)

Product Assembly

Assembling products for other people and businesses is a way for cash-strapped entrepreneurs to get into business with a minimal investment. There are hundreds, if not thousands, of products such as furniture, garden structures, and computers that require assembly by the purchaser, and it's never as easy as advertised. At some point, everyone has fought and struggled to assemble a product. Obviously, herein lies the opportunity—assemble products for other people and businesses. Get started for less than $500 in total investment, and market product assembly services to retailers that do not currently offer customers this service. You will need basic tools, such as a cordless drill, hand tools, and socket set, moving equipment like blankets and a dolly, and suitable transportation if you also offer delivery services. Retailers selling "assembly required" products will be your primary market as well as residential and commercial moving companies, because moving often requires furniture and equipment to be disassembled before the move and reassembled after the move.

AT A GLANCE

INVESTMENT: Under $2K

SKILL LEVEL: 1

RESOURCES
—Entrepreneur, small business portal, ♂ www.entrepreneur.com
—National Retail Federation, ♂ www.nrf.com

Vending Carts

Vending food such as popcorn, gift products such as sunglasses, and services such as a nail studio from pushcarts, portable booths, and fixed location kiosks is big business in the United States and elsewhere. All of these product and service providers have one thing in common: they all need a suitable cart, booth, or kiosk to display and sell their goods and services. Designing, manufacturing, and selling vending carts is a very exciting opportunity because there is almost unlimited growth and profit potential. Vending carts can be designed in push models, trailer-mounted models, knockdown models, and stationary models like the kiosks commonly found in malls. It is best to pick a specialty, at least to get started. You might specialize in completely equipped food vending carts or in designing and selling the unmanned kiosks commonly used in the real estate industry. There are lots of choices. Also consider specializing in a central theme, such as carts designed to replicate antique vehicles or kiosks designed to replicate spacecrafts; you are only limited by your own imagination. Selling vending carts, booths, and kiosks is best achieved by advertising in print and electronic publications related to the types of carts you manufacture, as well as by concentrating a good part of your marketing efforts on the internet because this is where small entrepreneurs commonly start their search for appropriate vending equipment.

AT A GLANCE

🏺 INVESTMENT: Under $25K

📟 SKILL LEVEL: 2

🏚 RESOURCES
—Cart Owners of America, ♂ www.cartowners.org
—National Association of Store Fixture Manufacturers, ☎ (954) 893-7300, ♂ www.nasfm.org
—Vending Connection, industry information and resources, ♂ www.vendingconnection.com

For-Sale-by-Owner Kits

Millions of cars, boats, RVs, homes, and businesses are sold every year in the United States by the owners, which creates a fantastic opportunity to capitalize on that market by producing and selling specialized for-sale-by-owner sales kits. As the name suggests, these kits are designed to help owners sell their items professionally, quickly, and for top dollar. Each kit should be specific to the product or item being marketed: real estate, recreational vehicles, boats, automobiles, motorcycles, and so forth. Kits should include a guide detailing how to prepare an item to sell, how to valuate the item being sold to arrive at a selling price, how to write advertisements and where to post them online and offline, how to negotiate with buyers, contract templates specific to the item being sold, and additional resource information specific to the item. Kits sold via the internet should be in e-book format available for immediate download while kits sold to consumers in other venues should be in print format accompanied by a CD with the corresponding electronic contract files. In addition to the internet, for-sale-by-owner kits can be sold at trade shows—recreational vehicles for-sale-by-owner kits at RV shows, car sales kits at auto shows, and so on. Kits can also be wholesaled to retailers such as bookstores and office supply retailers.

AT A GLANCE

🏺 INVESTMENT: Under $2K

📟 SKILL LEVEL: 1

🏚 RESOURCES
—Adobe, desktop publishing software, ♂ www.adobe.com
—Corel, desktop publishing software, ♂ www.corel.com

INDEX